# TO KNOW THE
# LOVELY NIGHT

The extraordinary life of acclaimed Australian scientist and writer,
MARY E. WHITE

**MARY E. WHITE AND BARBARA ECKERSLEY**

# ABOUT THE AUTHORS

Mary E. White - born in South Africa in 1926, raised in Rhodesia (Zimbabwe). She studied botany at Cape Town University and worked as a botanist in Rhodesia and Somaliland. She immigrated to Australia in 1955 and worked as a paleobotanist (identifying fossil plants) in Canberra and Sydney while raising a large family.

At age 60, Mary began her writing career, producing scientifically important books on the evolution of the Australian continent and its flora, and the environmental crisis after 200 years of unsustainable land-use practices.

When Mary died in 2018 she left an unpublished autobiography of her African beginnings and early married life in Africa.

Barbara Eckersley born in South Africa, came to Australia with her family when she was five. She grew up in Canberra and Sydney and has a BSc and a PhD. in physiology.

Barbara lives with her husband, Richard in Bundanoon, NSW surrounded by wombats, kangaroos and amazing bird life. They have three children and six grandchildren, 2 ragdoll cats, bees and chooks.

First published in Australia
by Nebula Books
Bundanoon NSW

ISBN:978-1-7635229-0-9

NATIONAL LIBRARY OF AUSTRALIA

A catalogue record for this book is available from the National Library of Australia

Cover design by Barbara Eckersley

In honour of Mary
With love and reverence

To my family, past, present and future.

# CONTENTS

Map 1. East Coast of Africa

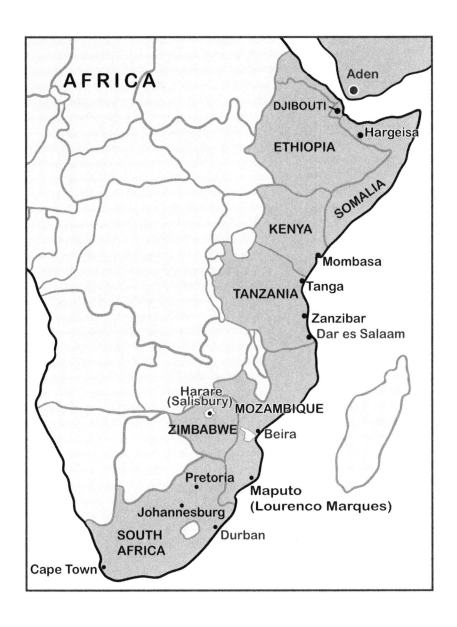

Map 2. Area of Somalia shown in Map 3.

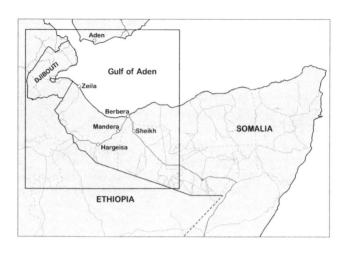

Map 3. Western Somalia

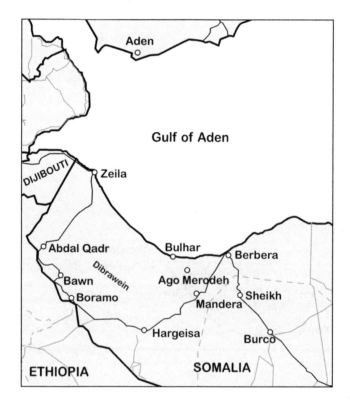

I feel secure, and privileged to be alive,
To know the lovely night, and be a part
Of all creation.

# INTRODUCTION

by Mary E. White

When I was writing **The Greening of Gondwana**, describing the co-evolution of the Australian continent and its vegetation through 400 million years of geological time, I became increasingly aware of a deep sense of my own belonging—as an infinitesimally small part of Life's Continuum; that the lineage of my DNA and that of my children and grandchildren goes back into the misty, watery beginnings when the Earth was young, nearly 4 billion years ago; and that all of us humans alive today, and all other living things, are here because every one of our ancestors achieved the Primeval Life-force's goal of reproduction. Sobering, humbling, but also deeply satisfying—no place for overgrown egos, only for gratitude at being allowed a brief glimpse of the wonders of this world and the awesome magnitude of the overall scheme of things.

In this autobiography I take a different journey of the mind – one where memory of most of the travelling is lost and only some of the stops along the way remain as captured moments—that being the nature of human remembering. These are small bits of time snatched from the speeding river that carries me inexorably from birth to oblivion. How sad that so little can be recalled; that only incidents remain and the thread of living, loving, happiness, gratitude for life and wonder at the endless bounty of nature is not preserved. If only it had all been recorded on film to be replayed and experienced once again—the travelling and not the small arrivals celebrated.

Some years ago I prepared a memoir, largely of the African part of my life, so my sons and daughters, and their descendants, might have more insight into the very different world of my generation and of the early part of their lives of which they have no memory. I did not know when I began compiling it just what a strange emotional and mental upheaval would result from the opening of the floodgates of my memory bank. I was amazed, even then, to find just what was stored on the hard-drive of my brain's computer. Perhaps what surprised me most was that I not only remembered events, but that some were stored wrapped in the emotions, colours, scents and context of their time and they came back unexpectedly and surprisingly alive.

What spurred me to write the original account for my family that is here expanded and brought up to date was a strange, coincidental, happening (a bit of serendipity?) that I wrote up as an essay titled:

## Eleven, Eleven

A few years ago, on the eleventh day of the eleventh month, I watched the TV ceremony at the War Memorial for the recognition and celebration of Australia's Unknown Soldier. At 11 o'clock the alarm clock in my kitchen went off uninvited, shattering the one minute's silence of a nation. It made me think of chance and coincidence, and I suddenly realised just how great a part chance had played in my being alive, just me, and how fortunate I was to have been born at all.

I have often, at times of quiet thinking, known that the odds against my beginnings were great — biologically speaking. That day, when I was moved by the sorrows of war and the deep hurt that remains forever within when one loses those one loves, I saw suddenly that had it not been for a soldier unknown to me who died, there would have been no me, nor my two brothers and sister. If it were not for my mother's loss of her first true love in the barbaric killing fields of German Southwest Africa in WW1, her children would have had a different father and the genetic mix

10

that is uniquely us would never have been created. It humbled me and made me sad to know that my gentle mother had to suffer such profound grief and misery along the way. Part of her heart remained forever with that young man who lies in an unmarked desert grave. She spoke of her joy at going to meet him again when she was close to death half a century later.

Because I moved so far away (eventually to the other side of the world) when I married, I never really knew my parents from a fully adult perspective and I'm very conscious of that deprivation. We would have had so much to talk about now and just knowing some of the mundane things of their past that had made them who they were would have enriched my understanding.

Though my children might not have thought about war and coincidence and their chances of being here at all, it was war that brought their father and me together. He came from Ulster, then a Northern Ireland part of the UK. He was sent to Southern Rhodesia (then an African colony of the British Empire, now Zimbabwe) to train as an air force pilot in WW2. We met in Bulawayo where my dad had taken a post-retirement job for the "duration". We were two people from opposite ends of the Earth whose paths crossed for a sum total of a couple of days before the war ended, yet that brief confluence shaped our lives from then onwards. Though I did not know it then, he had decided that he would come back one day to marry me. (And it was war, too, and the death of an unknown paratrooper at Arnhem that destined that I should not marry the person who was the object of my first serious love. Strange to think that such a distant and chance event could have determined the path my life would take, and that it would lead to a lifelong commitment to another love.)

So, on that eleventh hour of the eleventh day of the eleventh month, when for a reason best known to itself my kitchen clock rang its bell, I had reason to pause and give thanks. I wish I could have told my mother that I empathised and knew a little of the sorrows of war that had darkened her life and whose shadows had travelled with her thereafter.... The symbolism of so much that has been positive and happy arising out of the darkness of war

**merged with the symbolism of the recognition of the Unknown Soldier and touched me. ....**

Thinking about it since has made me realise that the greatest gift my parents gave their children was their love and reverence for life and their strong connections to the natural world.

Several years later, when I was asked to expand the private family memoir into an autobiography of sorts for publication, I found again how challenging emotionally and intellectually the exercise could be. Opening up that storehouse of memories, bringing the story up to date and seeing one's eighty-plus years of living in context and against a background of the changing world is a recipe for sorting out one's thoughts and beliefs. By adding bits and pieces of creative writing and letters that captured the moment when they were written, I have, I hope, enriched the content.

# PART I

## MARY'S AFRICAN STORY

# SOMALILAND 1953

Our camp near the Ethiopian border

# SOMALILAND STORY

A trace of aromatic wood-smoke on the breeze
Immediately evocative,
Taking me back on instamatic journeys into the past

## CONFRONTATION WITH THE ESA 1953

It was early morning and the deputation sent to kill us had arrived. The heat inside the tent was stifling and the glare outside was intense. A hush had descended on our part of the world and the silence and tension were palpable.

I crouched on the rough stony floor of our tent clutching my two tiny children. Our young dog was tied to the central tent pole. The presence of a woman at such an all-male occasion might tip the scales and the dog too, being just about as "unclean" as I was. The children, silent and awed, watched me, wide-eyed. They could sense the tension and my terror. Their complete trust in me unsettled me and I thought, Oh God, what am I doing here in this inhospitable, lawless country? How damnably irresponsible of me to bring these tiny children to this godforsaken place. We are all going to die— here and now; Bill, me and these precious babies— their lives only just beginning. There's no help to be had and it could be weeks before we are missed, and our bodies discovered.

Raised voices and the stamping of feet on the hard, parched dirt startled me and I put my eye to the gap in the tent flap. Barby in my lap, clung tighter and studied me seriously, her eyes large and dark under her ragged golden fringe and her thumb firmly

15

stuck in her mouth. I could feel her brittle calm. The dog whimpered quietly and strained against his leash—he too sensed the gravity of the situation.

Just outside the tent a group of about a dozen Somalis of various ages—all wild-eyed and woolly-haired, each with a long and frightful spear and most with a knife in the belt that gathered their tattered rags together, had formed a circle around Bill and our interpreter, Liban. The faces of the visitors were grim and all except the spokesperson stared at the ground. The knuckles on their brown hands that held their spears were almost white.

Bill greeted the assembly politely and tried to look relaxed. The interpreter interpreted; the belligerent leader started a loud harangue, we were invading their territory, we were not wanted there, we had been warned that if we did not leave they would kill us.

Bill explained what we were doing, that we were government officers, that we needed three days to complete our work and would then go; that if we found minerals or gold the local people would benefit.

The conversation went on and on, covering the same ground. Another Somali joined in and several in the ring showed their agreement by stamping their feet and brandishing their spears. The atmosphere was electric and deteriorating fast. The deputation would far rather get on with the business of killing us than waste time arguing.

I could hardly breathe. I was about to witness Bill's bloody murder a few feet from us and there was nothing I could do (being an unclean woman with no rights in the fiercely male world of the Somali) and then they'd come for us. I clutched Barby, barely two years old, to my chest and turned to gather David in close, but he was gone.

♠♠

Bill had been working in the remote western part of what was then the Somaliland Protectorate for several months, working on foot in the mountains and the difficult country along the escarpment. He had been covering some fifteen to twenty miles a day on survey work over very rough, wild, waterless country, gradually making his way westwards towards the rough track running down to the coast. When he reached this road he briefly left his camp and came back to Hargeisa where he collected the children and me so we could have a few weeks together. I knew it would be tough going but I loved the camping in wild and lonely places and found the landscape harshly beautiful. Bill also needed to map an area close to the Ethiopian border which could be only accessed by the remains of an old track which had been put in when the Ethiopian border was surveyed. It was only used by camel trains now, but he thought it might just be passable. If we could get a car along it he could complete his work in the area, and we could have another week together.

We camped in the crater of an ancient volcano, and on the bank of a dry river under the only thorn bush within miles. While Bill spent a couple of weeks working along the road making long walks across the bare semi-desert and covering as much ground as he could, the children and I played in the sandy tug (a dry river bed) and wandered about the stony, desolate surroundings. I usually collected plants and stone artefacts while on treks but this was particularly barren countryside.

Eventually Bill could do no more from camps along the road, so we agreed to try the old survey road even though it led into the grazing lands of the Esa.

"If you must go into the Esa country don't take your wife. And if the Esa play up, don't stop to argue." That was the advice given to Bill by a responsible government officer who knew what he was talking about. It was good advice, which Bill chose to ignore, with what might have been disastrous results.

At first the track was quite good but after a few hours spent digging ourselves out of the sand in a tug we were able to proceed only slowly for several miles. The track deteriorated badly as we skirted round the foot of a bare, shimmering limestone mountain, but we bounced on over the boulders and outcrops till, after about six miles, we were stopped by a narrow, deep gully. It was narrow enough to jump across but deep, and steep, and impassable. There was no timber available for bridging it and no way round, and we did not have enough time to think of digging out a gentler approach in the iron-hard ground. So, we pitched camp on its edge. We had not got very far, but at least Bill could do three or four days' work from there.

That evening we had our first encounter with the Esa. The Somali as a whole are a proud and independent race, often with fiery tempers. In their nomadic way of life, they wander from summer to winter grazing grounds, always prepared to defend, with force if necessary, any infringement of their tribal rights or encroachment on their traditional grazing grounds and wells. They could not be called lawless because they operated within their tribal laws and customs, but they showed a disregard of any other laws that interfered with these.

The Esa are an offshoot of the notorious Danakil people of northern Ethiopia. Their traditional grazing lands spread across the border into Ethiopia and French Somaliland, but they had had little contact with any government and took good care to maintain this state of affairs.

We had pitched camp and made ourselves comfortable in this desolate moon-landscape part of the world. The mountain nearby was white and stony with hardly a plant growing on it. The flat terrain around it where we were was little better. Just before dark a very agitated interpreter came to the tent to say he had had visitors who told him that they would not allow us to camp in this place and that they intended to send "a delegation to kill us all". The use of such words made it seem quite ridiculous, but the agitation of the man who was usually so level-headed and dependable had us anxious. Bill asked him to go back to the visitors and tell them that we would be pleased to see a delegation in the morning and that we would explain why we were here and what it might mean to them in terms of future wealth. This was done and eventually the interpreter came to say that he had passed on the message, but he still thought we should listen to the warning and move back out of the mountains.

That night was an anxious one. Every sound outside the tent held menace, the dog kept growling under his breath at what we hoped were hyenas moving about among the rocks nearby and twice in the night we heard the slip-slop of camels' feet on the track only yards from the tent. When we got up and looked out of a crack in the tent door we saw camel trains of several beasts, laden with dried skins, silhouetted against the white mountain in the moonlight. They drifted past, ships of the desert, almost soundlessly and the haud-cloth-wrapped men who walked with them were ghosts in the moon landscape. It was eerie beyond belief and at the same time strangely beautiful. We realised that we were camped on a smugglers' road and that under the loads of skins were the packages of khat[1] that was sold all over Somaliland and far afield in the Arab world. Everyone knew of the trade, no one could do anything about it, and there was no other export economy.

♠♠

Absolutely horrified, I realised that three-year-old David had got tired of being hidden in the tent and had wormed out under the flap and gone to find his dad. He pushed his way through the ring of legs and spears and marched straight up to Bill, took him by the hand and beamed at the assembled company. He was very small, very fair, completely confident and had the warm smile of an angel. Instantly the tension was gone. You could hear the breath being let out by one and all as they smiled and relaxed, leaning lightly on their spears. Small boys are what the Somali love best and this small boy who was obviously the friend of every

---

[1]  Khat is a flowering plant native to Ethiopia. It contains the alkaloid cathinone, a stimulant that is said to cause excitement, loss of appetite and euphoria. Khat chewing has a history as a social custom dating back thousands of years analogous to the use of coca leaves in south America and betel nut in Asia. (Wikipedia)

one of them changed the complexion of things. "Did you ride here on your camels?... Have you brought us a baby dik-dik?... Be careful not to poke your eyes out with those pointy sticks!" he babbled. The interpreter interpreted and everyone laughed and some of the warriors squatted down to child height to hear the questions better.

The rest of the discussions were informal. We could have three days to finish the area, or four if that would be better for us, and everything was all right. I would rather have packed up then and there and gone home, but Bill said that that would be giving in to the lawless and the government had to be seen to do what it said it would. So, I had sleepless nights when every sound was someone creeping up out of the darkness, and during the days the children and I stayed in the tent and did not explore the area or try to collect plants.

When survival is what it is all about and the land is as harsh and unforgiving as Somaliland, there is little room for sentiment. I had reason to be grateful that a little love, for boy children at least, still existed in the hearts of the Esa.

♠♠

Bill was a bit worried on one of those days when he was going around a mountain and came upon an ancient Somali woman, as mad as a hatter, with a few straggly goats. She fled from him screaming like one being murdered, and when by chance he met her again on the other side of the mountain still running in terror from him she started the terrible screaming again. He was afraid any locals would hear the yelling and think he was molesting her.

The Somali regularly abandoned the very old, mad and infirm in remote areas, leaving them a few goats, when they could no longer keep up with the nomadic group as it moved to summer or winter pasture. They were also said to leave many of the baby girls on hillsides to die (and feed the hyenas) because there was no need for more than a few women or girls to do the necessary tasks.

♠♠

We had moved to Somaliland from South Africa in 1952 when my husband Bill, a geologist, took a job with the Somaliland Geological Survey, part of the Colonial Service. We were based in Hargeisa but Bill's work of mapping the geology of the country took him out on 'treks', the word used for each field work journey, into remote and desolate parts of the country. In fact, most of the trekking in Somaliland was rough and through difficult and usually waterless country but when Bill thought it was safe for us to do so, the children and I would accompany him.

Travel in Africa, especially in those years—the 1940s and 50s—was far from easy. Distances were vast, even more so than in Australia where I was eventually to spend the greater part of my life. Roads were appalling, trains were magnificent but antiquated and journeys could take weeks, and air travel was prohibitively expensive. Our journey to Somaliland had started with a road trip from Salisbury in Rhodesia (now Harare in Zimbabwe) where Bill had been working with the Southern Rhodesian Geological Survey, to Pretoria in South Africa—a journey of over 1000km on shocking roads, with two small children. We stayed briefly with my parents in Waterkloof, a suburb of Pretoria, before boarding a train to Durban where we were to meet an old ship of the Union Castle Line, *Llangibby Castle,* which would take us to Aden. From there we would fly across the Gulf of Aden into Somaliland.

The few days with my mom, ZoZo, and my dad, was a very special time. David and ZoZo became firm friends. She took him into the garden at night to see the stars; introduced him to all the stray cats that came to be fed, and to the neighbour's dog, and doted on him and her "wild rose" Barbara.

It was a difficult and emotional time for me because we were going so far, taking the children away when I so much wanted to share them with my parents who loved them, and most of all because I could see that my dad was not going to live much longer. I knew I would not see him again when we left. I had always had a wordless communion with my dad and I knew, and he knew, and we did not have to say anything about it because there was nothing we could do about it. Sometimes one just knows things about the people one loves.

Though I did not think about it or analyse it at the time, I have since realised that all my life I had worried about my mom, about her health and about her happiness, and I felt a great responsibility for the welfare of both my parents. I knew that my mom in particular was full of misgivings about us taking two babies into such a remote and undeveloped territory, and I had to see to it that I never let her worry about us—hence the weekly (or bi-weekly) letters that I wrote throughout the Somaliland interval, and even when we were living in Australia. They were so full of detail that she could not worry, and she could share the children with me although we were so far apart. She kept all my letters relating to Somaliland and many of them had been sent on to my sister Joan in Zambia and had been returned. When ZoZo died the letters were sent back to me, providing a diary of daily activities and the progress of the children that enabled me to savour again the joys of young motherhood and even some of the wonderment. They also provided a diary record of daily life and activities in that backwater of the British Empire.

When we left Pretoria with our mountains of luggage, we were seen off at the station by my parents. ZoZo had the wisdom to bring toys to distract the children, and us, and keep everyone's mind off the parting.

# AFRICAN BEGINNINGS

Dad, Oupa, Ouma;    Ouma, Dad and ZoZo

# EARLY CHILDHOOD

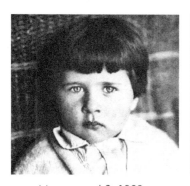 

Mary aged 3, 1929    ZoZo, Joan and Mary

The four Brain children at Fourways circa 1932    Fourways

# AFRICAN BEGINNINGS

I have come to realise that it is my African imprinting
That has facilitated a general communion
with nature everywhere
And has enriched my life.

## FAMILY BACKGROUND

I remember a quiet house with a long brown passageway down its centre, wood-lined; with shady verandas, vine-festooned like cool green caves, and a big, high window through which I was lifted to pick the purple grapes, blue-bloomed and cool and smooth to small and eager hands. And all around me, even now, when I recall that essence of my first-remembered place, was loving warmth and a deep sense of security which, then instilled, has been my everlasting core of peace and purpose. I realise now how fortunate I was to have been born to wise and loving parents, with a wider family that loved and reinforced the inner me.

That earliest memory was of the Lyndall house of my grandparents in Pretoria, visited on holiday from Stellenbosch in the Cape where I was born. I was almost two and it is an isolated snapshot, but so photographically remembered that polished floorboards, brass doorknobs and stained-glass panels in a veranda door are conjured up by the scent of summer sunlight on leafy grapevines. Scents so evocative. I have another snapshot with the smell of fig tree leaves and dry red earth, a wooden stairway ascending to a loft, and a feeling of a secret place where small brown birds came to eat the ripening figs. That's all I know, but I was told much later that such a place had been my favourite hiding place next to the kitchen door at that same house. And after that house was sold, my grandparents moved to the farm **Xanadu** near the Haartebeestpoort Dam, and Lyndall was demolished. When I saw the high-rise flats that had replaced it, filling the block, many years later, I saw inside my head the low-crouched, gracious house, a lawn where the Alsatian dog minded me when I was a baby, retrieving me when I crawled off the rug and carrying me back by the nappy. But those images came from photographs I'd seen and things I was told.

My grandmother, Elizabeth Aletta (Bessie) Findlay, (Ouma to us) was a most remarkable lady. When she was only twelve her father, who was farming in the Orange Free State and had been bankrupted by drought, shot himself. He left a pregnant wife and six children, of whom Bess was middle daughter. Two other children had died in infancy as was expected in those days, and two of the boys who were older than my grandmother were later killed in the Boer War.

My great-grandmother packed the children and all her worldly possessions including a crate of hens into an ox wagon and, accompanied by a loyal family retainer—a Bushman called Boesman— and two cows to provide milk for the children, she set off on a virtually cross-country journey towards Johannesburg. She and the older children often walked beside the wagon and I was told that her ninth child was born en route. The gold rush was on, and Johannesburg was a bustling town where she knew she could survive by opening a boarding house for miners. (Relatives had offered to pay the rent on a suitable house until she could afford to do so.) Her daughters Katy, Bess and Marguerite, aged fourteen, thirteen and nine, were the main labour force in the establishment.

I wish I knew more about those years. There is now no one alive who can verify the anecdotal things that I recall. All I was told was about my grandfather's courtship of Bess. She was seventeen, very beautiful and very competent. He was a rising lawyer in a firm in Johannesburg and was to go into partnership with a young relative of his wife when he married Bess and moved to Pretoria. (The law firm exists to this day.) We were told that when he called on his betrothed and she was busy with the family laundry in the evenings, he turned the mangle and was such a gentleman that should any female garment come through the wringer he turned his head away so as not to embarrass her.

The law firm did well from the start and Bess was soon living in style in a large house with many servants. The Lyndall house was apparently a magnet for the somewhat Bohemian assortment of poets, artists, writers and musicians who came to stay or dropped in for tea or a meal. Many were from Holland, France or Germany with connections to the family.

My mother, Zoe Findlay (ZoZo), born in 1893 at the Lyndall house in Pretoria, was one of the first female graduates of the South African College that later became the University of Cape Town. She had a privileged childhood with a father who was a successful lawyer and a mother who enjoyed the social position that the legal world entailed. She was of that flapper generation of emancipated girls so well portrayed in British television series, with their glamorous beaded, fringed and embroidered clothes, their wonderful hats and their gaiety.

On her mother's side she came from a line of strong and talented women, many real pioneers, and including the famous South African writer Olive Schreiner of *Story of an African Farm* fame. One of her uncles was Eugene Marais, the first ethologist who was generations ahead of his time (before Conrad Lorenz). He wrote *The Soul of the White Ant* and *My Friends the Baboons*. A manuscript of *The Soul of the Ape* was discovered and published more than thirty years after his death. Its content and that for a book on bees was allegedly plagiarised by Maeterlinck, to whom the manuscript had been sent for an opinion, and a court case that was never finalised was ongoing until all the participants were dead. I was told that when Marais' son Eugene, my favourite uncle, was born his father immersed him in deep water to see whether swimming was instinctive, and he was delighted to find that it was.

After completing a B.A. degree, my mom fell in love with a charming and, as judged by the family, unsuitable young man whose mother was an alcoholic (which I think was the reason given for his unsuitability). When he went off to war and died in the barbaric killing fields of German Southwest Africa she was shattered. Aunt Elizabeth told me of ZoZo's inconsolable grief and how such a confident, carefree and joyful person was completely transformed. She also said that ZoZo had known of the death at the time it occurred, long before news came, and that an elephant-hair bracelet that she wore instead of an engagement ring had leapt off her wrist and the soldier's picture had crashed off the wall. I know that I always believed that my mom was psychic, though I rationalised it by thinking that anyone who worried so much about everything must sometimes be right.

In 1919 the killer flu epidemic swept the world and Pretoria was not immune. ZoZo volunteered like so many others to help during the crisis. The young Ouma Smuts, wife of Jan Smuts who was to be famous as the Prime Minister of South Africa in WWII, was also a volunteer. When she was asked what role she would play in dealing with the problem of the orphaned children who were being accommodated at the Show Ground, she announced that she and Zoe would wash the nappies, surprising the organisers who had expected that she would pick a supervisory job. So, wash nappies they did, under the most primitive and frightful conditions, while babies and children died around them. Few families were untouched by the plague. Gargling and sniffing disinfectant up their noses and wearing handkerchief masks was the only protection. Long before the time of sulfa drugs and antibiotics only the strong survived if they had caught the infection, and luck or good immune systems protected the rest.

I am told that my parents met at a tennis party in 1920 and found that they worked in adjacent buildings; and that Mom came home and confided in her younger sister Elizabeth that she had met and instantly recognised the man who was going to be the father of her children. It was lucky for me, and my brothers and sister, because he was forty when they married, mature, wise, gentle and a father who taught without ostensibly teaching so that we were all fairly competent general scientists, botanists, entomologists and thinkers before we went to high school. For good measure I learnt from helping him how to lay bricks, tile walls, use a saw and other things not taught to girls. And my mom was as good a parent in her sphere, a homemaker in its fullest sense, and a practical person as well so my sister and I could sew and cook.

My dad, Charles Kimberlin Brain, was a Professor of Entomology at Stellenbosch University when I was born. (For me, his existence started with my first recollection of him in Salisbury, Southern Rhodesia, where he was appointed Director of Agriculture in 1929, when I was three.) He was born in England in 1881, eldest son of an industrial chemist who had told his bride when they moved into the family home after the honeymoon that together they would fill every seat round the enormous oak table in the dining room. This they did, with eleven children, nine of whom survived. My paternal grandmother, Mary Elizabeth, for whom I was named, was a strong-minded lady who, like others of her generation and class, revered and spoilt her sons and worked her numerous daughters like slaves until they found suitable husbands and could flee the nest. She had no respect for girls and when she received notice of my birth she replied by cable saying she hoped for better news of a boy next time.

Dad was apprenticed to a cabinet-maker while he was finishing high school, because, although he was to proceed to university, his father believed boys should have trades as well as academic professions. He was a brilliant student and won a rare scholarship to America for post-graduate work on the transmission of polio —investigating with the help of rhesus monkeys whether the disease could be transmitted by mosquitoes. He did not see military service in the First World War because his work was considered essential. I was to learn many years later that he had fallen in love with a girl in the U.S.A. and that it was only the impossibility of his affording the fare to return to her after he went back to England that had stopped him marrying her. She got tired of waiting and married someone else. He migrated to Cape Town to a science teaching post at a boys' school. He obtained the first ham-radio operator's licence issued in South Africa and he used to build his own wireless equipment. Later he joined the Entomology Department in Pretoria, whose premises were near to the Union Buildings and to the National Herbarium where my mother was working as a systematic botanist.

While my parents were engaged they bought land in what was then an outer suburb of Pretoria. After work, at weekends and on holidays, they built their own house, a beautiful Cape Dutch style cottage with high gables and a thatched roof. My dad and an African helper did the building while my mom helped where she could and she created the garden from scratch. They were never to live in their house because when they married my dad had been offered the professorship in Stellenbosch.

In those days, the university town of Stellenbosch was also the Afrikaner heartland. (I believe it is still somewhat of that per-suasion today.) The Dutch Reform Church with its narrow funda-mentalist doctrine, Afrikaans as the preferred language, strong racial prejudice against black and "coloured" people, preju-dice against English "rooineks", all created a closed and stifling environment for one as emancipated as my mother had always been. On Sundays everyone wore black, no cooking or work of any sort could be done, and after church the residents sat on bentwood chairs on their verandas, bibles at the ready, visibly following their church's pious instructions for the day of rest and holiness.

The town is a beautiful one among rugged mountains with their Cape flora, fertile valleys and vineyards. The house to which my mother was taken as a bride was in a lonely valley outside the town. It was old and ramshackle and rat-infested and was reputed to be haunted. Dad used to go off to work and my mom was alone, away from the work and comradeship that she had enjoyed at the Herbarium, and away from the extended family she had always had access to. She told me how she used to wander in the rundown apple orchard at dusk, waiting for Dad to return, and how people passing who saw her in her floaty white dresses thought she was the ghost and hurried by. How upset she was when Dad squashed a rat with her silver hairbrush on the dressing table one night, and how alone she was when she was expecting her first child and could share her thoughts and worries with friends and family only by post.

Sometime before the baby was to be born they moved house, into a depressing semi-detached old cottage in a back street of the town. By then they had bought land and when my dad was not at work he was building his second house — and pregnant women of those days were kept out of sight and told to rest. When the birth started, at home with a part-time midwife in attendance, the only doctor in the town was busy. He prescribed "Twilight Sleep", the wonder drug of the times, in the early stages of labour and went off to attend other patients. The drug rendered my mother totally unable to participate in the birth, and the baby, a perfect little girl, suffocated. My mother was devastated, suffering what we would now recognise as post-natal depression, and it is little wonder that she felt that Stellenbosch was totally alien.

A year later my brother Peter was born — in Pretoria in the safety of Lyndall. The Stellenbosch house that Dad built was completed, and a quick-growing hedge and a developing garden made a private oasis in a hostile town. But fate was still not kind. Dad fell ill with typhoid and for three months was at death's door. There was no money, no salary or sick pay, and the Pretoria family helped out. Each day the resident nurse announced, "he will not last the night." It was amazing that he recovered, albeit with a damaged heart muscle, and debts were eventually settled. After all that, my mother never had any real feeling of security and the migraine headaches that plagued her until she was quite old began.

Peter became the centre of my parents' universe. He was a beautiful child and very bright and they devoted so much time to him that by the age of three he had learnt to read and could identify all the butterflies and other insects in my dad's collection, complete with Latin names. Mom told me he used to ask her to draw the nervous system of a rat or the digestive system of a pigeon, things she had learnt at college, for him as light entertainment. When I told her it sounded as though he was probably horribly spoilt and precocious she assured me that it was Peter who did the demanding to know. As I have known some children who are just born that way I believe her — and Peter remained brilliant, with an amazing memory and capacity for research.

I have only a few clear memories of Stellenbosch. In one I remember sitting on a small wooden bench made by my dad, in the bathroom having an injury attended to. I had been persuaded to take a ride in a billy cart made by my brother and a rusty nail had gone right through the arch of my foot. I can draw an accurate picture of the room and all it contained; the memory being burnt into me with the iodine no doubt. I was Peter's devoted slave, following him about and probably annoying him and his friends, and he used me as a guinea pig in his experiments. He had a work bench with his own woodworking tools attached to the side of the garage and much of his time was spent building bridges from apple boxes to span the mill stream, a concrete channel about a yard wide, that ran through the back of our garden. When each new bridge was finished I was the one chosen to try it out, and I remember falling through into the running water on several occasions. I clearly remember being told not to be such a baby and that I was an idiot to go over an unsafe bridge in the first place when I howled loudly after each collapse. But I was obviously a slow learner because I remember later in Salisbury obediently putting my finger into a termite nest when instructed to do so and being told again how silly I was to have done so when it came out covered in biting soldier termites.

Happier recollections are of wheelbarrows, full of the highly scented trumpet flowers of a creeper that festooned the house, being tipped into the mill stream. Mom found the scent overpowering at night so we helped to pick off most of the open flowers each evening.

I have no recollection of my sister Joan's birth when I was three, but from mid-1929 in Salisbury onwards much more survives.

## CHILDHOOD

Joan, Dad, Mary, ZoZo and Bob;       Mary, Peter, Joan about 1939

Xanadu                    Mary writing detective stories

Perhaps because it was wide open savanna country in Rhodesia
That was imprinted when I was very young
I have found that a complete feeling of belonging
Comes to me occasionally
When I am alone in the wide-open semi-desert landscapes
Of Central Australia.

# EARLY CHILDHOOD IN SOUTHERN RHODESIA

Salisbury, now Harare, the capital city of Southern Rhodesia, must have been a very small town in 1929. It had reached a population of 10,000 (Europeans) when the Second World War broke out in 1939.

The journey of at least five days and four nights from Cape Town by antiquated steam train must have been a marathon effort for my mom, with a new baby and Peter and me. It would have been one of the very few times when she did not have native servants or a children's nurse to deal with all the menial jobs. I wonder what she did about nappies in those times before disposables and even before plastic bags, as the washing facilities on the train consisted of a fold-down washbasin in each compartment, and a dreadful lavatory at the end of the corridor in each coach, where a trapdoor opened to spill the contents of the pan onto the track.

The coal-burning trains spewed cinders that often set-fire to the dry grass on the railway embankment, and if you stuck your head out of the window you risked getting "smuts" in your eyes — dreaded and very painful. I know from later journeys which I can remember that because catering and facilities were so primitive on the train ZoZo would have taken along all the food, demijohns of boiled water, and milk in the big picnic baskets that went everywhere with us in those days. Towards the end of the journey as the food ran out we were allowed buttered toast from the dining car to supplement the rusks that were so much a part of my childhood. It was considered by my mom that food prepared on the train was too risky. Even the bedding supplied by the railways — crisply starched white sheets and rigid army-style blankets embroidered with the R.R. symbol of Rhodesian Railways — were considered dubious, and we carried great canvas bags of bedding. Mom's worries about the food may have been justified. Jokes were told about parties of heavy drinking men demanding ice with their drinks until a stage was reached where they were told that they could have no more because the corpse who was being transported in the guard's van would go off if any more ice was diverted their way.

The mountains of luggage that I remember included iron-bound trunks, and native porters at the station pushed carts laden with amazing piles of suitcases topped by prams and tricycles. The rattling and rocking of the train, its clatter and the wonders of Africa seen from its windows were endless delight to us children, but Mom was no traveller and always suffered motion sickness.

Though I do not remember the house in which we lived when we arrived in Salisbury I can see and feel its very small front yard, an iron-bar fence with a gate and a brick-paved path and a very small Sealyham puppy being put into my arms by my dad. That was Puppy who bore that undignified name all his life, and I suppose it was because of the special event that the dog's arrival in my life represented that I have my first recollection of my dad. I knew at that time that he went to office, and I was very impressed by the Club, one of the main institutions of the town, where professional men went after work. Its pillared entrance and, to me, enormous size instilled a feeling of awe. This feeling of being impressed by the opulence of the corporate world has occasionally flashed back to me with the warm-milk smell of a licky puppy, so strangely are our memories and impressions linked.

We soon went into another house, in a suburb called Avondale, starting a series of fourteen moves in twelve years. Some houses we flitted through briefly because Mom did not like them and as soon as something better appeared we would pack up and go. Dad had had more than enough of building his own houses. They rented out the Stellenbosch house he had built for some years before selling it and when I visited South Africa in 1983 after an absence of thirty years a strange coincidence occurred. The Afrikaans wife of a university lecturer whom I was meeting for the first time in Natal turned out to be the daughter of the people who had rented and then bought the house, and she and I were the same age and she had virtually picked up where I had left off. Her memories of the garden lay-out, fig trees, mill stream and so on started where mine ended.

For us children, all the different houses, gardens and neighbourhoods were fun. Gardens were large and family life and activities, making one's own amusements, were the general pattern. Friends came to play or stay by invitation, we were taken and collected and watched over. A series of European nursemaids joined the household from the time when we were settled in Salisbury, and the native servants — a cook, houseboy, wash-boy and gardeners, were normal in the colonial set-up of the times. Avondale, a semi-rural suburb on a hill outside the town at that time, had houses on large plots of land, a welcome relief from the cramped garden of the first little house that I suppose was all that could be found for us when we first arrived. It had a dark cellar and Peter and his friend Alan locked me in it one afternoon and I was terrified.

Mom was a great storyteller and had animals called Ippamopsis-Bahoolies in her stories. They were composed of the balls of fluff that live mysteriously under beds (or did in pre-vacuum cleaner times) and the cellar was home to these not always friendly creatures.

Peter was losing his baby teeth and we were told about the tooth mouse and were not all that convinced. The tooth, a letter and a bit of cheese were put out on the veranda for the mouse and we crept out at night with a torch and found the ginger kitten eating the cheese and that the tooth was already gone, but there was no letter. Next day the money was there with a reply, thanking Peter for the tooth, so we knew we were being had, but we decided wisely to say nothing in case the funds dried up for subsequent teeth. We had the same attitude to Father Christmas—better to play along with the adults than to jeopardise our presents. In that house I learnt a bit about what cats' whiskers are for when I gave the ginger cat a haircut and it promptly got stuck in a pipe under the driveway. Major digging released it eventually.

The house next door burned down while we were in Avondale and the policeman who lived there with his mother had a big hole burned in his helmet. That and the money that was burnt because it was kept inside the piano was a source of amusement and satisfaction to Peter and me. We did not like policemen because nursemaids threatened us with them. Though it was all a bit frightening, the fire engine and all the excitement made it worthwhile, and we were much less frightened of policemen after that, knowing that they had houses that burnt down, not like us.

Dad had a Ford car with a dickey-seat and a luggage rack sticking out at the back and Peter and I were allowed to travel in it, hair streaming in the wind, thrilled to bits.

When we moved from Avondale, we settled for several years in 10 Montague Avenue, a large house with wide verandas and a huge garden with trees to climb, paths to ride bikes on, a summerhouse and sweeping lawns. I expect the move was to accommodate Peter, who had to go to school at the age of eight, and travel from Avondale would have been a problem. Here we had a playroom with our own gramophone and records, and the first European nursemaid that I remember clearly. She, like all the others who came briefly and usually left under a cloud after some disagreement with my mom, had been trained at a special mother-craft school in South Africa. Nursemaids saw to it that we wore hats in the garden, picked up and tidied after us, did the children's laundry and mending and took us for walks. They had no authority and were very much background figures. I wonder if we gave them a rough time, knowing that our parents would always side with us against them in any dispute.

In a house so full of servants, Mom's responsibilities were supervisory, seeing that the dusting was done properly, the furniture polished, the routine shopping done. Arranging the flowers each day, making the cakes (after the hard work of creaming the butter and sugar and beating the eggs had been done by the cook) and giving the orders seems to have been full-time activity. A long sleep in the heat of the afternoon after the hot dinner at 1.15 pm was sacred and could not be interrupted by the children. We were collected from school by our dad, who took an hour's break from office for the midday meal at home. After that dinner, we stayed in our own shuttered rooms, reading, having a nap, waiting for the cooler late afternoon to go and play outside.

The public service hierarchy in a colonial town like Salisbury had the same sort of protocol as existed in other outposts of the British Empire. The wives of high officials called on each other in the afternoons, leaving cards. Then by invitation they met for tea parties (all female, minus children) and occasional dinners that included husbands. This was the formal entertaining. Friends mostly met for sundowners, which were elaborately catered for with cheese straws, sausage rolls, nuts and savouries with the whiskey and soda or other alcoholic drinks. Soda was made in soda-siphons that had replaceable cartridges to make the bubbles. The women played tennis and as most houses had their own courts, they rotated the location of tennis parties. These too were lavishly catered for, and Mom was famous for her date scones and her chocolate cake. Children played in the playroom and kept away from the adults, occasionally being brought in, clean and especially dressed, to meet the visitors.

Mom did a lot of shopping, returning with dress-boxes of clothes "on appro" — most of which were returned to the store after long sessions of "trying on" that we witnessed. When she felt depressed she used to go to the shops and buy another hat, and she used to have her hair done each week by a hairdresser who was an expert with hot tongs, because perms had not yet appeared. The grocery, butcher and any other domestic shopping was done by ordering on the phone or sending one of the "boys" to fetch and carry home; and everything was put on account to be paid in a monthly session that children were asked not to interrupt while cheques were written.

The native servants' quarters were just basic rooms enclosed in a hedge on the back boundary of the land, with the most basic of furnishings. Bucket-style toilets, one for Africans, one for Europeans, were also situated on the back boundary, enclosed by hedges. "Sanitary lanes" ran behind every property, allowing the sanitary cart and the "night-soil removal team" to carry out their task before dawn. The natives' "kias" were strictly out of bound, and we were not allowed to go to the toilet at night for fear a passing native would grab at us through the flap that opened onto the lane. One of the tasks of nursemaids was to ferry potties back and forth to the distant W.C.

As a child I simply accepted that white people were different from black people — that's how the system was set up and it was the wordless conditioning to the only environment that I knew that established what I later saw as racist attitudes. For privileged children like us, so different from African children, there was never any question that this was how it should be because that was how it was. It was not until I was about ten that I began to see the system as unfair.

I remember the birth of my younger brother Bob in 1931. Only weeks before he was due we three children went down with whooping cough. We were isolated in our part of the house and Ouma rushed from Pretoria to take over from my mom who was not allowed near us. The baby was to be born at home in spite of the risk of infection. On the day of the birth my dad took the three of us to the Agriculture Department offices and we played in the gardens there until almost evening, wondering why we were being kept there but thinking it was fun with lemonade and biscuits on tap — things never in our diet of wholesome home bakes and milk - boiled, with a hideous skin on top because there was no pasteurised milk yet and ZoZo had an obsession about germs. When we went home we were told that we had a baby brother, but we still could not go near him or my mother because we were in quarantine, so it was not very interesting.

We added a much-loved Maltese poodle puppy (called Poodley of course) to our family about then and Joan and I used to dress him in baby clothes, including bonnet, and make him lie all day in the dolls' pram, often forgetting him for hours. He never objected.

Peter had started school, which was mandatory at eight years old, and he was very superior and remote from us girls because he was busy making crystal wireless sets, morse-code senders, and other boys' things. He still used us for experiments—like making us try to get a coin out of a jar of water that he had attached to a battery and giving us electric shocks. Once when he was being scathing about us when we were skating on the lino of the long corridors in our socks I lost my cool and threw the bone handle from my baby brother Bob's pram at him, hitting him on the top lip. His lip burst open, exposing his teeth, and blood poured everywhere. I did not wait to see what happened next but fled and crawled under the car in the garage, lying in the oil-soaked red dust — and I remember being absolutely certain that I would be taken by a policeman straight to gaol. It was very hot and stuffy under the car, and nothing happened, and it seemed like forever, and I went to sleep.

I gather that Mom came back from the hairdresser (on her bike), found a bleeding child waiting with a distracted nursemaid who had lost me, and Joan and Bob howling in chorus. Dad was summoned and took Peter to have his lip stitched up (he bore the scar for the rest of his life) and the hunt started for me. When I woke, after dark, and emerged oily and covered in red dust I had been given up for dead, or lost forever, or kidnapped, and I was welcomed with tremendous relief and joy and not a word was said about the "accident". I knew it had been premeditated murder and felt guilty for years.

For some reason or other I once accompanied the nurse-maid to town on her afternoon off, and she took me to see the film *King Kong*. I had never been to a "bioscope" before and would never have been allowed to see such a film, so sheltered were we from the world outside, and I was absolutely terrified. I had to have a night light for months afterwards because dark shadows were giant apes, and I was next on the menu.

I have no idea why we moved again in 1932 from that house which was so suitable, but perhaps owners returned, and leases ran out. I have always had the feeling that it was just a sort of inner restlessness in my mom that demanded that she start anew, reorganise the furniture, create or alter a new garden. Because I have her genes I can see she was probably looking for new learn-ing opportunities and some sort of a career to add a dimension to domesticity and make use of her great intellect. She was a mar-vellous homemaker but with the availability of servants she proba-bly had plenty of time to think how things might have been.

When we moved to 2 Baines Avenue I was six and had to go to school. Having had no nursery-school experience, not because it was unavailable — children could go into Kindergarten at five — but because my parents thought home was the best place to learn, it was an enormous step.

Magic moments when time stands still
And being a part of the Biosphere and the Continuum of Life
Is enough.

# CHILDHOOD

There were two government schools in Salisbury in those days and a Catholic Convent for girls and its separate equivalent school for boys. The sexes were completely segregated from kindergarten to matriculation, sports played were different and the different subjects taught and the emphasis placed on them were in keeping with the clear distinction between the expectations of males and females. It goes without saying that schools were entirely white. Schools in the native locations on the fringes of the town taught basic reading and writing to some African children.

When I look at early education for my grandchildren today, or even consider the comparatively gentle introduction that my own children had, I see why it is that I have always had an overburdening need to obey the rules — any rules, regulations or implied obligations no matter how trivial. The teacher was an authority figure and we were all terrified of the headmistress and one large, very overweight lady whom everyone called Tomcat. We lined up in crocodiles, filed into rooms filled with rows of two-seater desks with inkwells, chanted our responses, learned by endlessly repeating spelling, mental arithmetic, tables, lists of products of Brazil or countries of the British Empire. History was all about kings of England, and geography was about faraway places. Nature study was a relief from the tedium though there was no attempt to deal with anything Rhodesian.

As an adult, in times of great stress I have sometimes found myself saying the seven or twelve-times tables under my breath. I was always anxious about anything concerning figures, never fully understood the basics, and to this day I remain mathematically illiterate.

Our handwriting had to be of whatever style was being promoted at the time, and several changes were made; our books had to be blot-free; the greatest fear was of being ridiculed in front of the class for errors or being sent to the headmistress if one had dared to sound rude or answer back. I certainly learned to spell, and to understand grammar, and nothing even then could dampen my love for writing stories and essays. By the time I was nine I was sending books of animal stories to my patient godfather, who responded with postal orders for ten shillings — a fortune to me and my first earnings as a writer. By eleven I had a whole book of detective stories with the hero called Mr Blandley, because I read everything I could lay hands on and my dad used to buy detective story paperbacks for his own light reading. Agatha Christie, Ngaio Marsh and others were my models.

School uniforms, in that subtropical climate, consisted of a woollen gym-tunic like St Trinians' with yoke and three pleats front and back, white long-sleeved shirt, black bloomers with legs that could come down to the knees if extended, black polished leather shoes with white socks for juniors, and black stockings with regulation black suspender belt for seniors. It was not until I reached high school that a summer uniform was introduced. Then for a few months of the year we wore a summer-weight tunic and short-sleeved shirt and pale lisle stockings. We had broad-brimmed Panama hats with a school hatband and badge; a regulation woollen, cover-all swimming costume with green top, blue waistband and black bottom, and for PE at school we took off our tunics and pranced about in shirt and bloomers. For tennis, the summer sport in which we had to participate, we had short white tennis dresses; for hockey in winter we wore the normal school tunic and black stockings, but shirt colour was determined by the team to which you belonged. Add regulation black raincoats ("Mackintoshes" — pre-plastic), regulation hard school cases, regulation pencil cases, fingernail inspections every day, regulations about haircuts and absolutely no adornment except blue hair ribbons — no bangles, rings and, heaven forbid — earrings — and you will see that the aim was complete uniformity.

In order to survive, the idea as I saw it was to be as invisible as possible, to make no waves, to never excel to a point where you would be noticed, and above all to do as you were told. I realise now, that the fact that my surname was Brain probably had a lot to do with this. Knowing how children tease and pick on each other, I was probably avoiding having them chant "brainy, brainy".

A fair proportion of the school students were boarders whose families were farmers or lived in small communities that lacked schools. The boarding-school houses were on the perimeter of the school's sports fields and policed like prisons so that no one entered or left without permission. I used to feel sorry for the girls there though sometimes a little envious because they were such a close-knit community and seemed to have lots of fun, mostly by breaking rules and defying authority.

Dad dropped us off at our schools before 8 a.m. on his way to office and picked us up at 1 p.m. (when the school day ended) on his way home to dinner, until we were old enough to ride bikes to school. After we had all had the main meal of the day together he returned to office till late afternoon and we had a rest in a cool, shuttered house until afternoon teatime — served in the dining room by the houseboy — biscuits and cakes, embroidered linen cloth and fine china. Because all eating was formal and around the dining room table with one or both parents, there was much time for conversation and information. Certain subjects like money, scandals or anything vaguely connected to sex were never discussed in front of the children, but everything else was, and any real education I acquired as a child was from my parents, at home.

From the time when we went to school we were increasingly involved in natural history with my dad and sometimes with my mom) After school, at weekends and during holidays we drove into the surrounding veldt[2] and collected plants, insects, and

_____

[2]  Veldt - open, uncultivated country or grassland in southern Africa, a wide grassy plain. It is conventionally divided by altitude into highveld, middleveld, and lowveld.

rocks, and observed birds, weather patterns, soil erosion and all the other things that interested my dad. When he could not identify a plant, Mom always could.

The Baines Avenue house had its own tennis court. Dad had a study off the veranda and used to play classical music on a gramophone. There was a thick hedge between us and the next-door house and my friends and I made a cubby in it and used to dry the skins of mandarins and keep them as our secret rations. We also ground up bricks into a fine red powder, mixed it with water and ate that too. From the time I went to school I had a special friend, and we were always together and gradually my sister Joan was left out of our activities. She and our younger brother Bob became very close. Girls did not usually mix with boys, hardly ever even with brothers, but a six-year-old neighbour who did not know the rules used to hang around and one day he grabbed me behind the hibiscus bush and kissed me firmly on the mouth. He ran away and I don't think I saw him again until about ten years later when I was no longer averse to boys or kissing. By then he was an unattractive teenager and I thought I was already grown up.

Then we moved to 2 Fife Avenue which was remarkable only for the boarding house next door where young men and women, who Mom said were "common", lived, drank beer and "carried on". My friends and I were dying to know what the carrying on was and we used to climb into the high trees next to the boundary fence and watch them. They never did anything but lounge about and sometimes had arms entwined or did a little bit of cuddling, so we did not know what made them common or what they were carrying on. That was another really nice house with an enormous garden, and I don't know why we moved, but after flitting through another unsuitable one we were soon in the best house of all. I think it was first government house that was made available to Dad, and it was available because it was intended for the Chief Justice and there either wasn't one or maybe he had another house. *Fourways* was next to the Prime Minister's property and on the other side of the road from the Government

House estate. It was a magnificent house on five acres of land that was divided into four paddocks — one for the house with its rose garden, tennis court, avenue of mango trees, aviary and jacaranda trees; one for the vegetable garden and orchard full of guavas, custard apples and oranges, where gangs of low-security African prisoners, watched over by a guard with a rifle, used to do the heavy work several times a year; one that was just a grassy field with the garages and servants' quarters in a corner; and the wonderful back paddock where a mango orchard had been allowed to go wild and melt into a forest of large trees. It felt so remote to us kids that when we camped there it was like being in our own world.

There was an enormous Australian chestnut tree that was exciting to climb, and huge belombre[3] trees that were dangerous because the wood was so soft that branches could break. When we camped in the back paddock during school holidays we made elaborate houses out of canvas tarps with walls of old curtains. There were always lots of old curtains because most house moves required new ones. We used to take food with us to our camps and think we were quite independent, though supplies used to filter in from the house. The polo ground was next to our boundary, and we used to watch the games being played there from vantage points in high trees. Polo and cricket were the sports in that very British colony, and what was going on in the Mother Country was the important news.

It was at *Fourways* that our menagerie was at its greatest. To the dogs and cats and birds that had always been around, were added a lamb that had lost its mother and had to be hand reared, rabbits, guinea pigs, chameleons, fantail pigeons and all sorts of special birds in the large aviaries. At one stage, I had twenty-one charges that needed my individual attention before school. I loved them all and worried about them and going away, even for a few days, was something I would have preferred not to do. I still remember how sad I felt when we left for a short holiday

---

[3]   Bela sombra or Belhambra—'*Phytolacca dioica*

to visit the Zimbabwe Ruins and I was worried about leaving my charges to be fed by the old retainer, Shilling, who had been our houseboy ever since we arrived in Salisbury.

The house was remarkable in that it had five pantries. There was a butler's pantry next to the panelled living room for Mom to arrange the flowers in; an open pantry off the kitchen and three locked pantries for stores, drinks and cool-storage of vegetables and perishables. The ballroom/dining room was a huge, high room, panelled in white-painted wood. Our dining room furniture and a few couches occupied only a small part of it. There were many bedrooms and wide verandas with tubs of bright geraniums, and an outside toilet; and there was a rondavel in its own garden for guests. The mango trees used to bear so heavily, every kind from big green Durban to small red kidney-shaped fruit, that wooden boxes that had held two 4-gallon cans of paraffin were filled with ripe fruit and delivered to friends. They were always left rather apologetically because there was such abundance and mangoes were not as highly prized then. Friends who had an avenue of avocados had a similar problem with over-abundance and the rotting fruit used to turn to green slime under the enormous trees. When war brought shortages of imported goods and there was no face cream available, avocados were used to make substitutes.

I went to high school while we were at *Fourways* and was taken to piano lessons — which I hated. Peter and my mom were both very competent pianists and ZoZo had been a singer in her youth. It was soon obvious that lessons for me were a waste of money.

Our Christmas holidays from Salisbury were mainly family ones when Dad came along and drove us to Pretoria to stay on our grandparents' farm, *Xanadu*. The journeys were long (over 1000 km on terrible roads) and difficult, in a series of Fords, Buicks and Terraplanes[4], none bought new and all liable to tyre troubles, broken springs and mechanical problems. Dad and Peter could fix

---

[4]   Terraplanes were manufactured by the Hudson Motor Car Company of Detroit, Michigan between 1932 -1938

anything, and we all knew about carburettors and blocked fuel pumps and vaporising petrol. We travelled, heavily overloaded, with the six of us in the car, with mountains of luggage in a big canvas bag on roof racks, strapped on the luggage rack, and around our feet. The necessary (to Mom) demijohns of safe water and baskets of food under the kids' legs were all just part of such expeditions. A regularly car-sick mother and occasionally car-sick children must have been no fun for my dad. We used to stay over-night in Umvuma and sometimes also at Louis Trichardt to break the journey for Mom, and I never remember Dad being anything but pleasant and patient, or the journeys from my point of view being anything but exciting.

Rhodesian roads, outside the towns, were "strips"—essentially single-lane, with two narrow ribbons of tar on a gravel road base where the median and marginal parts were mostly rough, loose and eroded. Passing an approaching vehicle required each to vacate one strip and brave the unstable terrain.

*Xanadu* was a wonderful place. It had a long low farmhouse set in beautiful gardens; a poultry farm where Ouma had her 10,000 black Australorpes; the cattle and the fields of lucerne and corn for their feed, and a dairy which were Oupa's part of the farm; huge barns full of hay, and tool sheds, machinery sheds, generator rooms, windmills and dams. The river that ran through the fields on its way to the Haartebeestepoort Dam had quiet reaches with willows and a punt; the Magaliesburg Hills behind the farm were within riding distance when we saddled the old horses and the couple of nearly derelict mules that were there for grandchildren to enjoy.

Best of all, there was a swimming pool (a water reservoir) and it had the famous "golden syrup" engine in a shed next to it. Oupa was somewhat eccentric, and this engine was his pride and joy. Its long belt used to slip off the flywheels until he discov-ered that Lyles Golden Syrup, in green and gold tins, "By appoint-ment to the King", cured the problem. Much of our fun on the farm holidays involved the swimming pool and Uncle Eugene (son of Eugene Marais the writer).

Lots of stories were told about Oupa's eccentricity — how he could never buy only one or two of anything needed for the farm. When he died the work sheds contained hundreds of taps, tools, barrels of nails and screws, parts for engines long dead — enough to restock several hardware stores. He is also reputed to have attended to a cow suffering from advanced bloat by using a brace and bit to perforate its swelling belly when no vet was available. The cow went down like a balloon whose air is released and with much the same sound, and it died. He cured another cow that had cut an artery and had blood spurting from its neck by stuffing cement from a handy building operation into the hole, and this time the treatment worked. When the flesh had healed the plug fell out and the cow was as good as new.

Oupa continued to work as a solicitor until he died; the farm was his hobby, and his part did not pay and was kept going by his legal practice. He used to sit at night at his desk with the green leather top reading Latin and ancient Greek and I suppose Peter owed him his interest and ability in such literature, as I do my much less developed one. He was so courteous to us, telling us about Ulysses and about the Medusae with their hair made of snakes, and we loved him. He could never turn away anyone in need and used to buy books of tickets that entitled the homeless to a night's lodging and a good meal at the Salvation Army Hostel. These he gave to the old drunks and lost souls who came regularly to his office.

There were usually cousins spending part of the holiday at the farm. Dick Findlay was a competent artist from an early age, and I used to paint with him, though his expertise and my bungled efforts were not in the same class. He went on to become a famous watercolour artist, his bird and plant series on South African stamps a lasting tribute to his talent.

Many of the small-holdings on the road to *Xanadu* had "poor white" occupants and some of them came knocking on the door at the farm. Ouma protested bitterly and in vain whenever Oupa asked them in, plied them with tea and cake and sent them off with a few pounds (Sterling). Ouma would then spray for fleas and wash the cushion covers and nag about seating such unsavoury characters in her lovely drawing room.

Ouma's poultry business was a thriving success and she supplied major hospitals and a long list of clients with eggs and dressed chickens. During our visits, she and my mom used to get through great piles of darning and mending, sitting in the huge drawing room while the children had the run of the farm. When the sponge cakes and all the other home-baked things for which she was famous were being made I remember sitting on the table next to her and being given the bowls to lick out when I was very small.

The natives who worked on the farm all lived there in round thatched mud brick cottages (rondavels) each on its own plot of land on which they grew mealies (sweet corn) and vegetables and kept a few hens and goats. Their extended families lived with them, and they were even paid pensions when they were too old to work. The women worked in the fields at certain times of year, weeding, and two were house servants, doing the ironing and helping with the cleaning—though there were houseboys, cook-boys, garden boys and all those other "boys" needed to look after the poultry business.

Oupa was regarded as an unnecessarily generous employer because of the way he ran the farm and looked after his people.

Just before WWII a young German lady came to work for Ouma, supervising the housekeeping and helping with bookkeeping. She was shy and nervous and her English was not very good and she used to go for long, lonely walks. No one knew where she went on her days off when she went into town. When the war started everyone became paranoid about spies and subversive activities. There were deep divisions between Afrikaans and English-speaking citizens, with a considerable proportion of the former supporting Hitler's regime. Whispers about Frau Winkelman started. Could she be reporting on traffic going to an army camp on the other side of the mountain or on aircraft flying up the valley towards the bombing range beyond the dam? When she committed suicide on the slopes of the Magaliesberg no one was told about it and the secret was kept for several years. On the farm it was thought she had found a way to disappear because of the enquiries officials had been making.

Thinking about her now, I can imagine her loneliness—she could not have gone home if she had wanted to, and she was facing incarceration because of her nationality.

Every second or third year our Christmas holiday was a visit to the sea. We travelled by train and Dad did not come, except for once that I remember when we went to Sea Point near Cape Town. I think it was a disastrous holiday because we stayed in a private hotel that Mom had booked into and which proved to be far from the beach, run by unpleasant people who provided dreadful food and fed the nursemaid who had accompanied us the left-overs scraped from our plates and reassembled on hers. Peter, who must have been eight, got lost when the nurse took Joan and me back to the hotel for breakfast, and I remember the acute agitation until he was found hours later.

Other holidays at the sea were always at Muizenberg, staying at the old *Ocean View Hotel* that was one of my mother ZoZo's holiday places when she was growing up and was still there when I was at university.

One year we went to Hermanus in the Cape (over 2,500 km). Ouma had hired a house there and an aunt and her children were there too. It was a dreadful holiday for the adults as everyone came down with chicken pox. Our cousins and their mother arrived with it, and no one escaped. I remember being so sick that I was delirious, got up in the night and dressed my calamine-painted body in my mom's smart new coat and skirt and wandered off, thinking that I was going somewhere with the Mormons and Brigham Young. I had been reading a book about their journey to Utah. I can still recall how real it felt and how carefully I dressed so as not to offend the Mormons because as a heathen (even then!) I must take special care and not be rude.

That was a strange holiday in other ways too, because there was a girl staying in a house nearby who could have been my twin sister. We were so similar in appearance that her family and mine and all our friends and acquaintances mistook us for each other. We never spoke, both being so embarrassed, and it was weird to be confronted by one's mirror image. The chicken pox was almost a blessing as it kept me out of sight for a while and then the healing spots made me recognisably different.

We had to vacate *Fourways* when I was twelve. A Chief Justice arrived, plus large, fat, garden-party-organza-clothed wife who was fanatically interested in boxing and wrestling and used to sit in the front row at prize fights and "forget that she was a lady". We were told in hushed tones how she completely let the side down, yelling "kill him, knock his block off" in her excitement.

When I visited my old home town that had become Harare in what had become Zimbabwe in 1983, I found that the land that had been the four paddocks of *Fourways* and the wonderful old house and outbuildings had been totally cleared. Instead of the forests of trees, the gardens, the house and driveways and other buildings, there was emptiness with a short dry grass cover. Because the old Government House on the other side of the road was now the Presidential Palace, all surrounding areas that might have concealed guerrilla forces or irate citizens had been laid bare. I wept for the vandalism that epitomised the alien place that my spiritual home had become. What has happened in the years since, of course, makes the clearing of one block seem trivial.

We moved a few streets away to a comparatively small house that Mom hated. I don't know if she had some sort of health problem, but she had insomnia and when she did sleep she said tubes came through the window bars like octopus limbs to invade her. She had us all scared. When she found out that the ground on which the house had been built was in a part of the town where a considerable massacre of natives had taken place long ago, we packed up and fled. Her insomnia and dreams disappeared, and she was convinced that it was the evil energies of that fateful place that had caused the problem. So once again we moved and 22 Fife Avenue was a pleasant house and memorable for me because there I raised Bess the baby duiker, a small-medium sized antelope and two baby parrots found in a nest when a tree was cut down. It was also memorable because war was declared, and all our lives were going to be affected in different ways.

I have a clear and photographic memory of the sitting room, all of us there eating Cadbury chocolate after our lunchtime dinner, and the wireless was tuned to the BBC in London. We listened to the speeches and Mom wept, remembering the horrors of the First World War and fearing for Peter who would soon be called up in this one.

My brother Peter was in the first batch of students who sat for the Cambridge Certificate exam instead of the matriculation. His transitional year did so in fifth form. By getting a high score in it a matriculation exemption was given and students could proceed straight to university. There was no age barrier to university entry though most students even then stayed on for another year at school.

Peter went to Cape Town University in 1940, just after war was declared, and when he reached eighteen and could have been called up for military service (there was conscription of all able-bodied men from eighteen to forty) he was allowed to complete his B.Sc. degree before he joined up and was posted to a Signals Corps and ended up in Italy. He was involved in very early Radar work that was all top secret.

## WAR YEARS

A Baobab tree

Mary and Geoff

A hornbill (Photo Shantanu Kuveskar)

## UNIVERSITY DAYS

University of Cape Town

Mary graduating

And the magic of the wide, wild veldt is all around us,
Lapping like a sea at the fringes
Of our illuminated island

# WAR YEARS AND UNIVERSITY DAYS

Although Rhodesia was so far away from Britain, it was a colony and the whole white population of the country felt involved in any war that affected what they called "home". Most Rhodesians had probably never been there. All the eligible men were mobilised and started to leave. There was a general call for women to step into jobs that had been vacated to keep things going.

Mom announced that she was going to apply for a job, and she was so infuriated when Dad and Peter asked her what use she thought she could possibly be, that there was an eruption at the dinner table and for the first time that I can remember she stormed out.

Next day she registered at a typing school and in a few weeks she had a secretarial job, at first at the Correspondence School headquarters (distance education having started by this time) and later in the government legal service. She was to become a legal secretary and conveyancer very rapidly and it was not long before the men in the house could see that she meant business.

I remember clearly how I felt when I came back from school one day and she was not at home to receive me. We were long past the resident nursemaid stage by then, and she only worked school hours to be there for us, and this day she was delayed. I felt upset, slightly indignant and put upon. How could I still have been so self-centred at thirteen?

When Italy came into the war all the African colonies felt endangered. In Salisbury, so remote from everywhere, we dug a very deep slit trench in the back yard and had plans to get into it if planes came to bomb the city. Why it should be safer than a house with the hit and miss aim of a night bomber was never explained to me. It used to be said years later that the Italians did not enter Kenya, Uganda or Tanganyika because when they looked over the borders and saw the roads they thought they were tank traps.

After about a year and with mosquitoes breeding in the trench we filled it in and planted sweet peas, for which deep trenching was the suggested optimal preparation.

Our lives went on much as usual during the war, but with restrictions and rationing of petrol, and many things in very short supply. Just about no manufacturing was done in Rhodesia and the Union of South Africa was feeling the pinch too. Silk stockings (before nylon) became a luxury given to girls by American servicemen. Tobacco exports boomed because of demand for the forces. Anyone adult who did not smoke was a rarity.

The colonies were used as training places for the RAF; and there was an influx of evacuees from Britain. I clearly remember the conversations of ladies over morning tea bemoaning the fact that the British migrants did not understand the natives and were ruining them for everyone else. How scandalous it was that a woman someone knew had called out from the bathroom to a native servant to bring her a cake of soap, and he had handed it in through the partly open door while she was in the bath! And women were wandering about scantily clad in front of houseboys and letting them wash intimate articles of apparel — things that we Rhodesians would never do. On top of that, the wages they were paying their servants were undermining the whole system. That and the communists who were already causing unrest among our natives and making them cheeky and lazy was an awful state of affairs! The golden age of isolated colonialism was fast coming to an end.

My sister Joan very nearly died from mercurial poisoning when she was eleven. She had dandruff and a friend of Mom's recommended a solution he had obtained from the chemist to cure the problem. It had to be rubbed into the scalp and washed off with a special soap. No one knew that it contained lots of mercury. It cured the dandruff, but Joan had a massive haemorrhage and had a special calcium remedy flown from the USA which may be what saved her. She was looked after at home because Mom fervently believed that people only went to hospital to die. When she was very ill she woke and told Mom that she had had a dream in which she met a girl called Jean in a pine wood, and the girl said she was her sister. Mom nearly freaked out, babbling to us that Joan was dying and that the baby girl who had been stillborn had come to collect her. We had never heard about that baby until then and it was pretty scary stuff. But the dream marked the start of a recovery, and the strange matter was never referred to again.

Dad was by this time very much involved in putting together a Flora of Southern Rhodesia. He had been collecting specimens on all our expeditions over the years and was in the habit of working for long hours at weekends at the Herbarium that was an outside building at the Queen Victoria Museum, in front of the Girls' High School in Moffat Street. I had had a private collection of pressed plants since I was a small child, and identifying the plants, mounting them and labelling them, as well as drawing them, was one of my absorbing occupations. While Peter was away at university I moved into his "outside" room that was part of an enclosed veranda and I used to have my collection, drawings and all the other things connected with my interest in nature around me. And it was close to the animals and birds that I loved and looked after. I was not interested then in man-made things, or in the idea of travel to see cities or other cultures. And nothing much has changed for me in that respect.

My dad travelled a lot in the course of his work, visiting the Research Stations he had established and the special farms where Africans were being taught about land management, giving him the opportunity to collect plants from all parts of the country. When he was at home the family trips we took into the veldt with him were still the highlights of my childhood, even when they were no more than visiting a piece of railway embankment that had recently burnt because cinders from the train had set fire to the dry vegetation. There we would find the wildflowers that followed such fires, bringing bits home to identify and sometimes to paint.

I remember one not-so-ordinary foray into the veldt. On this occasion we wandered into a grove of M'hobohobo[5] trees, attracted by the profusion of golf-ball-sized yellow fruits among their enormous leaves. The ground was covered with rotting and fermenting fruit, whose alcoholic propensities were well known among the Africans who made a potent brew from over-ripe fruit. The place was alive with birds, squabbling among the branches as they ate the fruit, and a few blue-tummy monkeys swung away through the trees when we approached. On the ground, among the fallen yellow globes, lay three huge hornbills. Two appeared to be dead, their ridiculous heavy beaks bent at strange angles on their scraggy necks. The third sat more or less on his feet, a pathetic, bedraggled, beak-heavy object. As we approached he ruffled his feathers, opened one eye and attempted to stretch his neck and raise his head, and he sang a sad little drunken song. He was the only completely lovable drunk I have ever seen. He looked debauched and wise, yet infinitely foolish, and the song he sang was far from that prescribed for any self-respecting hornbill. We could see then that his companions were not dead but were merely sleeping off their excesses and we christened the three Sotto, Blotto and Sotto-Voce. We did not like to leave them sprawling on the ground in their helpless state. Their awesome beaks were more hindrance than defence. When old Sotto-Voce attempted a few rolling steps, he tipped over on his nose and had to be untangled and set up on his feet again.

We wiped the sticky M'hobohobo juice off their beaks and whiskers and cleaned off the attending ants that were already exploring among their feathers, and though we handled them gingerly at first, expecting to lose fingers if they regained their senses, the only response was unmistakable snores from Blotto and Sotto, and additional fragments of melody from Sotto-Voce. And a snore is a very strange sound to emerge from the horny nostrils

---

[5]  Mahobohobo tree - *Uapaca kirkiana* sugar plum or wild loquat

of as bizarre a creature as an inebriated hornbill. When we had cleaned the birds we left them in a nest of dry grass in the shelter of a rocky outcrop where they would not be baked by the sun, away from the fallen fruit. We returned the next day to see if they had survived, and there was no trace of them — no tell-tale feathers to show that they had met a violent death. Presumably, they had recovered and returned to their usual haunts — hornbills with awful hangovers, hunched in quiet shady places nursing their beaks.

♠♠

In the second year of the war, my dad's contract with the government suddenly came to an end. It had been renewed every five years and he was to find that in spite of the promises he had received (and because he was unbusinesslike and left such things to work themselves out) he was not eligible for a pension. Anyone who joined the Service after the age of forty was not eligible, but he had been assured that when the time came his situation would be reviewed and he would be looked after. The whole structure of the Agriculture Department was to change. There would no longer be a Director, and instead there would be a Minister of Agriculture. A young bureaucrat was to fill that new post. Dad was asked to work instead on a project connected with tobacco farming at the Trelawney Research Station, which was a considerable drive of several hours away from Salisbury. Although such things were never discussed in front of the children, I imagine that the change meant a big cut in salary, worry about finance for the future, and for my mom, who was a great worrier, the beginning of a feeling of great insecurity. Luckily she was fast becoming qualified to earn, though pay for part-time women's work was poor.

We moved house again, probably for financial reasons, going to a small modern house in a new suburb with the first electric stove we had ever had. This 13 Bates Street house was rented furnished and some of our things were crowded in too, the rest going to the house that was supplied to Dad at Trelawney.

Dad was away except for infrequent weekends; Peter was far away at university; Oupa's death in Pretoria at this time of upheaval was shattering for my mom; war was telling us that the world was not the friendly place that it had always seemed; and I was aware of all the tensions because I was at last growing up and feeling a world outside myself.

A baby blue-tummy monkey and a tiny black Cairn terrier puppy for me to mother were my main interest at this time—the former going to a farm later where it was able to return to a troupe that lived in the wild, and Benjy moving with the family to Bulawayo later while I was at university.

We had a couple of school holidays at the Research Station. Dad was working on the life cycle of the tobacco aphid that was a serious problem for the tobacco crops. He was to find where the insect over-wintered when the fields were empty and how to control it. He found eventually that a sort of native spinach growing wild in the veldt and often abundantly near the native quarters between the tobacco fields was the main culprit and that by eliminating it the problem of infection of young tobacco plants each season could be much diminished.

Trelawney was a wonderful place with its huge tobacco barns where the golden leaves hung in bunches from long poles on racks and fires had to be kept burning day and night to dry them. The African "boys" who had to be on night shift sang or played on Jews-harp sort of musical instruments, keeping themselves awake and frightening off the spirits that populated their nights. From our beds in the rambling old farmhouse that Dad lived in we heard the faint music, and the faraway drums and shouts from more distant native kraals.

Three white families lived on the station, and it was a friendly place. What made it very special was that night-apes (or bush babies) lived in Dad's house. They were the most beautiful creatures with their enormous eyes. They were nocturnal and emerged from their boxes on top of cupboards in the fully screened house at dusk. A special "piccaninny" was employed to catch their food each day. Armed with a jam jar, a fly swat and a butterfly net he spent all day catching grasshoppers, katydids, cicadas and beetles and the jar was put on a table for the "nagaapies" to help themselves. The insects were alive, having been stunned and not killed by the collector. The lid was left loose, and the little animals learned to lift it up, reach in and grab a wriggling creature and replace the lid. They were very intelligent and amazingly acrobatic. They could leap from on top of a high cupboard, land on the rim of a wineglass without knocking it over and fly off up onto a curtain all in one swift move. Mom was afraid of them because they used to leap onto the head of anyone passing by and seemed to know that she was afraid and pick on her as she walked along dimly lit passageways.

The house was also home to an interesting species of small bats that came in through some small hole in the eaves. They used to swoop about just above our heads before going off to hunt outside at night. Peter wanted a rare sort of flea that inhabited bats for a university assignment so he and my dad made catapults, loaded them with orange peel and managed to knock a bat down for long enough to catch a few of its fleas (and to get well bitten) before the bat flew off unharmed.

Once when we were travelling to Trelawney to spend a school holiday there, with three children, parents, old dog Puppy, Benjy and four grey Persian kittens in a grossly overloaded car, we had a head-on collision with a farm truck. The road, through granite sand country, was two deep ruts and a large sump-bumping median ridge and coming round a bend straight into the setting sun Dad saw the oncoming vehicle too late to do anything. All the occupants of the truck, all Africans, were drunk. Those on the tray shot off and picked themselves up and disappeared into the bush. Both cars had been crawling along so the damage was to radiators and the injuries were bumps from flying forward. Mom had just put the sun visor down and hit that, otherwise she might have gone through the windscreen. Dad was bruised by the steering wheel, Bob in the back banged his mouth on the back of the front seat, and Joan and I were mainly bruised round the legs by all the luggage. Poor old Puppy developed dropsy afterwards, his heart being affected by the bumping he had had, and the kittens had to be rescued from where they had fled into the bush. We were lucky that no one was killed.

The few days that we spent on the station that time were unhappy. Mom's concussion kept her in bed, and everyone was very sore and sorry, and when the car was fixed at the nearby village garage we went home.

I wrote the Cambridge Certificate in 1941. I had had coaching in maths at the very last moment and all the other subjects were easy because somewhere along the way I had learnt how to study and how to pass exams. Now I could proceed to university. My friends all stayed on for the extra year that was advised to prepare for tertiary education with bridging instruction in the subjects that would be studied. I am sure I was only allowed to go on so young because 1942 was to be Peter's degree year and after that he would have to join up, and it seemed a good idea for him to be there for me in my first year.

Looking back, it surprises me that in an unsettled period like that with the Forces using Cape Town for R and R leave they let me go at all. I would not have wanted either of my daughters so far away from home under those conditions, so young. The recent, 19.02.2012, celebration of the 70th year anniversary of the day that Darwin was bombed by the Japanese brought back many memories. However, that event that was so significant for Australians was presumably just another remote wartime horror for people in an African Colony of the British Empire!

On the day that I turned sixteen in February 1942 — 22.02.1942 — I caught the train to Cape Town with Peter, to register for a Science degree, majoring in Botany. For as long as I could remember I had known that one day I would be a botanist like my mom, and that and a nice husband and a houseful of children was all I had ever wanted. I was elated at being allowed at last to put school and home behind me and start on making my own life.

Long journeys by steam trains across Africa from Salisbury to Cape Town had a magic that no other form of transport can compete with. Five nights and four days were a sort of limbo, disconnected from the ordinary, about to enter the realms of the new. Friendships blossomed, and everything was Technicolor — stopping at small stations and sidings, hearing the crunch of footsteps and the dream-like voices of people catching the train in the night; seeing the time-worn face of Africa unfold before one's eyes. Like disembodied spirits we could watch and not be involved. The tribal people came to the train in Bechuanaland to sell their hand-carved wooden ornaments. We saw the poverty and the hunger at times of drought when small black children ran alongside the train as it moved off holding out their hands and begging for food.

Students like me became part of a close-knit unit, travelling the long distance in groups so that whole carriages on the trains were reserved only for us at the times when university was starting or the holidays were beginning. When I went into Women's Residence in my second year I found that the Rhodesians carried on this grouping and that they shared flats in the residence, excluding any non-Rhodesians. We felt we were different from the South Africans and that Rhodesia was the centre of the universe.

♠♠

The University of Cape Town in 1942 was still as its architect had designed it. All the buildings on the magnificent site on the slopes of Devils Peak were of the same construction and appearance. It fitted in on the side of Table Mountain, beautiful, tasteful and looking as though it belonged there. The sloping site meant hundreds of steps between the levels. Wide avenues of granite stairs up the centre from the level on which the Residences stood, across the level with all the Faculty buildings, and up to the Athenaeum-style Jamieson Hall with the enormous Library block on one side and the Students' Union on the other. Up behind, among the pine woods, were the golf course (more used by lovers than by golfers) and parking areas. There were very few cars and a student with one (or even access to one) was a rarity. Everyone came by train to Rosebank or Rondebosch and there was a bus service up to the De Waal Drive that ran below the rugby field at the bottom of the main university property. Walking was the usual transport, and because of the location much was decidedly uphill. On the lower side of the De Waal Drive the university property extended almost to the railway line and in those days it had a famous rose garden, oak woods and the tennis courts. Near the bottom were the Registrar's office and houses for the Chancellor and a few high-up university people. As it expanded greatly later the additional buildings that sprang up around the original core were a jumble of styles, heights and modes of construction. Concrete fortresses, steel and glass towers, they were out of keeping with the rest, resulting in a sprawl that jars and conflicts with the beauty of the mountain.

The boarding house where Peter had lived throughout his university time was next to the Rondebosch railway station. I joined him there, and had a narrow, dark room, more like a passageway, that opened onto a partitioned balcony overlooking the tennis court. The boarding house was run by Mrs Gertrude Trollip — this was her real name, not one I dreamed up. The student group at "Maseru" consisted of Peter, a very handsome friend of his called Ian, two girls who were also at UCT, and me. There was a young mother with a small child whose husband was away in the Navy, and a young accountant; and for a while a physicist who was working on top secret radar or something like that. All the other permanent boarding house people were old—some almost senile.

Apart from the many rooms in the rambling old house there was a comparatively modern annex in the garden with about a dozen occupants, and there were two rondavels that were very superior, self-contained, accommodation for two couples. The house was next door to the old Dutch Reformed Church, and we used to watch the black-clothed flock going back and forth on Sundays. I think in retrospect that the food and even the student accommodation were very sub-standard, but we were a young and happy group and all that did not matter. We had lots of fun at meals, played tennis and probably were an irritation to the older inhabitants. It was a long walk through Rondebosch village and up the very steep Stanley Road to the university. There was a café at the top of the road on the corner with the De Waal Drive that was much frequented by students — and called *The Rob*—where we used to eat toasted sandwiches and drink cokes.

I remember often walking along Stanley Road in a group of friends and all of us completely overcome with mirth—what about I do not know. Those were completely happy, carefree days and the serious attitude, bordering on shyness, that I realise had been my public face at school, had flown. I loved the learning in the freedom of a university where it was up to me and everything was relevant to my interests; the social life of masses of friends, boyfriends, dances, outings to films; trips to the sea, walking and climbing on that most beautiful Table Mountain; and the falling in and out of love that went with the territory.

My serious boyfriend Bob joined up and was sent to Italy at the end of that first year, but his family had adopted Peter and me as regular members of their household by then, and I continued to visit for years afterwards, long after I had stopped thinking of Bob. Peter and I used to walk the several miles to their house at night, through pine woods and quiet streets, and with a brother as escort I was free to be out and about after dark, going there or just going for walks as groups of young people did through the university suburbs.

The war was very much part of the fabric of things, though it seldom came close emotionally. We had young sailors, army and even airmen staying briefly at our boarding house on their way through the Cape, and they added interest; and the working at canteens that all of us girls did a couple of times a month, making fruit salad and waiting at tables in the city, were added excitement. There was one frightful tragedy that touched us all and brought war home to us, however. We had had a girl boarding for a couple of weeks whose fiancé had been killed. She was returning to her studies after an interruption, and she was quiet and withdrawn. We did not get to know her and went about our carefree ways. One evening she threw herself under the city-bound electric train that our young boarding house group was planning to catch to go to a City Hall concert. We watched the drama at the station, not realising who the victim was, and we even saw the awful, scattered body bits when the train moved back. She had been so beautiful, so young, and we all felt such guilt at not knowing she was so desperately unhappy.

At the end of that year Peter joined up and was soon sent to North Africa and then to Italy, and I returned to Salisbury where the family was getting ready to move again. Dad had completed his work at Trelawney and had accepted a temporary post at the Bulawayo Museum as Herbarium Curator, which would enable him to complete his Flora. I returned to university and moved into Women's Residence, joining the Rhodesian contingent there, and I was based there for the next four years.

On holidays to Bulawayo, where the family lived in a large and spacious flat above the Library, opposite the Museum, I met Geoff, a geologist who was an instructor at the RAF training base at Lockhart near the city. (I had more or less decided not to include this account in my reminiscences as it was just a private episode. But having re-read it in all the letters recently, I realise it typifies the wartime years and the very different world and values in which I was growing up, and it was certainly part of my emotional development.) Geoff used to spend all his spare time at the Museum where he had become a friend and colleague of my dad. He had been invited to the flat and had become my mom's favourite visitor. She told me, years later, that she saw in him the reincarnation of the man she had loved who had been killed in WW1 and that was why she had been so supportive of our friendship, hoping that things might work out for *us* in *this* war, a generation later. He was thirty, I was seventeen and we fell hopelessly in love. We had the approval of my parents because they trusted him and knew he would not let them down so I was safe and could remain a teenage romantic of the sort that hardly exists today — in a relationship that was all about love and commitment but **certainly no sex before marriage**. We had a typical wartime "romance, all dreams and hopes for a future. He was from Yorkshire and married — had been since he was nineteen, and he had been living apart from his wife for several years before he had been posted to Rhodesia. His wife was living with a parachute regiment commander in Britain. He was lonely and displaced, and I was a starry-eyed girl. Like so many romances ours was doomed by circumstances largely beyond our control not to work out, but it coloured my life and added immeasurably to my happiness until he was sent back to Britain towards the end of the war.

A long silence, with no letters to me or my family, followed Geoff's return to Britain. He, honourably, had made no promises to me, but I hoped and worried and tried to continue as though everything was going to be all right. Eventually my mom ZoZo was told that his wife was having a complete nervous breakdown because her partner had been killed in the Arnhem parachute drop and she had tried to commit suicide. There was no one, no family, no friends to help her and Geoff had no choice but to look after her and take her back into his life. I was such an idealist that I wanted no part of what I thought would probably end up a messy divorce so I wrote a goodbye letter and moved on.

I have realised, with the insight that comes with age, that what I learned from it enabled me to choose wisely and find great happiness, later, in marriage to the right person, so it determined the course of my life as an adult to a very large degree.

I had met Bill, whom I was later to marry, under similar war-time circumstances at the Museum during 1944. He was training to be a pilot with the R.A.F. and, having just completed a B.Sc degree in Geology in Belfast, Northern Ireland, also came regularly to the Museum. There he met my dad, and like so many young men far from home in those days he was brought over to the flat to have a meal and meet the family. We became good friends, but my heart was elsewhere then and it was only when he came back to Rhodesia to a job with the Geological Survey that we met again, fell in love and decided to marry.

I graduated in 1944 with a B.Sc degree in Botany and Zoology and the Botany Medal. I was lucky enough to be given a junior demonstrator-ship that enabled me to stay on for a M.Sc. year without being a financial drain on the family. Mom was working at the Bulawayo Supreme Court and Dad was completing his Museum work that year. When I was looking for a subject for a thesis I had the good fortune to be advised by Dr A.L. du Toit, South Africa's famous geologist and a "father" of Continental Drift, who was a friend of my botany professor. He suggested that I should do a thesis on prehistoric plants because there were no palaeobotanists in Africa, and he supplied the material for the thesis. He burrowed in the deep recesses of the pockets of his greatcoat (he was a very elderly by then and a frail, ant-like gentleman) and he pulled out a much-crumpled envelope from among the pipe tobacco, sealing wax and bits and pieces. In the envelope were the fossil cuticles of Triassic plants that had jumped off the rocks that he was splitting to find fossils at Bethlehem in the Orange Free State some years before. So, I did a thesis on *Dicroidium* cuticles[6], the Botany department structured a special course in Palaeobotany for me, and, though I did not know it then, the direction of much of the rest of my professional life was determined.

I received my M.Sc. degree at the end of 1945. At the same time, my family left Rhodesia for good and went to Pretoria. There they moved in with Ouma in the house in Waterkloof to which she had gone after selling *Xanadu*. She had tried to go on living on the farm for some years after Oupa died, and her son George and his family had even tried living with her there, but things had not worked out and she had bought her daughter Baba's house in town.

Dad worked for a couple of years as a consultant to the Union Government on soil conservation. Mom went into a legal firm as Secretary/Conveyancer and Joan started her nursing training. Bob would finish his schooling in Pretoria and later go on to Cape Town University; and Peter was to return from war service and start Medicine at UCT, plus a wife and a baby girl shortly afterwards, living in ex-service accommodation and battling with a young family and very little money.

The university in 1945 was being flooded with returned soldiers and it was even more fun being there, with escorts who

---

[6]  Dicroidium is an extinct genus of fork-leaved seed ferns that were widely distributed over Gondwana during the Triassic. A cuticle is the outer protective layer of a plant and fossil cuticles are useful in identifying fossilised plants and provide important information on palaeoecology and palaeoclimate.

had cars, were older and frequented nightclubs, and who were more mature than students straight from school. I loved the life and when my demonstrator-ship was extended, and I obtained a generous bursary from a Scientific Research Organisation that was equivalent to the CSIRO in Australia, I decided to stay on and start working towards a Ph.D. The Botany department scientists were part of a team producing a new *Flora Capensis* and I worked on the floral morphology of the family *Thymeleaceae,* of which daphne is a member.

Bill returned to a job in the Southern Rhodesian Geological Survey in 1946 after completing an Honours year at Queens University, Belfast, and he came to visit us at Christmas in Pretoria and again the next Easter. He had applied for the post because he was hoping to persuade me to marry him. He was very persuasive and I soon decided to hand back part of the scholarship, to the great surprise of the donors, as it had not had strings attached requiring that it result in a doctorate. I sent the thesis in six months early, was told that with some minor additions and alterations I would be able to receive the degree in December — and I returned home to Pretoria because I wanted to spend a little time with the family before going off to get married. I was no longer interested in submitting the thesis. I had had all I wanted of university and a new and exciting phase of my life was beginning.

Looking back on those university times I realise now that the UCT was virtually an all-white institution. I recall two "coloured" students in the Science Faculty who kept very much to themselves. That's how it was, and I do not remember ever thinking about apartheid or whether it was appropriate—the education of non-whites was such that it was unlikely that any would get to university. When I receive the Alumni news from UCT these days and see the "black" domination of everything there, my memories of the place have a dream-like feeling of unreality. How the world has changed—in this context for the better. And how I must have changed too from a "privileged Rhodesian", a race that no longer exists, to a "Gaian, privileged to be an insignificant part of Life's Continuum" as I have described myself!

## JOURNEY TO SOMALILAND 1952

Mary, Barbara and David in Dar es Salaam

The beach in Mombasa                Aden airport

Aden

# SOMALILAND STORY

*Young red M'sasa leaves dancing in and out of darkness*
*In flickering firelight*

## JOURNEY TO SOMALILAND

The train journey from Pretoria to Durban went very easily, the children were exceptionally good. The countryside after the first night was most beautiful, very green and lots of water in the rivers and ditches. There was one farm where there were hundreds of brilliant dwarf Erythrina[7] blazing in the green grass and masses of daisies.

The Royal Hotel in Durban was a perfect place, full of atmosphere, with the best service and food. It was an old building with many additions of all ages and had paved courtyards and mosaic floors which made it feel almost Indian and full of charm. The hotel was in the middle of the shopping area and near the sea but unfortunately nowhere near the bathing beaches. Our room was large and comfortable and very pleasant with oldish furniture. After lunch we went to the docks to see if we could get the luggage onboard but were told it had to be done when we boarded the next day, so we took a bus to the beach and had a couple of hours playing there and watched the *Stirling Castle* leave the port. David had almost forgotten the sea and at first wouldn't go near it, then suddenly went quite crazy and pad-

---

[7]  Erythrina is a genus of flowering plants, including trees, in the pea family

73

dled and fell in the water and ran on the sand like a mad thing. Barbara wouldn't paddle but dug and shouted with glee and chased the pigeons.

After two days in Durban, we boarded the old *Llangibby Castle* on 20th November 1952 and sailed in the evening, very excited to be embarking at last on our great adventure. Our cabins were most comfortable, each with a window onto the deck, so we could sit outside and still hear the children. Our stewardess was a Mrs Clive and the steward gloried in the name of Twiddy. We unpacked and got the feel of things and enjoyed watching the ship being eased away from the dock and the tugs pushing and manoeuvring. Barbara called the tugs wowos and was wildly excited about them; David watched with concentration and did not miss a thing.

The next day our ship called at Lourenço Marques in the colony of Portuguese Mozambique.[8] After a brief stay we continued on, meeting an unpleasant rolling swell, to Beira. The children were rather unsettled, David especially holding onto Bill and being impossible at times, obviously not knowing what was going on and feeling insecure but by the second day they had settled down and the nonsense had stopped. They woke at 5am as usual and we'd go out on deck and play till breakfast, theirs being at 7.30 and ours at 8.30. We had several sessions in the nursery with a rocking horse and other lovely toys, but a quite hopeless nurse was in charge. She was often not there, and when present she sat and read and periodically shouted at anyone causing a disturbance, so we couldn't leave the children there alone. We had meals in relays and the food was excellent. However, apart from the dining room, the service was not as good as we had been told to expect on Union Castle ships.

ZoZo had told me that I should see if the purser was like the ones in books, ripe for romance, but though I eyed this one when I came on board I could not do more. This one was fat and

---

8    Upon Mozambican independence in 1975 the city became the national capital and was renamed Maputo, serving as a main port for Zimbabwe and Malawi.

rather feminine with rimless glasses and a lisp, and he had pink legs. Hardly a likely candidate for onboard romance, I thought! However, the doctor was a friend of mine from U.C.T. and we shared a table with a delightful woman from Borneo, and considered going there if Somaliland was not all we hoped for. We also spent a long time with a most charming couple en route to England, who were full of encouragement and enthusiasm for Somaliland. The doctor had been to Hargeisa briefly as well in the air force and had pleasant recollections of the place. He thought the country abounded in interest from every angle and gave me the name and address of someone who had published a flora of Somaliland. All very reassuring and exciting.

Two days in the dirty, busy harbours of Lourenço Marques and Beira showed us a little of the squalor and poverty of busy ports where garbage and all waste from ships of all sorts was thrown overboard. Beira was redeemed by the flamboyant trees that were ablaze everywhere, those in the shopping area pruned to stumps with bundles of red flowers.

Arriving at Dar es Salaam, a fortnight after leaving Durban, was like entering the world of Joseph Conrad. Baobabs down to the edge of beaches; ramshackle tin buildings and broken wharves on low islands; the wreck of the *Koningsberg* and other hulks rotting in the shallows; and boats of every size and means of propulsion rushing about, ferrying people and goods from all the other ships anchored in the bay. The harbour was surprisingly clean. Special dhows collected the rubbish from ships, and none was thrown overboard. We went ashore in a launch and shopped in Indian bazaars for Christmas presents to send back to family in Pretoria.

Letter from Dar es Salaam, Monday, 2nd December 1952:

…This is the most perfect place one could dream of. There is a winding river entrance to the harbour and coconut palms, casuarinas and something called the Indian false almond trees that have vast leaves, growing on the white sand. We are anchored in the middle of the bay, as are all sorts of other ships, and launches come for passengers, rowing boats for the intrepid, and barges for cargo. There are coral islands and everywhere the real South Sea Island look of palms and vivid colours. The flamboyants are ablaze with glory and there are Peltophorum[9] trees along the streets as well.

We gave the children breakfast on board and then went, plus large pram, on the first launch so as to be ashore before the worst heat. It was exciting going on the small boat with natives in the Somali costume of white nighties and fezzes. We walked around shop-gazing and wondering all the time at the perfection of the place. It was hot, but that did not matter. Every available inch in town was planted with trees. The main streets were tunnels under flamboyants and cassias and the roads had a narrow tar strip and the rest was coral—brown and not very romantic look-ing—but coral nonetheless. The shops were lovely and the Indian bazaars full of ivory, brass and mats etc. We bought you, ZoZo, a cashmere scarf as it's easy to send and we got stamps for Dad. We had tea at a large hotel and returned to the ship in a rowing boat so the children could have a rest before lunch.

We received a charming letter from the director of the Somaliland Survey saying that he had only just got our address and they were all looking forward to our arrival. He said two young geologists straight from university had just joined them. We were to fly from Aden and our heavy stuff would follow by boat, taking about a week. There was a small house ready for us to start in and we were to stay at the Club until our things caught up with us. The director said he had five children, one 22 months old, and that he had given up geology from 1936 to 1951 so he was rusty and needed Bill to fill in the gaps. It was a welcoming and reassuring letter, and it was so exciting now that more of the future was com-ing into focus.

♠♠

---

[9]    Tree of Freedom, Siar tree or yellow flame tree, Copperpod

Two days later we were in Zanzibar harbour, anchored far out in the bay. I did not want to expose the children to the heat in the crowded streets with their oriental smells and diseases, so Bill went alone and took photographs and bought the obligatory elephant book ends that still adorn my office more than fifty years later.

We had a day at Tanga and went ashore in a battered old launch. It was very hot and though very picturesque with huge tropical trees and flowers we simply had a quick look around and came back to the comparative comfort the ship. The trip back was in an even more battered launch, and we had first to call at an old Greek tramp steamer also lying in the bay. We sat at the bottom of their gangway while a lot of filthy lumps of ice and loaves of bread were carried up — and what toughs the crew looked and how ancient and battered the ship. It was quite exciting, and I told Bill that ZoZo would have been horrified at the imagined risks we were taking in case they kidnapped us all.

Letter from Mombasa Thurs.11th Dec 1952

What a paradise Mombasa is. It is in an estuary so that the mainland almost completely surrounds it. The mainland too is unbelievably lovely — they can keep the South Sea Islands after this! White coral sand, coconut palms, and blue sea with white breakers on the reef is dream-like. The island is green and has baobab forests, palms, flamboyants in flower, African almonds, cashew nut trees and masses of other vast green trees. We were in Kilindini dock for five days. A clean harbour but hot, and with the loading of the ship there were hundreds of natives on board for that and re-painting the ship, so we did not want to be on board too much in the day. We had two long visits to a place called Tudor House on the island where there is safe bathing and an excellent hotel. It is on a raised beach with somewhat precipitous descent to the sea through frangipani, bougainvillea and all other tropical flowers. We bathed and had picnics there and it was heaven, and we delighted in the beauty and peace. The giant mango trees never cease to amaze me. They are up to at least 80 foot and covered in fruit which was not ripe or I'm sure would endanger the passer-by.

We spent a perfect day at Nyali Beach on the mainland—the most picture-like place of all—an endless gleaming white beach edged with palms and the sea a sheltered lagoon with the reef and white breakers in a semi-circle about a mile out. There was a goggle-fishing expedition to the reef which we'd have done anything to be able to take part in, but it would take three hours and we could not both go. Bill would not leave us, and I would not go alone in the Arab dhow — which was foolish, and I regret it now. There was a beach café and we had taken sandwiches from the ship, so we had a whole day there. There was a paddling pool under the trees and the children had a glorious time. We went by taxi and had to drive across the island and over a toll bridge to the mainland. It is all so perfect with the rich tropical vegetation. We were there during the hottest month of all but the heat was quite bearable.

We did a bit of shopping. I went on my own one morning as it is no good trailing the children along. I bought a Cole of California dress for myself — boned strapless top, elastic back and big circular skirt in white with dark green spots, and a little dark green bolero with white spots; also a pair of Clarke walking shoes which I had forgotten to buy in Pretoria. The shops were nice but expensive. We hope to do Christmas shopping in Aden as it is duty free.

We were sorry to leave Mombasa but quite glad to be on the last lap. I spent yesterday feeling seasick as we ran into heavy swells and rollers and the Avomine tablets take a time to settle one down. I'm fine again today. Bill was very good, taking the children to meals and even washing nappies as I could only cope in the fresh air on deck. Altogether this has been a most glorious voyage. It seems to have gone in a flash and I am sorry it is nearly over.

♠♠

From Mombasa it was five days to Aden, and the ship refuelled there, so it tied up to a buoy on the pipeline and we went ashore in a launch with all our luggage ready to fly into Somaliland.

Mary, Barbara and David under a thorn tree
with the Club in the background

The Hargeisa house

*I feel again as I felt then,*
*Young and happy and very much in love.*

# ARRIVAL IN SOMALILAND

The port of Aden and its immediate surroundings, located in the south of Yemen, was still a British Crown Colony in 1952. I was travelling on a South African passport and I remember my hostile reception at Customs because of this—a first introduction to the different world we were entering where the North Africans and Middle East people of all the different races were anti-European—whether paternalistic like the British Colonials or apartheid-contaminated like South Africans. Bill was travelling on a British passport, and the children were recorded on his, and hatred of the UK was less, and brownie points were scored for at least having the children on that document! I could see that it was going to be a new experience to be part of the unwelcome or actively disliked fragment of population, outnumbered by the hordes in whose countries we were coming to work.

We were driven to the airport and that was all we saw of Aden, but enough to make me wonder how anyone could live there — all dead rock and picturesque dirt—and I was beginning to wonder what awaited us in Somalia. The hour-long flight across the sea to Berbera was calm and we all dozed.

Berbera airport was outside the town so we couldn't verify if Berbera looked and smelt like a goat pen, as one of my dad's friends had told us to expect. There was nothing at all at the aerodrome at Berbera, only a pre-fab hut, fine white gravel and low bush, and that whole coast was a real desert. We saw no real escarpment flying up to Hargeisa. We had expected an abrupt rise onto the plateau, but we looked down on country that seemed to rise steadily, with hills and plateaus and waterless rivers, and a lot of flat-topped thorn trees—very African and reassuringly familiar.

We were met by the Chief Geologist, J.A.H., who had only just received our wire in time to meet the plane and book us in at the Club. Everyone was friendly on the plane and at the airport and it felt good to have arrived at last and to be starting on an adventure.

The airport was on top of the watershed, and we came down through the hills to the Club, the centre of the small European settlement, skirting the main Somali town. The administrative offices and European houses were about two miles from the magala (native township). There were thousands of camels coming in to get water in the town, baby camels too, to the delight of the children and me. Seeing it all for the first time was like looking at sepia pictures of stony desert, silhouettes of flat-topped trees, Somali wrapped in pale shrouds, little wild-haired children chasing goats. These photographic images I can still recall in complete detail.

In my letters to my parents I always emphasised the positive so that they would never worry about us, but even now, looking back, I remember all the hardships and problems (the times when the children ran high temperatures, and the spectre of meningitis and polio was there to terrify one at night, and no medical service apart from the most basic clinics) as unimportant and all the Somali experience as full of interest and satisfaction. That's what youth does for one, and in my case the wondrous joys of motherhood coloured all my living at that time.

♠♠

Hargeisa—our part of it at least—had a lot of charm. We lived among flat-topped *Acacia spirocarpa* trees like those in Erich Mayer drawings in my grandmother's home. It was winter when we arrived in December and quite dry, so the ground was bare and most of the thorn bushes were leafless, but the big trees were dull green, and it felt fine — like alluvium country in the Sabi Valley or near Bulawayo in Rhodesia.

The Club was a series of two-roomed cottages under the thorn trees on the banks of the dry "tug" — the vast sand river running through the valley. The river flowed for only a few hours at a time at odd times all through the year, the valley lying just below the main watershed of this part of Africa. It carried water below the sand and holes were dug to make ponds where animals drank, humans filled water containers and did their washing. Seepage from surrounding dry tug beds carried in all the bacteria and stuff that resulted from use of the place as a sewer.

A water reservoir on top of the hill near the European township supplied water to houses and offices for two hours a day, supplementing rainwater tanks. The tank was filled when the river flowed, and by rain in season. During the dry winter, very heavy night-time dew helped plants to survive.

The trees were full of birds — glorious hoopoes with their distinctive crown of feathers, go-away birds and starlings with calls just like their relatives in southern Africa, and hundreds new to us, so that bird watching was an absorbing pastime. To me, everything seemed full of peace and time did not matter much.

The main building at the Club was a large old stone place with arched doorways and a stoep — all homey and comfortable. A lion cub and a baby cheetah were being hand-raised by the manager. It was said that many casual visitors like locust officers swore off the grog when they were suddenly confronted by these creatures jumping up onto the bar to socialise with the clients.

We lived at the club for some weeks while we waited for our big luggage to arrive. Transport of such luggage by dhow from Aden to Berbera and by worn-out rattle-trap truck up the escarpment to Hargeisa was to prove a frustratingly slow process and a lot of our goods arrived water-damaged or broken. While we were waiting to move into our allocated house, we employed a young Somali to start clearing the thick bush from our garden and leave the trees only, so we could plant vegetables at once and make a flower garden.

Tours of duty were only fifteen months, with three months back "home" in the UK, travel paid. It was a generous arrangement as the living conditions and climate were surprisingly pleasant and benign in Hargeisa, everyone looked really well and children thrived. But regulations were the same as in awful places where such short tours were necessary for survival.

A different house was allocated for each tour of duty, so people were always moving through the dozen or so houses that comprised the Colonial Office township. Basic government issue furniture was supplied, and residents brought all the furnishings and household items that made the houses into comfortable homes.

We were told on arrival that it was obligatory to have servants, as many as possible (to uphold the prestige of the British Empire—and because only servants could shop and bargain in the native town). We immediately employed a "sweeper"—a 'piccanin' to wash the children's clothes and to do the sweeping that was infra-dig[10] for a Somali. (The caste system among servants dates from the time when the Indian Army came to fight the Mad Mullah. The locals quickly found a tribe of untouchables and those now do the sweeping and the other unclean jobs. The house boy would wash clothes, but nappies had to go to the sweeper). A sweeper was paid thirty shillings a month, and a first class cook about five pounds sterling, and a house general about four pounds sterling. Servants were supposed to provide their own food entirely and eat nothing from the house, so labour was not expensive. The cooks did everything, all meals, snacks, bread, soufflés and even cakes. I hoped Somali hands were clean because they were supposed to wash them before they could pray six times a day.

I made a trip with neighbours to the magala (native town) to open an account at the one general store that supplied everything one could think of. The town lies in a valley between rather flat-topped hills. What a town, what a confronting experience!

---

[10] Shortened from the Latin Infra Dignitatum - Beneath the dignity of

No concessions to Europeans at all and quite unlike anything I'd seen before. The houses and shops were in rows with broad roads of sand between them and pepper trees planted on the sides. All the buildings were low and white with narrow arched doors and no real windows. Picturesque locals in national dress lounged about in thousands. Surprisingly, there was little smell and it all looked rather biblical with tailors and cooks working on the roadside, elders lounging on bentwood (!) chairs, and children begging for annahs.

The main shop catering for Europeans was owned by Jirdeh Hussein, a Somali of unusual enterprise who had just been awarded the MBE, who went to England for the Festival of Britain and who was going again for the Coronation, no doubt with a seat in the Abbey. He was a most charming man and black as black of course. Amazingly enough one could get just about everything in his shop. One entered through the narrow door marked "Friday Shut" in a double storey, flat-topped house like all the others. Inside there was a high wooden fence with a gate about a yard from the front wall. Locals had to stand in that passageway and what they bought was handed to them through the bars. The superior Europeans could enter through the gate into the room behind that was crammed solid with everything. There were store rooms beyond and that year, 1952, for the first time, Jirdeh had imported toys and knitted jerseys. There was cloth of all sorts, depressingly Manchester, and not of much local interest; hardware, toilet things and all groceries. A small branch of the big general store that operated in the magala was located close to the Club, selling some of the basic groceries and important needs like alcohol and soda water—for what would a colonial operation be without sundowners?

Having servants to do the housework and all but the most ladylike gardening, I had time to enjoy my children, to sew and make all my clothes and the children's, make wonderful pure wool carpets and rugs, some of which, with their successors, are still in use in my house, experiment with painting and drawing, collect plants and read the books that we ordered from London.

There was a lot of social activity, and several families with young children so there was much pushing of prams along dusty tracks through thorn scrub to visit and play at each other's houses. Small antelope known as dik-diks abounded and were a delight to see in the bush but less welcome in the vegetable garden that had to have a thorn fence.

When it became known that I was a botanist and had had a lifelong contact with herbaria, I was asked to take over the very rudimentary collections of plant specimens and create a Herbarium for the Agriculture Department. Carpenters were organised to make suitable cupboards; mounting sheets and labels and all the paraphernalia were ordered from Kew, and I created a small Kew Gardens Herbarium there in that unlikely place—and had great pleasure and satisfaction in doing it. All the officials who travelled about became collectors and I made many friends. I found out more than twenty years later, when an ex-agricultural officer visited me in Australia, that my herbarium was still going strong and ever growing—whether that still applies after all the turmoil that has affected the country since it ceased to be British Somaliland I do not know.

My diaries and family letters from this time tell of social occasions. The first Christmas party, while we were still at the Club and waiting for our luggage to arrive was a happy occasion and typical of the sort of recreation available. With a young geologist who had just joined the Survey, a forestry officer and an agriculture officer, we went in two jeeps eight miles up the dry tug bed until we were beyond the concentrations of camels and goats. We camped under giant *Acacia spirocarpa* thorn trees and made a fire. We made toast on the radiator grill of a jeep laid across the coals as it was too hot by hand, opened tins of all sorts and had beer, orange juice and lots of tea. It was a most delightful day full of laughter, and the kids had a wonderful time too.

The whole tug bed in this valley was under the trees and very picturesque. Lots of *Cissus*[11] climbers and occasional giant

---

[11]  Perennial plant of the grape family, commonly known as veldt grape or devil's backbone

*Ziziphus*[12] trees. There were stone age implements by the dozen — mostly rejects. On the way home we visited a locality about two miles from the town where there are tall alluvium banks with pebble bands which we could see should make interesting hunting. As a result, Bill contacted the famous archaeologist Desmond Clarke in Nairobi who was working on the prehistory of the whole country and offered our help. Throughout our time in Somalia we were collecting stone implements and recording information, and everything was eventually sent to him and, I believe, used in his *Prehistory of the Horn of Africa*.

While we were waiting for the luggage to arrive so that we could move into our house, a camp cook was taken on so that he would be available to leave with Bill as soon as we were settled in. There was little for him to do while we were living at the Club but in typical old-man Somali fashion he tried to run everything, and it was an unwanted addition to the frustrations of waiting for our luggage.

I wrote to my mom:

Bill's cook is driving me mad, trying to run me and everyone else and it is talk, talk, talk, and he is quite impossible in town. I think he will look after Bill because he really can cook, and he is used to being almighty. I find it hard to accept that Somalis are used to wiping their faces on dish cloths, drying cups on rags that belong to them and were last seen round a leg of raw mutton; dusting in the bedroom with filthy hankies removed from the laundry bag; and wearing tea towels round their necks as a sort of adornment. And they are noisy—being nomadic people used to talking over miles—they shout worse than South African natives — and it is bedlam, unless you know the word "amus" which means "shut up".

---

[12]  Spiny shrubs and trees in the Buckthorn family *Rhamnaceae*

I think things will go quite easily when the frightful cook takes himself off into the blue with Bill and our routine here can be worked out.

♠♠

Our luggage arrived suddenly, late at night in early January, and we were able to move into our house. We got up at dawn the next day and packed up at the Club and a lorry came to move everything to the house. It was a hectic day getting in, and an upsetting one as such a lot was broken or damaged.

We had seen the crates being unloaded from the railway lorry at Durban and watched as the boys dropped one over the edge of the tray, picked it up and trundled it off as though that was quite in order, and we knew we'd find things broken.

One of our trunks had been dropped into the sea and rescued, in getting it from the dhow at Berbera. Much of our crockery in other boxes was broken and other things damaged—sad because we had only kept our favourite things when we packed up to go to Somalia. Our few good bits of furniture were left with my parents and given to my sister by them when she married and went to live in Northern Rhodesia. In the strange way that things sometimes happen, a drop-leaf table and six chairs in a beautiful South American timber came to Australia when Joan and family migrated years later, and eventually came back to me, after Joan's death, bringing a host of memories of the early days in Salisbury.

We opened the big crate first and found that the microscope had got very shaken and looked bad in spite of being in a locked box and well packed in, and the same for the sewing machine. They luckily proved to be quite all right once all the screws were tightened again. The wireless had two controls broken, our nice table lamp with the pottery bottom was shattered as were most of our wedding gifts. Everything had been so carefully packed, but when one big thing broke it made room for everything else to move. It was a bit shattering — a well-chosen word — but it taught us something and we had heavy wooden boxes made with compartments to take everything that we possessed, so that when we moved each time it was not such a heartbreaking business — and it made the packing easy too. It shouldn't have upset us so much, but we had kept so little and couldn't help feeling a bit sorry. No ordinary breakage was covered by insurance, and we couldn't replace anything in Hargeisa anyway, so we just had to forget about it all.

Bill's first trek was postponed for a few days so that he could get us settled in first, and he worked like a slave to get everything right, developed film of the voyage and organised his gear for going out. The house was really very pleasant. I made curtains and chair covers and we had bought an Indian mat and a sort of imitation Persian carpet in glowing reds, blues, and yellows on the voyage that made the living room look lovely.

The house was entered by the back and the lavatory was along a path to hell-and-gone in the thorn bushes so the children's potties had to be carried out through the lounge — but that was the only defect we could find. There were two kitchens, one with an enormous Dutch oven built out on one wall and the other with a blue-flame stove (ethanol fuelled) and a sink. The cook had the big one; I had the other. It was freshly painted and though mud brick and not very well built it was nice. Floors were plain cement, rough and not polishable, which was just as well really. The furniture was not very smart and all rather crude, but it was nice to have PWD (Public Works Department) furniture for the children to cut their teeth on and not my own. All windows were burglar-proofed with wire mesh and all doors had good locks, so we felt quite safe while Bill was away.

Jama the house boy was an old faithful, concerned for our wellbeing and eager to learn. (We found out that he was a twice convicted murderer who paid the victims' families in camels and was therefore exonerated. He, like all the others smoked khat and was occasionally off his brain but was just wild-looking and quite gentle when not intoxicated.)

Everything in the house was locked away from the servants and I had a big key ring with dozens of keys. When Barby was about eighteen months old she used to borrow the keys and she'd bustle around with them. When asked what she was doing locking and unlocking cupboards, she told me she was doing "green work".

As soon as we were settled, Bill went off on his first trek. The Chief Geologist, J.A.H., had informed us on our arrival that it would be necessary to find gold or other mineral wealth as soon as possible, otherwise the Survey would be shut down and everyone would be transferred to another Survey in another part of the Empire. There were three months left of the field season before the summer and the rains, and Bill had to be away for most of that as there was a great deal to do and only a little time to do it.

The children and I did not attempt to go on trek with Bill while he was getting the hang of the country. Families left behind were provided with a police patrol and the houses were fairly close together, so security was not too much of a worry. We were told there was hardly any crime, except petty thieving, and no serious offences as the Somali were Muslim and devout.

One night when I opened a curtain I was confronted by the squashed face of the night guard pressed hard against the glass, and it was an unpleasant shock. He had been watching me through a crack in the curtain and from then onwards I was far more worried about guards than burglars.

I was completely happy, and it felt good to be alive. Hargeisa was a pretty good place to live. In January it was really cold at night with such a heavy dew that it dripped like rain from the eaves till the sun came up. The early mornings before the sun got above the hills around the valley were clear and gloriously fresh and cold. Then heavy low cloud came up with the sun so there was a mist until about nine, or at least it was overcast. The days in winter were not hot, even in the sun, and there was usually a fresh wind which felt like a sea breeze. We all felt completely fit. The children's colour was glorious and their appetites would have done my mom's heart good. Dr Baird, the chief M.O., told me that it really was the best climate for children and they all thrived. Tropical diseases were practically nil, and everyone was very healthy. In summer it got fairly hot and a bit oppressive before rain, but no worse than Pretoria — and winter or summer temperatures varied from 10 - 32 degrees C so it was not a trying climate. There were no mosquitoes and preventive measures were adequate and only very seldom did one hear of malaria, and that only in a rainy year.

Water was officially at its shortest in January and for the next two months till rain came in March. There was a big reservoir on the hill behind and supply to the houses was from 7-9 am daily. Each house had a storage tank as well as the 44-gallon tank of hot water and 44 of cold which supplied the bath, so there was no shortage in the house. All it meant was that water had to be carried to the kitchen and to the garden, except during two hours, but was always available in the bathroom provided one did not waste it. Washing of clothes was done in the garden from the storage tank.

I used to get about three pints of milk delivered daily for 1 shilling and 30 pence, and that was boiled in a double boiler and was more than enough for the children and us. I had a tin of powdered milk as back up. Fresh vegetables of all sorts came to the door each day and were cheap. We got paw-paws, oranges and bananas too. There was a shop in the European area near the club (a branch of Jirdeh Hussein in the magala) and it was within walking distance from home. It had all foodstuffs. There was no difficulty about shopping—one's boy did that — he could bargain and get everything for half what we would have had to pay. For things such as khaki material to make Bill's bush shirts I'd make a special trip to the magala with one of the neighbours.

We spent a lot of time playing in the sandy tug as it was safer than the rocky garden where there were scorpions. We once killed a scorpion when making a rockery, so I tried to impress on the children the importance of running to tell me if they saw a scorpion. However, David would batter the unsuspecting arachnid to death and then run to tell me, so they were not allowed to

dig among the rocks. The snakebite serum I ordered came broken so I had to order more—the postal service and all transport in
Somalia seemed to be inordinately rough.

When Bill went out on trek it took a couple of days to settle
into life without him, happy and interested in everything around
us. I missed Bill but even at odd times when the longing was bad
I never for a moment wished I was anywhere else, and I couldn't
be lonely with my children. I wasn't the least bit nervous at night
without Bill. I had two police watchmen on the premises, and it
wasn't a nervy sort of place. There were no strange sounds in the
night, and it was peaceful. At night I'd have supper, lock the servants out and sew and read and I was perfectly happy. Barbara
was restless at night with teething and usually slept in my bed for
part of the night. David sometimes would climb out of bed and
wander in to me in the dark but would go happily back to bed
if I said it would soon be morning. He was such a different child
here—much more settled and secure. Perhaps it was because I
was not harassed and had time to play and sympathise with him
when he needed it. For so long Barbara seemed to take most of
the time not taken by chores and David had to go to Bill in an
emergency but was now quite content with me.

The garden was taking shape. The bush all around was full
of dik-diks which would go bounding about and thrill us, and we
had to put a thorn zariba[13] round the vegetables or they would
all be eaten. The birds were wonderful — dozens of hornbills, hoopoes, painted and glossy starlings, bee-eaters, drongos, bulbuls,
pigeons, doves, larks and shrikes. I had plans to build a cement
birdbath.

One day I was invited to Government House for lunch.
Surprisingly, it was a most delightful and informal excursion. I left
the children with Margorie H, and they seemed happy and confident. I was excited to be going out on my own and dressed
up for the occasion, wearing a little grey hat covered in flowers.
However, I needn't have bothered as no one else was wearing a

---

[13] Zariba—a thorn fence fortifying a camp or village

hat, so I removed it and Lady Reece the Governor's wife said she was sorry I did so, as it was such a treat to see such a pretty hat! I knew an Italian couple who were there as well as the Berbera District Commissioner and his wife who I had met at the Club. I was seated on the right of the old Governor who, in my youthful arrogance, I thought was stodgy, lacking in personality and a bit of a bromide. The rest of the party were gay and talkative, and I felt completely at home.

Government House was an unpretentious house, old and rambling and a bit like a Rhodesian farmhouse under big spreading thorn trees on the banks of the tug. I was not worried about the children and felt emancipated—perhaps it was the wine and sherry. During lunch a small goat, apparently a pet one of the sons, wandered in. The Governor wanted it to stay but Lady Reece insisted it be taken outside as during a previous lunch it had eaten part of a visitor's dress without her noticing. Altogether Government House was unlike what I remembered of Salisbury—no ADC or secretaries. Lady Reece welcomed her guests personally and I went home feeling I wanted to ask her to our house for tea!

The kitchens in Hargeisa houses were very primitive. After a couple of months I gave up trying to use the antediluvian blue-flame stove. A good Somali cook could produce the most perfect meals using charcoal braziers and camp ovens made from petrol tins, so I made myself a camp oven out of the two halves of a petrol tin, embedded it in coals on the kitchen floor and started baking. About every third day I made rolls, plaited loaves and plain loaves — and we enjoyed fresh hot bread. The charcoal was brought by camel at 3 shillings a sack, and we used about four sacks a month, so fuel was not expensive.

I was completely enchanted by my children but missed my parents and felt guilty for not being able to share them with them. Bill was waiting on an enlarger that his parents were send-ing from Northern Ireland so we could send photos as a small compensation for being so far away. Barbara was changing rapidly from a baby into a little girl who reminded me so much of my sister Joan. She was so bursting with love that she had to walk kissing my hand and when she was restless I'd take her into my bed and she'd reach up and put both warm fat arms round my neck and pull my face onto hers and go to sleep like that. She was so gentle and yet so full of life. She'd fight with David, and he'd retaliate though he seldom started the fights, but could play angelically with him.

When Bill returned for a few days it was perfectly glorious having him home. Separation really made me appreciate him to the full when he came back, and I hated his having to leave us again. He didn't like being away either, but he was working hard and very interested in what he was doing. He was making excellent progress on the work mapping the geology of vast areas and was quite prepared to put up with a bit of loneliness when necessary. He said what amazed him was that although he was in semi-desert and there was no water and not a leaf anywhere, the humidity was so high at night that his plane-table sheet on which he was drawing the map was like a sponge and useless for work. Even in Hargeisa where it was still winter and nights were cold and days pleasant and not too hot, the dew dripped from the eaves and there was sufficient moisture for a line of plants to establish themselves in the drip line round each house.

I was busy setting myself up with a desk and all the furniture I needed as I was now officially the botanist with the Agriculture Department and was being paid for the work I did establishing an Herbarium. I could work about three or four hours a day in my own time, and largely at home and I drew 20 pounds a month. I was very content.

One day I gave three-year-old David a screwdriver to stop him pestering me while I was busy, and he completely demolished his trike. Luckily, he had a good idea of how to put it together again. He looked after the toy Morris Minor that Bill's family sent him rather like Bill looked after our MG, Susan — taking it out to admire and run it a little, and then polishing and wrapping it in tissue and putting it carefully in the wardrobe.

As time passed and we spent more time in the countryside I became aware of the appalling state of the Somali landscape and realised that South Africa would be like Somaliland before too long. Desertification, encroachment of the deserts, destruction of vegetation by goats and camels and for fuel by man, and torrential rains causing massive erosion, were all common to both countries.

Camp under thorn trees

Bulhar beach

Camels moving our gear

## LIFE IN HARGEISA AND ON TREK

David and Barbara identifying plants

Mary and kids collecting plants

'Archaeologising' in a cave

Stone implements

Barby and David with tortoises

*The lovely night is not a sleeping presence,*
*Very much alive, it sings its symphonies*

# LIFE IN HARGEISA AND ON TREK

I worked nightly on the Herbarium and found it stimulating and interesting. During the days I sewed for the kids and made myself new dresses for Bill's return. I quite often had visits from a couple of the Agriculture and Locust officers, and I'd take the children out to visit friends most days.

In the early mornings with dripping dew and light mist there were often as many as four dik-diks in the garden — always at least one. All day long there were little brown squirrels, called dimmagalas in Somali, and hosts of birds including yellow neck quail and sand grouse. Our plot was largely wild thorn country, and the thick vegetation was the result of being fenced and safe from overgrazing by domestic animals.

Bill came home after a few weeks on trek, looking sunburnt and well and with such a vast area mapped. He had two days at home before we all set out together on his next trek. It was so nice not to have to be separated again and was heaven having him home. Our departure was delayed because Bill had a bout of colic. Gastro-enteritis with acute pain, fever and all sorts of horrible symptoms was the one scourge in Somaliland. All our water had to be boiled. To brush teeth with unboiled water could result in an attack. There was a specific remedy which we all carried, called Berberitis Mixture, because it is much used in Berbera where gypsum in the water aggravates the disease. The mixture contained morphine as well as kaolin.

Our first camp was on the Guban[14], the sandy coastal plain, about 100 miles from Hargeisa. We drove the Vauxhall we'd bought from the local policeman to Berbera where we left it in

---

[14] Guban—Coastal plain in NW Somalia, running parallel to the Gulf of Aden between Zeila in the west and Berbera in the east

the Public Works Department store and picked up the light truck which was sufficient for the camp. We had a glorious swim at Berbera on the coast before going to make camp some ten miles from the sea. Berbera did indeed smell like a goat pen, or rather worse. But the aroma in the magala! The inhabitants lay, wrapped completely, head and all, in white cloths, and slept in the roads, and from the smell might well have been corpses that no one had come to collect.

We took the coast "road" from Berbera to Bulhar and drove along it for about twenty miles. Parts of it were passable, parts bad, and the rest very bad. We only got stuck once in the sand at the inevitable coffee shop where there were many people to push us out again. All the time Bill was away he'd send messages like "based at La Ferug" or "Sheikh Abdal" and I pictured a small town with a couple of European buildings, perhaps a few pepper trees, and an oasis effect. In reality one goes through nothing or less than nothing in the desert and then suddenly pass two huts which are permanent, and not the round nomadic homes of mats etc. but made of old tins. Around and in the huts are dozens of people and a smell of camels and goats and that is all — and sometimes a police hut with brick walls and a highfalutin name written on it.

We met the camel men at Sheikh Abdal. Bill had ten camels to fetch water and to carry the heavy tents and stores. That meant five camel men. We'd sent our heavy stuff a few days before by truck and it was waiting at the police post there. Bill and the five boys with us were greeted like long lost brothers by the five camel men and the three office boys who had gone with the kit, and the hullabaloo was frightful. By means of the interpreter he then gave instructions to the camel men on where to take the stuff. Some of the men were local and knew the country and he explained what hills they were to go to and which tugs to cross— landmarks that only the locals would know. The children and I sat in the shade of the "police station" and played happily with stones and it took a long time with each and all having their say, mainly all at the same time.

Then the kit had to be sorted — essentials to go with us in the lorry and the rest by camel across country. We went around the other side of the mountains and up from the coast, while the camels came across country on a camel track. The view at Sheikh Abdal was superb with escarpment mountains all around and the basalt tableland in front, and there was a strong breeze blowing from the sea thirty miles away. Bill was remarkably good with the Somali, and patient — and believe me it took patience when they all knew everything and had to let you know it.

Somali 'coffee shops' were said to be everywhere up and down the country, and I pictured something like a shop. But it turned out that very few Somali had the energy to cook and they all "ate out" in a filthy zariba which looked like all the rest but was called a coffee shop. Inside there was a charcoal fire and an assortment of tins for cooking, and the flies covered the chapatis to a depth of inches!

We went on a couple of miles beyond the coffee shop and tried to get down to the sea shore to camp but there was soft sand and dunes and we hadn't time to make a road. The sea looked lovely. That part of the real Guban was beautiful with salt marshes miles inland, and salt bush in parts, then patches of dunes with bushes and grass, and open park-like country with desert grasses and odd trees. We camped in a pleasant place on what proved to be a raised beach and it was full of wonderful fossil shells; vast ones with spikes and horns, giant oysters and all sorts of small ones. There are apparently three raised beaches at 20, 250 and 600 feet. We saw them as wonderful material for a scientific paper and hoped one day to come back and investigate them further. We collected specimens for an hour or two one afternoon. There is one little gastropod we named the Barbara shell as she found the first perfect little one. It is a tiny shell with ridges on the spiral. She is as keen a collector as the rest of us.

The children were wonderful on the whole journey and loved all the activity of making camp. We could hear the sea clearly all night and it was probably better camping where we did as there would have been no shelter on the beach and no wood for fires.

Every three days or so as Bill finished mapping an area, we moved camp with the help of camels, staying near the coast and Berbera for about a fortnight and then moving up towards Mandera as the weather got hotter. David was enthralled by the whole business of loading and unloading camels and making or striking camp and talked of little else. There was a doctor in Berbera, always a reassuring thought, and good shops although we took enough fresh fruit and vegetables for a fortnight and only went to Berbera at the end of the month to restock.

I took a press for plants, although it was a bit early for many of the plants, as well as knitting, hand sewing, embroidery and books. It was not luxury camping as we were limited in weight with camels and a small truck, and water was precious. I had organised a boy to look after the garden and watch the house, and there was a watchman on day and night while we were away. I had planted a lot of vegetables before leaving and was looking forward to a healthy productive garden on our return.

Our second camp in the area was reached by driving some ten miles up a tug. Parts of the tug bed were hard and good, others sandy, and other parts full of rocks and erosion channels. Though we did not get stuck we had to go back and make several detours. The Bedford behaved well, and we pitched camp for four days at the farthest point we had to reach, then worked down the coast again. We were in a valley between limestone ridges and were relying on the camels meeting us there, but there was no guarantee they'd find us. The countryside was no country for the faint-hearted to trek in! Though we came quite easily along the tug I'd never have thought it possible to come so far by first appearances. Our navigator was an old Somali camel man who said at Sheikh Abdal that he could get us there by car (to a place not on any map at that!) and we had to leave it to him and have faith — and he did get us there. If one asked such a one "How far?" he'd answer "many miles" or "beyond the Araweina coffee shop" or something — and knowing what a coffee shop was, one was none the wiser.

We had a very pleasant, comfortable camp with a big tree giving shade for the children and I was well organised. All our water had to be brought by camels about ten miles but that was nothing for them. We kept Hargeisa water for drinking as the local water was full of epsom salts.

Our third camp was on the Berbera-Bulhar road—eleven miles up the Ago Merodeh tug—such a lovely address! I managed to collect quite a few plant specimens, which seemed little less than miraculous in that dryness. These were *Cassia, Tephrosia, Indigofera, Acacia* and a few other herbs and grasses. We saw quite a few gerenuk and dik-diks but no other game. On Sunday we got up with the first streak of dawn and packed up. While we had breakfast the men carried everything out of the tent and took it down. Then everything except a few lighter odds and ends was loaded onto the camels, and they set off slightly after we did at 7am. Loading the camels was fascinating for the children and me. There was one very surly one who was almost impossible to work with. He would not lie down to start with, he growled like a lion and tried to bite all who were busy with him, and he'd stand up and try to shed his load before they were ready. All the camels smelt to high heaven!

We left camp and drove down the tug about six miles and then Bill and the field-men climbed a nearby limestone mountain to get the lie of the land and the children and I camped in the tug bed for a few hours, collecting plants, walking about, playing and having tea. I had three very trusty Somali guarding us and we were never left alone. I didn't even walk out of sight of camp without an escort befitting my great dignity! When Bill came back he had tea with us and then we continued on down the tug, passing the camel train about half a mile from our planned camping spot.

We were in such a perfect camp that we were sorry to have to move, but Bill could not do much from it and time was short, so we had only two days there. Our tent was four minutes' walk from the sea — and what a perfect sea! We could be on the beach only in the late afternoon or early morning because it was very exposed and glary and hot. We bathed both afternoons and the children and I were on the beach as much as possible. All day long a strong wind blew from the sea, keeping the tent cool and delightful. It was a real seaside holiday. The only drawback to the beach was the crabs — giant fiddler crabs, inches high and simply huge. They hunted in thousands along the edge of the waves but were very timid and did not worry one, though if you sat still they came near to have a look, and they crawled all over our clothing and stuff. As well as the huge ones there were literally thousands of smaller ones ranging from ones like small spiders to spidery large ones. The whole beach was a honeycomb of crab burrows. I had always had an aversion to crabs, but they proved to be harmless, and I survived. There were land crabs as well all over the dunes and leaving tracks through our tent at night — luckily I did not see those.

We had a glorious time on the beach. The water was warm and as the beach sloped steeply our bathing consisted of sitting in the sand and letting the waves come up and wet us. The children were mad with delight. There were lovely shells, but all the suitable ones were occupied by hermit crabs, so we had to get a few out to be able to collect any at all. But the little shells along the tidelines were perfect for the children to collect. We were all brown and feeling very healthy after all the fresh air of the past ten days, and with the sea to top it all.

The two days in the last camp on the raised beach were spent collecting fossil shells, coral and echinoderms. It was a most superb collecting ground and needed weeks to collect along the whole length. We considered taking local leave to do it all later. The kids loved the collecting, and we had a vast weight of material. Some of the shells were about 8 inches long and incredibly thick. There were whole mussel beds, and odd places where there were thousands of small shells, and the actual beach was cemented into a grit in which all the sorts could be seen. Bill chipped out some perfect ones and we managed to get good examples of each type even though most of the large shells were broken. We were looking for flakes to be able to date the fossil beach by, but found only a few poor ones which might have been much more recent as they were not embedded. The age of the beach is given to some extent by the fact that there was no basalt in the deposit, and the age of the basalt (very young) is known.

I was very content in those camps in the middle of nowhere. While Bill worked on his maps, the children dug in the sand under big thorn trees. I collected plants and, freed from household chores, immersed myself in the landscape, nature and my children. I started teaching David to write by drawing letters in the sand in the tug.

To me, Somaliland was a glorious country. I realised that its beauty was in the eyes of the beholder as it was not a soft kind of beauty. There was a stretch of limestone country outside Hargeisa where the ground was covered in white stones from cricket ball to football size and the vegetation there was thorns and Sanservieria[15] and nothing between — but even it had a fascination with the blue hills of the escarpment as backdrop. Coming down the winding passes of the escarpment was rather intimidating. The view from the top before one started to descend was unbelievably grand. We were working in an area where basalt from an ancient volcano had flowed out in a sheet, covering the land and filling up valleys. Seen from afar it was a tableland of black rock with deep ravines cut through it, sitting up in the middle of the coastal plain. Parts of the plain before one reached the real Guban or coastal strip were deserts of sand dunes each with a spreading thorn bush on top, and there were high basalt ridges along the road where the basalt had run down the sides of the limestone which it covered, so that it looked as though there were oil seepages — black on white limestone. Many prospectors had been to see if oil really existed.

At the end of the last trek we moved into a house in Berbera—a Colonial Service rest-house available to employees of the Geological Survey—for a brief holiday before going out on the next leg of the trek.

The rest-house was a touch of luxury. There were several, each a high two storey house and only the top floor was used at that time of year. Each had a garden full of big trees and there were birds that sang all day and came right inside. The upstairs

---

[15] snake plant, mother-in-law's tongue

in the house we had was a vast room with open sides with green tilted shutters of crisscross wood. This was the living room with easy chairs and dining room furniture. There was also a large bedroom and a sleeping porch where we put our camp beds as they looked more comfortable than the peculiar beds supplied. There was a bathroom with a vast stone bath and unlimited water (full of epsom salts) and a lavatory of antiquated design, but functional. The kitchen was downstairs.

The house overlooked the bay over the tops of the trees and there were dhows in the harbour. A sea breeze blew all day, and it was quite cold inside. At that time of year Berbera was heaven. The magala no doubt still smelt, but it was a mile away and the European quarter was delightful. The trees were unlike anything we'd seen in Somaliland. Apparently, the seawater extended under that part of Berbera, and very brackish water was found four feet down, but it obviously suited the trees. For four months of the year Berbera is too hot and the Karife—a strong southeast wind that blows on the southern shore of the Gulf of Aden—makes Berbera too unpleasant and most locals leave and go up to Sheikh in the mountains.

There was a swimming pool as well as the sea, tennis courts, and an open-air bioscope. We had a wonderful rest, and the cook would go out at dawn and bring a huge fish from the boats for our lunch.

We had baths, showers and hair washes at dawn in the big stone bath and left feeling clean and rejuvenated. Our camels and heavy stuff had gone over the hills to El Anod from our last camp, where we were to meet them.

Letter from Camp at El Anod. 10th March 1953

Just a note to send up with the runner to Hargeisa tomorrow, too late for the plane I'm afraid. We are all thriving and are now camped on the inland side of the basalt plateau and about thirty miles from the sea and forty from Hargeisa. We made camp here early in the afternoon, after a rough camp for lunch a few miles away while a way was found down to this point. We will move a bit further on tomorrow.

The children and I are loving every aspect of the camping. We will go back to Hargeisa in 10 days if things work out as planned and will be there for six weeks before the next trek. Barbara talks such baby-talk now. She is a completely undemanding personality. When she stands in her place at table shovelling in her food competently she does not do it asking to be looked at and told how clever she is like a boy does. She gives a feeling of quiet strength and completeness incredible in such a little thing. She practises standing on her head all day and mountaineers up everything. David loves the camping and wakes with the first light and asks "are we moving today" as they love best the days when we get up before it is light and pack up and the camels come to be loaded.

Abbi the revolting verbose cook has left, and peace has descended on the camp. His absence is not noticed at all. His kitchen help did all the work I now find, and I have only to supervise a little. Abbi never stopped being noisy, was lazy and resented advice, scattered hair in the food, rolled frikandels (meatballs) on his hairy, sweaty chest and was simply too tiring. He even chanted when doing the washing up as gangs of mine boys do in South Africa.

Letter from Camp beyond El Anod. 15th March 1953

A runner is going to Hargeisa tomorrow morning so I'm hoping this will catch the mail this week. I'm using the book you sent already as I am busy collecting and identifying plants all the time, and this new camp to which we came on Thursday has Somali "Sabi stars" — a different species and too beautiful for words. The plants have only about an inch of trunk above ground with succulent grey stems and a crown of very narrow greenish-grey leaves and then the sprays of flowers. The plants are often a foot in diameter with about 20-30 brilliant flowers and lots of buds. Growing as they do on dry desert sand they are spectacular. I found a lovely one and got the field boys to dig it out. Underneath there is a group of roots to get surface water, then a sort of tuber a yard long and a foot or so in diameter at its widest point — like a huge dahlia tuber. It ends in a thick tap root which probably grows down for ever. Taking the whole contraption home will be a problem. I think I will get our 'boy' Jama to hold it like a baby.

Here too there are small very gnarled and twisted *Commiphoras*[16] growing to about six feet with scarlet fruits; and a scrambling acacia with very thick thorns and flowers like little white balls with rust-coloured pollen. This whole valley is eroded, topsoil gone and almost desert. On the lines of the tugs there are a few *Acacia spirocarpa* (flat-topped thorn trees), but for the rest it is bare ground with groups of aloes and *Sanservieria* and small "sheep bushes". These are woody *Indigofera* and seem to be dead — yet sheep graze them and grow fat.

One thing that looks definite to me is that the country I have seen is in an appalling state because of erosion. One seldom sees gully erosion, but sheet erosion has left just about nothing. The goats which roam in their millions are destructive enough without the Somali who are the end. There is not a single tree or bush which is edible which has not been damaged and nearly killed, and there are more dead bushes and trees than an army could make if they destroyed systematically for a month. The Somali cut down the branches of all the larger things, leaving them hanging from the trunk for the goats to get at the few leaves they bear. Vast flat-topped acacias are just a trunk and branches drooping from the top. It is an everyday sight to see a man standing heaven knows how on top of a vast tree, chopping it to bits systematically. And though the rainfall here is fair — about fifteen inches I think — it does no good. It falls in a few heavy downpours and is gone off down the tugs carrying trees and boulders for a few hours and then is seen no more. In these valleys the gradient is 100 foot per mile which seems amazing — but this area is part of the flattened scarp which elsewhere goes up sheer for 3000 feet.

---

[16] Genus of plant in Frankincense and Myrrh family

I find it an exciting country to collect in because everything is unexpected and also one is not overwhelmed by diversity and the picture is simple. I think after rain one would get a lot of annuals, but a study of this perennial part and how it can survive and support all the sheep, goats and camels is enough for a start. There are a number of birds at camps at waterholes, and a few at others. We see gerenuk, dik-diks, monkeys, jackals and little else.

Bill is remarkably fit and happy these days. Even in this heat, which is getting quite intense in the sun now, he walks about twelve to fifteen miles a day over the roughest ground climbing fair-sized mountains. Though he is weary and hot when he comes in he works on his plane-table in the tent all afternoon and is recovered by evening and goes for a short walk with us. We are going in to Hargeisa on Friday or Saturday. Bill will have to come out again for a few days to show the country to Dr Shaw who is one of the directors from London.

The children are really good about this camping life. They sleep all night, have a rest in the day, eat well and are adorable. They make mud pies most of the time. David was really a full-fledged member of the expedition by the end of the time, doing his share of the packing up in the mornings of moves, discussing the move with intelligence and loving every aspect. On very bumpy tracks both children sang loudly so that the bumps would cause loud notes — and that caused mirth. In fact, often without their enjoyment of it all it might have been a sweat for us. When we came to a tug they were all agog hoping we would stick fast because the digging and pushing and palaver was especially for them, as far as they could see.

Barbara is so easy-going and took it all in her stride; she amazed us both. She is an alarming companion on a journey because she seems to be fast asleep and suddenly gives the most prodigious scream (of delight) if she spots a camel or a buck. There are great numbers of buck — a gazelle called gerenuk, dik-dik, and a large, almost white gazelle. And lots of dimmigalas (squirrels), meerkat, baboons, monkeys and birds. The children explored around each camp with us, collecting every plant and taking them to a camel man to get the Somali name. As a result Barbara, (encouraged by David), identifies every plant she encounters, pointing an adorable finger at it, putting her head on one side in thought and then pronouncing "adarr" or "afad" or other words which are actually, or sound like, Somali words.

I cut Barbara's hair yesterday as it is still impossible to hold it back with a clip or ribbon and she was peering out of a forest. She is almost fair now — light golden-brown hair and black long lashes, sunburnt with a pink flush, like an apricot's rosiness. David's remark of the day was "those blasted flies drive me mad. No doubt I had better go outside and dig in the tug." He and Barby still fight like cat and dog part of the time. She is very kind-hearted and if one has a scratch or a cut she comes over time after time to kiss it better, with a quite indescribable expression on her face, head on one side, nodding sagely. When Bill staggers in each day after the walk she rushes round offering him things and handing him surprises — special stones she goes to collect, crusts of old bread or anything to make him feel welcome.

Bill finished the mapping the area in about four weeks, and we stayed with him till the end. We then had about six weeks in town before going to the Boramo district. We enjoyed being back home as much as we enjoyed being on trek. We left our last camp on "Theyen Road" and moved up to the main Hargeisa road about 25 miles from Hargeisa so that we would have all the part on rough tracks and with tug crossings behind us. The last camp in the blue was not a very nice one, no trees of any sort, just sheep bushes in a valley between the mountains, but we had only two full days there.

We did not get stuck at all on the way back to Hargeisa in spite of having to re-cross all the tugs we'd made ways across before. The thing with the sand in Somaliland which is different from the Sabi is that one doesn't go on the same tracks again as the sand is softened, not compressed, by going once. Bill's trials-driving stood him in good stead in that sort of bundu-bashing[17] and I held both children tight as we charged at all the obstacles — all of us exhilarated by the performance — and knowing that if we got stuck it didn't matter much as there was gear of all sorts behind us to get us out of trouble and lots of labour.

In all the three months Bill saw only one small snake on a koppie[18]. We saw none, no scorpions, no spiders and just about no insects apart from flies, and moths at the lamp at night. There were no mosquitoes. The only criticism I had of the country is the goats which were everywhere so that every inch of the ground had a faint (or not so faint) aroma—and camels as well adding their powerful stink. Our camp on the main road was very pleasant for one night, in a thick mass of *Sanservieria* and aloes with big trees, such as occurs on the few spots where there is still river alluvium. There was so little soil on the whole area that we covered that I trembled to think what the country was heading for. All the valley systems were juvenile and overstocking by goats of all things and wanton destruction by Somali didn't help. There were no difficulties with water at the time—we had as much as we could use. It had to be fetched by camels from waterholes where it was often soupy and always dubious. Very often, even thirty miles inland, it was so salt that one could not use it for tea or drinking. Why it was salt there was mysterious as we were on granite most of the time. On the Guban the water was all full of salts, so we carried two baramels of water for drinking only and refilled at Mandera where the water was good.

We put Dettol in all water we washed ourselves in. There was enough water for two fills of the big zinc tub at night — the children went first, then one of us in that water and the other in a clean bath. It was surprising how easy everything was. I found that I had to be methodical, and everything had to have a place and be put back there after use, and I had two sessions — morning and evening— opening boxes and trunks and getting out all the things required so that there was not endless burrowing in boxes,

---

[17] Bundu-bashing - South African slang for driving off-road in a wilderness
[18] Koppie – a small hill in a generally flat area

bent double under the sloping tent edge. The children had basins of water to throw on the floor of the tent not covered by the mat, and they dug and made roads there nearly all day. There was not always adequate shade outside and they preferred being inside with me.

We had left the camp at dawn and arrived in Hargeisa at about 9am. We were all rather sad to leave though Bill was tired and needed a change, and we really had had a good spell in camp. The camp was left to be packed up by the headman and the big lorry was sent next day to collect the tents and heavy equipment. It was so exciting getting home. We had heard that there was no water in Hargeisa because the reservoir was dry and rationing stricter than before, so I had steeled myself to find the garden dead. But by some error our water had not been turned off and the garden boy watered well, and the garden was thriving. Shrubs had grown inches, *Tecoma*[19] in flower, geraniums vast and starting to bud, chrysanthemums in flower, and all seeds up. We were eating spinach from the garden, and carrots, tomatoes and cabbage would be ready soon.

The children were wild with glee over all the old toys; the trike, the cars. It was chaotic for a while. We went by car to get supplies, and all felt bilious after a feast of chocolate, biscuits, sweets, and fresh meat. It took most of Saturday to get straight, and then I sorted my herbarium collections and made a dress for Barby as she had grown inches in the four weeks. There was a thunderstorm about in the afternoon but only about six drops of rain. The rains had started around Boramo and we expected the tug to come down any day and then water would be easy.

After tea we went out about ten miles in the car to where there'd been heavy rain and went down into a sort of erosion tug and collected man-made flakes. It was divine after the rain, and we all got really muddy — and it was an interesting flake area which needed more investigation.

---

[19]  *Tecoma capensis* Cape honeysuckle, family *Bignoniaceae*

# TO KNOW THE LOVELY NIGHT

Letter from Hargeisa, 31st March 1953

This is such a nice house, and the garden is full of birds, and visiting dik-diks and squirrels. Early in the morning there is an awful racket with quails and go-away birds all yelling, and parrots too. Each has a peck at the vegetables, but one can't really mind when we find dik-dik prints inside the fence that is supposed to protect our plantings. This first week at home has been busy and I am conscious of feeling exceptionally well after what was the first restful holiday for some time. The children were so little trouble and with sleeping all night and having little to do for them in the day I'm back to the stage where housekeeping and cooking are a pleasure and not something to be done with minimum energy and interest. I'm trying new cakes and biscuits daily and still baking bread and buns. We've put up new curtains in the dining room — cream background with vivid primulas and cornflowers. I've also embarked on the vast job of making tailored, box-type cushions for the Morris chairs. I got a huge sack of "goa" kapok, and when the cushions are made I will make the loose covers with piped edges from hopsack linen. I will not start herbarium work until I get all the sewing done. I've made Barby six little dresses with very full skirts, small yokes and peter-pan collars and sleeves gathered with sewing elastic. She looks like an angel and has grown so fast she is now up to the top of David's ear.

I had an interesting day last week when I went to the District Commissioner's court to give evidence in the case about my stolen laundry. I think I told you that we caught a little Somali who had taken clothes off the line, and he had had an older companion who had got away and hidden some of the stuff in a hollow tree not far from the house and had sold some in the magala. We got everything back eventually, because our houseboy found out through the grapevine what had occurred. A DC's court is not like what it must be in a European court, and I was pleased to be asked to go to sample the new experience. I was sworn in and everything I said was translated. The magistrate, Roberts-Shaw, was charming and I was the only other European. An exhibit in court was the ripple-cloth sheet which was recovered in the magala and I had to say how I knew it was mine. The little boy we'd caught was only 8 and quite unrepentant. He said he had not done anything although he had been caught with his arms full of washing. The other was 18. He has been in gaol for nearly two months waiting for trial and has been fattened and cleaned up a bit and he had no complaints, having never had it so good in his life before.

Dr Shaw, the deputy Director from the Colonial Office in London, has been here this week and we had him to dinner on Sunday night—cold chicken, decorated salads and trifle. He is very nice and has been especially nice to Bill. He and Bill went to Boramo yesterday for the day and had a pleasant trip, coming back to beer at 7pm.

The children and I are out most mornings for a few hours as they must have company. We go to the neighbours' or they come here in turn, so that there is someone here each morning when we are at home. We have also had visits from our agriculture officer, geologist, and other friends this week — so you see it is pretty social after being in the tent. But we will be ready for the next trek next month. It is still cool in Hargeisa—hot in the sun by midday but cool in the house and cold enough for eiderdowns at night.

As I write a starling is picking up crumbs under the table and a hornbill, two bulbuls and more starlings are at the door. They come into every room all day, and we love them. Only we can't leave a tray of cakes or anything uncovered, or they'd be gone.

Letter from Hargeisa. 1st April 1953

We have had a wonderful few days of absolute deluge. On Saturday, after complete drought and the ground like iron, water rationed to a barrel a day, and the garden just surviving and stinking of dish-water, the heavens literally opened, as they seem to do in these parts. The main tug in the valley came down at about 7 pm with a roar that could be heard here all night, and there was a tug on either side of our house, and we went to sleep while they chattered like English streams. The hillsides we live on are all cut by small water channels and a heavy storm on top brings them down as rivers. The roads are washed away and if it wasn't for large banks dug round the garden it would be gone too. Every car on the roads was stuck and anyone unlucky enough to be on the other side of the main tug had to leave the car and walk over the new suspension bridge. The water comes down the main tug like a torrent and the tar road-crossing is like a spillway. Vast boulders and trees come past, and the noise is wonderful. Bill took the car out to see the tug (we have tar to our gate and could negotiate the small rivers) and then as the children were asleep and I simply had to see it, I went for five minutes, had a look and hurried home. This certainly is a country of contrasts, and we like it more and find more to interest us as time goes on.

I've had a spurt of gardening since the rain came as I want to clean it up and get things planted to get the full benefit of what rain there is. You can almost see things growing and turning green. The place is suddenly crawling with vast tortoises about eighteen inches long and they delight the children. The flying ants and pests at the lights are the only drawback. We now have tiny black and white house swallows building in the scullery and flying through the house all day. They fly swooping round the rooms and out of the doors and are quite unperturbed by us. They are rather noisy, and they are also a source of danger when one gazes up open-mouthed as the children do! The starlings and bulbuls continue to walk about all over the house pecking at fruit and eating anything left uncovered.

We have been archaeologising and have found some good factory sites full of interest, and I've made progress with the herbarium. I have also decided to have a try at re-doing my doctorate I have decided how to approach the subject differently to simplify it and cut out the need for elaborate apparatus. And I hope to rewrite my MSc. thesis as Professor A. has offered to publish it. It will all take time as my days are very full, but I think it is worth having a try.

# MARY E. WHITE AND BARBARA ECKERSLEY

Letter from Hargeisa, Tuesday, 7th April 1953

Over Easter we made a trip out to the nearest beauty spot, Biyo Daaie, a waterfall and pools in a steep limestone and basalt gorge 42 miles away. We didn't know the road properly and did a dozen or so miles over boulders on a frightful track at one stage, ending up in a large Somali encampment to find we had taken the wrong turning about ten miles back. So we had to do the bad part again. Apart from that the road was good — a sandy track where one has to watch for stones and tree trunks and gullies, but quite easy. We left home early meaning to be at the water for early tea, but with going the wrong way were much later. We left our cars at the top and went down the gorge about a mile to a place where the water falls about 30 feet into a deep pool. It is a simply perfect spot. Getting down there with the children and the loads was quite a job as some of it was very steep, but we managed, and it was fun. We camped at the edge of the pool under a shady fig tree and wished you were there to enjoy it too. The limestone of the walls of the fall and of the sort of cave behind the big pool are all stalactites and there were cascades of *Cocculus pendens* (a woody vine) falling over the cliffs. On the stalactites, maidenhair fern grows in profusion and the water drips out of the walls into crystal pools on the rock ledges. In the water's edge there are rushes and the ground among the rocks is a mat of sedge and kweek grass with tamarisk bushes.

There was one minor mishap when Barby fell over backwards into a pool in all her clothes. Bill said he saw her go in as if in slow motion and lie on the sand at the bottom before he had her yanked up by the leg. She was shocked, as were all present, but was soon comforted. We swam right under the fall and the water was not very cold as the tug above is shallow and runs across rock which warms it. We had champagne with our picnic lunch and were to have had the top tier of our friend Elizabeth's wedding cake, but weevils, worms and all manner of fungi had got there first, and under the immaculate icing it was alive.

Coming back was easy as we knew the road, but we had to waste fifteen minutes when a tyre burst with a crack like a gun. The children slept most of the way back. David missed all the fun with the tyre and was indignant when he found out.

I spend whatever free time I have at the Herbarium, re-arranging it on the latest Kew system. It was in an awful muddle with no regular system, and it was impossible to find anything. I've now got new covers and mounting sheets on the way from London and will have a really good herbarium in time. I will soon be familiar with the whole Somali flora. Bill and I are working with John Lawrie on "vegetation arcs"—patterns on aerial photos where the vegetation is in arcs. We plan complete ecological analyses of the areas while in the Boramo district which we are due to start in next month.

The water shortage is still acute as there has been no rain to speak of in the higher parts which supply the tug. The wells are dried up in the day by the camels and stock being watered and water under the sand does not rise up enough to be pumped to the reservoir till the early hours of the morning, and then the one pump can't do much before the camels start again. We have ample, but none to waste, and to keep the garden going we use every drop from washing up and baths. So far we are just hanging on. Rain is expected in April, and we hope for a good season.

Bill seems content here. He is busy with something or other all the time. Geology, archaeology, pottering in the garage, making birdbaths, a swing for the children and fixing up a darkroom.

We have been going out to all the small tugs in the area collecting stone implements. There are so many everywhere, and the tugs are attractive with the acacias coming into leaf and flower in spite of the drought. There is a plant which you would love — a sort of convolvulus which grows as a bush about four feet high and four feet in diameter with grey, leafless stems covered in pale mauve morning glories. We picked a bunch yesterday thinking it would never do in water and we found that it makes a new crop of flowers each night so that it is freshly beautiful each day. It is startling to come on a bush of such perfect beauty in completely dry desert. The thunder clouds are building up daily and the rain is due. There has been some around but none in Hargeisa yet. We get a 44-gallon drum of water each day delivered by lorry as the mains are off until there is more water in the tug sand. We manage quite easily, and the garden is just alive. The rains must come soon. It is hot in the day, but not excessively and nights are still cool with dew dripping from the eaves.

Somaliland is being visited by the Duke of Harar[20], heir to the throne of Ethiopia, and there is a big flap on. The police band is going about playing martial music with some painful discords but lots of gusto. Flags are flying, and everyone is making a fuss. He's blacker than the ace of spades of course, and it's quite an education. He was met at the border by the Chief Secretary and other high officials in a fleet of cars and escorted into Hargeisa. A tent had been put up a few miles out where he could go to tidy his hair and apparel and get his breath before the triumphal drive into the metropolis. The Governor and all officers turned out in tropical kit, including helmets with plumes, and tomorrow His Highness is going to watch the polo. We usually watch as we know the riders and it is something to do, so we are going too, as no doubt all of the rest of the 150 inhabitants will do, not to mention the high up Somalis. It is all very amusing and full of local colour.

The doctor's wife has just had a daughter and David says he wants a new baby too, so I think it is time to get a puppy as two babies is enough for now. We may get a spaniel which is available but wonder if it is wise with constant rabies scares, going out on trek, and home leave every fifteen months when someone has to keep the dog and the children might pine. No doubt in a little time we will have a menagerie like there was when I was a child.

Have I told you the fun we have with goats? With the drought all the stock from miles around is brought to drink at the tug wells and there are flocks of sheep and goats coming and going all the time, and camels and the thinnest cattle too. They are not supposed to graze in this area as it is a "closed" area at the moment,

---

[20] Duke of Harar: Prince Makonnen Haile Selassie - Second son of Emperor Haile Selassie and Empress Menen Asfaw

but with no food anywhere the grazing guards don't do much to stop them. My big vegetable garden has survived the drought by much careful planning of where each drop of water will be put. The goats are watched by small Somali girls, and they are very keen to let them stray into gardens because a full stomach is worth any anger. I've got tired of seeing the goats being chased to my fence in the hopes that they will get through. After losing a few cabbages I caught a goat by the ear and tied it up, and when the owner came I threatened dire penalties if it strayed again. That did not help so next time I caught two and sent them to John Lawrie to put in the Pound. For a while that helped, then last week the whole crop of cabbages was eaten, and three little girls stood grinning at the fence, so we caught four goats and sent them along and a grazing guard came and rounded up the whole flock. Since then there hasn't been a goat in sight but there are also no vegetables to worry about. The delight of the children when they hear a goat is perfect, and the welcome they accord to the camels which bring the charcoal is tremendous.

Letter from Hargeisa. 27th April 1953

After the heavy rain a week ago, this place is heavenly — green with amazing growth everywhere. Every inch of the ground is covered with seedlings of all sorts. I suppose it is like the desert ephemerals and they have to come up when there is water. There are tortoises about in hundreds too. Bellaloo[21] bends right down to peer in at the big ones when they are inside their shells and has long conversations with them. I have visions of her getting snapped on the nose. We had a small one for a day but let it go. With so many animals around I do not want to start keeping anything in a cage. The painted starlings sing quite beautiful songs at night, even the doves coo at night when there is a moon.

Yesterday we had a palaver with an ostrich egg. We bought one from a Somali and I planned sponge cakes and omelettes.

---

[21] One of the many names for Barby—Bella, Bellaloo, Lulu, Lulabelle, Bella de pant, Panta-lulu

When we cracked the shell and punctured the thick membrane we saw blood. So, we opened it carefully and there was a little ostrich almost ready to hatch. It was alive and I am kicking myself for not acting more quickly and saving its life. We were all interested and upset and by the time I decided to tie off the yolk sac it had lost a lot of blood. We wrapped the chick up and put it on a hot water bottle. It was such a perfect little thing, feathers and all, and it seemed such a waste. Finally, we told the children it was going to run off into the bushes to find its mother and they were quite happy about it. If I ever have to act midwife to another ostrich I will know what to do and it should be possible to hand-rear it as they must be very hardy.

There are coucals[22] by the dozen here and their calls are all around all day. Every time I hear one I think of Waterkloof at 5am and am quite homesick. We look forward to your letters and all the news. I can't tell you how much or why I like this place. I am at home here as never anywhere up to now. Bill's contentment and endless interests are largely responsible as far as I am concerned. He is fit and full of energy and is submitting a paper to be read at the International Conference in June.

I have just discovered that Barbara has removed all her clothes and is stark naked. I've taught them to undress themselves, and this is the result. Fat and adorable and full of the devil!

When the Duke of Harar was here Bill had to be official photographer. The polo match was worth watching and one man fell off to the delight of the children. David now plays polo, riding his trike and wielding a wooden spoon and Barbara has to retrieve the ball.

The children and I have been working really hard in the garden. The morning glory is in flower all over the stoep. We are all so brown that I'm almost ashamed of my back. I wear sun-top dresses and look like a Capey[23]. David and Barbara have been revelling in the rain. They are mud from top to bottom all day and they are out in the rain a lot too, yelling and dancing with delight.

---

[22] birds of the cuckoo family
[23] A resident of the Western Cape or of Cape Town

They have a bath full of water and digging implements under the thorn tree at the back door and spend all afternoon bathing and making mud pies. I have to rinse them off in the garden before I can let them into the house. When it rains they strip, unaided, and charge out under the edge of the roof to get the hardest deluge.

Barbara has such a passion for all things living. I seem to remember feeling as she does when I was small. David loves them but is detached. He is very independent and goes alone to visit neighbours along a little track. He walks with his hands behind his back like one of 90. I watch from the house without him knowing.

We met the District Commissioner of Boramo who is called ffrench-Petah and who is as incredible as his name. He is small and slight with long curls in his neck and a face like a clown. He has an alert cocky manner and uses expressions which one feels are really too much! He even wears pants with a sort of flap at the front and two points on the hips with buttons there, quite unlike anything I've seen. He sways back and forth on his toes when he talks, giggles, but is very nice indeed. He has a wife and two children who we hope will visit us in camp.

You will be amused at how the Somali mind works. A ram was born with five legs, hermaphrodite and revolting in all sorts of other ways, and the proud owner asked permission of the Governor to fly it to England as a present for the Queen. The owner and the ram are now in Aden, the ram under a blanket and all who want to look are charged 50 cents. I wonder if the Queen would have been amused.

# ENGAGEMENT AND A TRIAL GEOLOGICAL FIELD SEASON

Bill and Mary's engagement

Bill and Mary

A badge Mary made for her shoulder bag reads:
Per Expeditionium ad Matrimonium

# AFRICAN BEGINNINGS

Tintintabulating frogs talk to the busy stream
Which chuckles, gurgling, among the reeds
And round-rolled pebbles.

## ENGAGEMENT AND A
## TRIAL GEOLOGICAL FIELD SEASON

When my numerous family members heard that I had decided to marry a young geologist and live in a tent in the wilds of Southern Rhodesia, they reacted in their characteristic individual ways to the news. My father was delighted because he knew the life would suit me, and he liked the geologist and would himself have wanted to map uncharted territory had he been younger. My mother worried about what we would do if we became ill, with no doctor within hundreds of miles; about snakes, and wild animals, and unreliable drinking water. She hoped that a long engagement might make me decide in favour of one of my more conventional suitors — a nice doctor or a university lecturer perhaps, who would supply a more settled future.

My grandmother was relieved that the man was from Ulster and that there was no risk of contamination of my children with black blood. She was also a little disappointed as she could not do her usual genealogical investigation to satisfy herself of the suitability of the applicant. She had embarrassed me previously by working out the pedigrees of my escorts even before they had shown serious intentions. She had a vast knowledge of the ramifications of most of the best South African families and knew which had "a touch of the tar brush", as she so elegantly put it. She warned each of her very numerous grandchildren in turn of the dangers of producing a pitch-black baby with peppercorn hair in accordance with the sins of the father being visited on the children even unto the sixth generation. She was unaware of the genetic impossibility of this threat, and so were we. Her interest was kindly, and I had great affection and respect for her as a matriarch who held a whole tribe together, but now I am horrified by her racist attitudes which were typical of the place and times back then.

Ancient Aunt Katy was so pleased that she had bought that purple toque at a sale some years before, as it was still as good as new, and would be just right for a wedding — but on second thoughts she would probably not attend because her waterworks were so troublesome these days. However, she immediately went to hunt in a cupboard for a suitable gift among the hundreds that she had been given in the course of a very long life. She re-wrapped all presents she received even before the donor departed, making a note on the gift card of the contents, and kept them to give away again. Some relatives claimed to have given and received back the same present repeatedly for years, others were said to give what they wanted for themselves, and to hint unmistakably when their birthday came around. A most conscience-satisfying method of obtaining little luxuries that they would never have dreamt of buying for themselves.

Strange Aunt Georgie, who was then about ninety, was deeply shocked because I called at four o'clock in the afternoon. She had retired for the night and her house was shuttered and dark, because for years she had been getting up progressively earlier in the mornings and going to bed correspondingly earlier in the afternoon. She would, however, have been deeply hurt if I had not visited, and she forgave the insensibility of the very young who are out and about until all hours of the night. Aunt Georgie was in the habit of staging death-bed scenes whenever

124

she considered she had been poorly treated by her family. She regularly arrayed herself in pure white draperies and reclined on a velvet couch, having summoned her family, by phone and well in advance, to hear her final wishes before she took off to pastures new. Because she was so old and frail no one liked to risk denying her the pleasure, just in case she really did die this time, and there was usually a good turnout and a happy family gathering. They came bearing cakes and rusks, and even sherry and brandy for *medicinal purposes*, and the party left the old lady refreshed and rejuvenated. She would bustle about for days afterwards, making life impossible for her old, unmarried, daughter who lived with her, and for the old native servant who had waited on her devotedly for fifty years. She went around sprinkling grains of sugar in the very corners of the stairs and other inaccessible places so that she could check up whether the cleaning was being thoroughly done. As a cleaning day was liable to start at 3am. and no one might be abroad in the middle of the night at four in the afternoon, it says much for her charm and character that she had managed to survive to such a ripe old age and still be treated with affection.

Only two relatives really offered me advice. Uncle George warned me that tents are great incubators, and time proved him right. My newly-acquired-by-marriage Uncle Bob's recipe for a happy marriage was always to sleep in a double bed, and never to welcome a husband at the end of a long day at the office with the information that one had been on one's feet all day and the children had been impossible; and always to make him feel welcome when he arrived home and save the worries until he had had time to relax. Of course, Uncle Bob (and most of the men of his generation and also of mine) would be regarded by today's generation of young adults as a male chauvinist pig, but it was good advice and I followed it as well as I could for all my married life. I had been brought up with a clear view of male and female roles and simply never analysed it, accepting my role as a wife and mother as the ultimate fulfillment, which I found it (during that phase of my life) to be. I have realised, looking back at things, that why this was so was because I had been so fortunate—finding the right partner and loving him so completely that I still think of him with deep and abiding love though he has been dead for more than thirty years.

None of my family or friends had any personal experience of geologists or their way of life. If they had, I'm sure I would have received conflicting advice from all quarters. I was to find that the pursuit of geology is a calling to those who love it and are good at it, and it imposes a lifestyle and certain constraints on geologists' families.

Everyone decided it would be wise to try a sample of a field season before getting married, in case I found it quite impossible to adjust to life in the wilds. An expedition was planned for my two brothers and me to join Bill in the Sabi Valley (now Save Valley) in Southern Rhodesia where he was currently mapping. Elaborate preparations were made and my mother insisted that we should go armed with a .45 Webley revolver, a scout whistle to indicate our whereabouts should we become lost in the bush, snake-bite outfits, first-aid kits, mosquito nets and heaven knows what else in the way of unlikely equipment which she considered necessary for our safety, or indeed for our very survival. By the time we added food, tins of rusks, containers of reliable water, natural history collecting impedimenta for my brothers, botanical presses and books for me, cameras, binoculars, clothing and the rest, our ancient family Terraplane was sitting low on its springs. Passengers, the necessary afterthought, were far from comfortable.

Fortunately for us, my mother's attention was distracted shortly before we left by the arrival of a letter from England from a man called Hector Payne who claimed to be my father's step-nephew. It informed the family that he was arriving hard on the heels of the letter as an immigrant to South Africa, and would be accompanied by his wife Ida, and the girls (number and age unspecified). They were coming to stay with us until they had decided on a suitable habitat. This was momentous news indeed, because nobody had heard of Hector before, and as for Ida Payne — the name was of course too improbable for words.

To tell the truth just about all of my father's family were totally unknown to us. When he had married my mother he had been so appalled by the complexities of her family and the numbers involved, that he took a perverse delight in withholding all information on his own. In fact, they had been married for twenty years before my mother found out that her father-in-law had been quite an accomplished and highly paid industrial chemist. She had assumed, from a chance remark that she had misinterpreted, that he was a coal miner and best left out of the conversation. He worked on chemistry of clays used for ceramic manufacture for blast furnaces and did not go down the pit daily with a miner's hat on and his lunch in a little tin box as my mother said she had visualised. In South Africa there was considerable snobbery about jobs that should be done by a native, the absence of natives in England being regrettable in this context.

So, while my mother planned Uncle Hector's visit and shuffled everyone around to accommodate his family, we were able to pack up what we considered necessary, and there was less drama than would otherwise have been the case. We were relieved to know that we would be away when the Hectors arrived as the preparations for, and speculation about, their visit was beginning to pall. My brothers amused themselves by impersonating Hector on the phone to my mother while she was at her office, causing a great panic, followed by indignation when she realised it was a hoax. After three such incidents, her confidence was so undermined that when the family finally arrived she thought they were imposters. We were away on our trip by then and she thought that they were university friends of her sons' who had been persuaded to come to her office to trick her again. Their appearance did nothing to dispel this misapprehension—Hector wore long baggy shorts, short socks and sandshoes and carried a linen hat; Ida had a very short, tight cotton dress, and bobby-sox with high heeled shoes; and the two busty girls were encased in very tight, tubular dresses and had pigtails tied with ribbons. They were fourteen and fifteen and looked quite unlike local girls of that age. When my mother was finally persuaded to come to the front desk to meet her visitors, she collapsed in helpless mirth, playing along with the supposed imposters until it suddenly dawned on her that they were genuine. They were utterly bewildered, and I wish I knew what they thought.

My mother was a woman of tremendous charm and she managed to turn the situation round, though later, at home, when they handed her a present of a brass alarm clock she pitched it into a chair on the other side of the room to her (and their) amazement. I'm sure that they had grave reservations about her sanity. That did not stop them moving in and staying on and on, until finally they had to be asked to move on so that the family could return to their own rooms.

♠♠

Our trial expedition was an unqualified success. We drove the 600 miles to Fort Victoria where we met Bill, staying a night in the local hotel and proceeding next day to the camp. The tents were in the middle of nowhere on the banks of the Chiredze River. There were no roads, only a track to a sugar estate and onwards linking a mission hospital and a few remote ranches. We traversed the country in all directions from the base camp while Bill continued with his mapping. Much of the country was granite sand, with granite boulder koppies liberally sprinkled. The vegetation was savannah, with long, tall thatch grass and clumps of trees. There were dried-up vleis (swamps) with shorter grass and sedges, and areas of Mopani[24] forest on red sand patches where the slender tree trunks were sometimes so close together that a fat man could not have walked in a straight line through them. The river banks had dense forest, with enormous trees and lianas and a wealth of plant species.

---

[24] A leguminous tree Colophospermum mopane, native to South Africa that is highly resistant to drought and produces very hard wood.

The abundance of game was one of the highlights of our visit to that unspoiled part of Africa. Impala in herds of hundreds bounded away as we approached. Royal kudu and sable were glimpsed in the dappled shade of the forest of Mopani trees. Lions roared on the river at night and their huge pug marks were found in the wet mud surprisingly close to the camp in the mornings. We found a lion's daytime lair under a thorn bush in a grassy area near a koppie. The grass was flattened, there was hair from his mane on the thorns, and there were fresh bones that he had been chewing. There was an all-pervading smell of male cat and we hurried by with many a backward glance, no doubt watched by him from the safety of the koppie.

Elephants were everywhere and we could hear the crash of falling trees as they grazed a roadway through the veldt, and we deviated from our intended path on several occasions so as to avoid them. Once we found ourselves in a patch of woodland in which the huge grey shapes of silent, immobile elephants could be seen. We decided that discretion was the best policy and headed as quickly and calmly as possible up the nearby steep koppie. We thought we would be out of their territory there, and we were all very anxious, not to say panic-stricken, when right at the top we came on heaps of steaming dung and knew that a steep pile of boulders was no barrier to an elephant. We waited for an hour there, wondering what would happen next, and presently the herd wandered out of the thick shade and off towards the river, and after a decent interval we descended and headed in a roundabout way back to the camp.

Zebra had been declared vermin in the Sabi Valley that year as their multitudes were said to be eating all the grazing, leaving none for the cattle that the few settlers had in the area. The first cattle ranchers had taken up land in the area a few years before. They had lost some cattle to the lions whose territory they had invaded. They declared an all-out war on the lions and hunting, trapping and poisoning had decimated the lion population. That it had also upset the balance of nature was soon apparent. Zebra, the lions' favourite food, had never had it so good, and the increase in zebra numbers posed a far more serious problem than the lions had done. The government even employed native zebra hunters who were armed with incredible old blunderbusses. They were paid a bounty for zebra tails and some control of numbers was achieved. Nature readjusted the numbers in time by sending a pestilence that killed zebra in thousands shortly afterwards. Whereas under a natural system, lions had killed the weak and ailing, thus stopping the spread of disease to the healthy in the herds, the sickly now lived long enough to infect more of their kind.

We visited one lonely ranch in a remote part of the mapping area one day and were shown a hippo-shaped doorway. When the house was being built in the traditional pole-and-dagga way used in the wilds, where the only building material imported was corrugated iron for a roof, an inquisitive hippo had come up from the river and chased the farmer into his house. The mud in the walls was still wet and the hippo had tried to force his great bulk in through the doorway after him, luckily without success. The sides of the door bent to the hippo's shape and stayed that way. There were large numbers of hippo in the rivers. They congregated in the deeper pools and there was one such pool near the camp where a very dangerous and aggressive male hippo lived. The pool was near a native village and the young boys had been tormenting the beast by hurling stones at him and rushing away and up trees when he lost his temper and pursued them. It was a continuing sport and doomed to end in tragedy, and meanwhile we made long detours around that area as we were by no means as fleet of foot as the boys and had no desire to encounter an irate hippo that might be grazing in the vicinity.

We identified hundreds of different birds, and my younger brother was collecting for a museum and had a list of species to bring home. He shot them with a 22 sports gun, skinned them expertly, turning them inside-out and retaining the skulls, and treating the skins with white arsenic. As there was only one camp table his mess of arsenic and entrails had to be cleared away before a meal could be served. He failed to get a specimen of the big grey lourie or go-away bird that was everywhere in the big trees repeating its raucous and unfriendly cry. He aimed at, and was sure he hit, several — but only a solitary downward-spiralling feather rewarded him in the absolute silence that follows a shot in the veldt. It was not till days later that a putrefying stench showed what the trouble had been. The go-away bird clings tightly to its perch when it dies, and hangs till decomposed, and the only way to get a fresh specimen is to shoot it in flight.

Guinea fowl in flocks abounded and kept us in meat. Each day the same flock appeared at the same time in the early morning near a large termite mound close to the camp. One shot would take care of dinner, and though the flock flew off it always reappeared as regularly as clockwork next day, apparently not associating the bang with the disappearance of one of its number. An occasional buck had to be shot, reluctantly, to keep the native cook and field boy in meat.

There was another geologist from the Geological Survey working in an adjacent area. He had his wife in the field with him, and they came over to our camp to celebrate Bill's birthday and our engagement on 07.07.1947. We cut a huge, iced cake, which had been an important part of our provisions brought with us from Pretoria. I was convinced I would love the life, and that I had made the right choice, and we decided to marry exactly a year from that day.

The visit to the field camp was all too brief and all of us wished it could have been longer, but I had to return to finish a thesis, and my brothers had to get back to work and school. If our vehicle had been laden on our outward journey, it was equally encumbered on our return, even without the food that we had used or left behind in the camp. We had packs of bird specimens, and some smelt awful, though I was told not to complain. We had a considerable weight of rock specimens, and botanical presses full of drying plants; and some strange relics like a buck skull and large animal bones that we had found; and large round baobab fruits and the enormous pods of the

German-sausage tree[25] whose poisonous fruit up to 60cm long resembles a sausage in a casing.

As we approached home we joked about Hector and the family whom we were sure must have arrived in our absence. We decided it would be nice to make a spectacular entrance, rushing in and blazing away with the 6-shooter and blowing the unused scout whistle to set the scene. Only deference to our grandmother's advanced age made us decide to arrive quietly. We need not have worried. Our appearance out of the night, dust and dirt encrusted, with our strange assortment of inappropriate clothing and equipment, and the chaotic and weird contents of the car, made a great impression on our totally urban new relatives. They were still bewildered and feeling their way after my mother's strange reception on their arrival. It was patently obvious that they were still in that awful state of wondering whether they or we were mad.

No one had thought to tell them where we were or the nature of our expedition. I think it put new life into Hector to feel that the savage Africa that he had secretly hoped to find might still be there for the finding. He confessed later to having been disappointed when he arrived in Africa. He had left England feeling that migration was a great and brave step into the mystery and romance of the darkest continent. He had visualised my dad — "Uncle Charley"— as going on a Stanley and Livingstone type of adventure when he had left England about thirty years before, and he hoped things had not changed. He had imagined Dad as the sole white man and upholder of the British Empire in the heart of Africa, being offered a choice of the black chief's favourite wives. And now he had come to Africa to find life in our quiet suburb as well-ordered as England, even if his relatives were eccentric. Perhaps migrants these days are better prepared for what they are going to find; or do some like poor old Hector still carry their improbable dreams inside them in spite of what they know must be true? He settled down to live exactly the same life as he

---

[25] *Kigelia Africana*

had lived in England, but with the bonus of better weather, and he stayed. But Ida and the girls, who I'm sure never knew what he had dreamed was in store for them in Africa, and they would never have come if they had known, returned to England and their small safe corner there with their familiar friends and predictable family.

If my family had hoped that I would decide that the comforts of city life were preferable to a life of heat, dust, flies and considerable physical hardship, then they must have been a little disappointed. They were too generous-hearted to try to dampen my enthusiasm and accepted that the choice was mine to make.

Mary's sister Joan

Perhaps that is why Africa has a presence,
"Gets into your blood"

# WEDDING

Bill and I were married as planned on his birthday the next year. Our family habit of escalating the simplest arrangements into a performance of complexity and massive disorganisation ran true to form.

It was decided that a small family wedding could be best achieved by moving out of the house that we shared with our grandmother, and hiring a large, cold and uncomfortable house in an adjoining suburb. We duly moved, plus two dogs, two cats and cages of assorted birds, a few days before the wedding. The dogs and cats kept disappearing or becoming involved in hectic fights with neighbours' animals. The family car, that was to be lent to us for our honeymoon, broke down and we had to do all the fetching and carrying of food, drink, hired crockery, wedding cake, and the host of other errands in a 1922 Silver Ghost Rolls Royce. This wonderful car, named Lavinia because of the lady with flowing drapes who decorated the peak of its radiator, had been acquired for Bill by post after being discovered as a car enthusiast. It had been up on blocks on a farm, being used as a chicken coop, and its interior was still not very hygienic. Its engine had started without hesitation after ten years' rest, but because among other things, it had only back wheel brakes, it was deemed unsuitable for us in Rhodesia and was passed on to my brother Bob.

Bill came by train from Rhodesia two days before we were to be married. He knew no one and I am sure the upheaval and hectic activity, which all sorted itself out in time for the event, must have left him as bewildered as Hector. My brother Peter was to have been best man, but he had contracted hepatitis and was very ill, being looked after in the house by my sister Joan who was a nurse. He was on a drip and confined to bed and a substitute had to be found at the last minute. The boyfriend of Maricelle who worked with me at the Pasture Research Department, where I had been employed since leaving university the previous September, offered to help out. None of us had met him and he added his bit to the dramas of the times by standing too close to the radiator in the vestry and setting fire to a trouser leg. An all-pervading stink of burning wool followed him, and us, down the aisle.

My mother was all but out of action with a migraine headache that stayed with her all the time she was in the strange house, and it must have taken great fortitude to carry on as she did. I was too happy to think much about her at the time, and she did not complain. We hoped that as the day was a Wednesday some of our vast family would not be able to attend. Over a hundred made it, and it was a clear, warm, winter morning and the reception was in the garden. The vase of fresh violets that decorated the top of the cake leaked and all three tiers were flooded but found just in time before the icing dissolved. The stove fused and the hot savouries had to be served cold.

A major disaster had been narrowly avoided the night before. I woke to find my male cat busily marking his territory in the strange house by spraying my room. My wedding dress was hanging on the wall ready for the morning and it was missed by inches. As it was, the smell in the room was so overwhelming that it was impossible to spend the rest of the night there. I hung the dress up in a breezy passage and migrated to share a double bed with my mother and sister. None of us slept much. I was delicately perfumed with male cat, and we all found the situation hilarious. We hoped fervently that the smell adhering to my hair would have abated by the time I had to go to the church.

We drove off on our honeymoon in the family car after the reception and stopped in a wood half way to our first destination on the way to Plettenberg Bay (a mere 1200 km drive) to have the picnic that my mother had packed for us. She had put in a bottle of champagne and Bill said afterwards that he took the middle bridge over every river that we had to cross to get to Parys.

Fortunately, it was not until the end of the third day's travel, when we had negotiated the winding mountain passes in the Cape and were safely installed at the Beacon Island Hotel, that our car troubles started manifesting themselves. No fewer than three of the Buick's wheels tore themselves off, leaving a ragged circle of metal round the studs — an alarming, original and potentially hazardous complaint. On each occasion we were just moving off after a stop when the wheel crunched off. When we went to a garage with the first, the young mechanic said, "bloody God, man, I never seed that before," and when the second and third events occurred, at decent intervals when we were just beginning to believe it could not happen again, we repeated his words of wisdom and were overcome with mirth — though the financial strain put on our very limited budget was no laughing matter.

We spent two idyllic weeks at Beacon Island, exploring the coast, the mountains and the forests. Some of South Africa's best scenery is round that Garden Route region, and it was out of season, and we had it largely to ourselves. We drove back to Pretoria, left the car there and took the train to Salisbury (another 1000 km plus trip). There we had two days in a hotel and then set off to the Sabi Valley again to complete the field season that Bill had interrupted to marry me.

The area in which we were to live from August to November was so remote that many of the tribal natives had not seen a white woman, and we were to have no contact with Europeans except for the isolated occasion when a government official called at our camp on the way to a distant outpost or to assess the desert locust problems, or to examine native cattle for disease. It was a wonderful way to start a marriage and a wonderful experience for which we were both deeply grateful. So little of the world remains untouched and unchanged by modern man, and it was a privilege to be part of the teeming life of that natural kingdom.

And exerts a spell
That draws its children back nostalgically
If ever they have known
Its secret ways?

# GEOLOGICAL FIELD SEASON
# IN THE SABI VALLEY

Compared with today, field work for geologists in 1948-49 was an adventure and real pioneering stuff. There was none of the back up like radio contact, or base camps, or even consideration for the well-being of the geologist or his family. We supplied our own basic medical kit and the nearest clinic, staffed by a native first-aid assistant, was fifty miles away from some of our camps. There was no thought of return trips to a city during a field season. A six or seven month stretch, or longer if the weather held, in an unmapped area, remote, with the most basic equipment, was the norm. Such mail as we received was brought by the rare visitors passing through the area. The geologist had to be his own mechanic and good at improvising in all situations. I remember an occasion when a springy branch had to be used to replace a broken spring of the old-fashioned suspension of a vehicle and times when sumps had to have holes in them repaired after a fashion; and bits of engines that were kept working by tying them up with wire.

We carried a 44-gallon drum of petrol and had to replenish it from a dump in the general area that was supposed to have fuel at all times. We were to find, however, that the supply was uncertain and there were worrying times when we were waiting for petrol and could not even move camp or go to the very remote native stores to replenish stocks of tinned food. Once, our food had dwindled to rice and black tea and we sampled bamboo shoots from the wild reeds that grew in the Sabi River.

We employed two Africans, a cook and a field assistant, and we took a stock of basic foods, including the main rations for the servants as laid down by regulation — "mealie-meal", beans, sugar, a little tea and tobacco. We were expected to keep them in meat by shooting buck as required. We were issued with an army rifle for this purpose, and Bill had a duck gun of his own that was used for obtaining a regular supply of guinea fowl.

A geologist had to be self-reliant and self-motivated. There was a saying that you didn't have to be mad to be one, but it certainly helped. It was expected that when he returned at the end of the field season he would bring back a geological map of his area ready for publication. In the case of the Southern Rhodesian Geological Survey, our generation of geologists was considered to have it easy because the Director and his generation had been the real pioneers. They had travelled in ox wagons, taking their family, a cage of chickens, a milking cow, and a gun and disappearing into completely uncharted territory for a year or more at a time. Our equipment from the government consisted of a three-quarter ton utility, a tent for us and one for the "boys", camp beds, a table and chairs, and a plane-table and the paraphernalia needed for making a map of the area.

The journey from Umtali (now Mutare) into the mapping area was long and hot. Our new canvas water bags had not been soaked sufficiently and dried up, and we were not carrying any other water as we were to camp on the Chiredzi River. We had set off later than planned as the shopping for supplies was delayed by problems with form-filling to obtain the servants' bulk supplies. The unmapped tracks deteriorated progressively and by evening when it was getting dark we were proceeding anxiously along one so overgrown and little used that Bill was uncertain that we were on the right one. We were aiming for a single, prominent, rocky hill on the banks of the Chiredzi. Since the middle of the afternoon our way had taken us through forest in which elephants had been snapping the trees and creating havoc. Huge piles of their dung decorated the track on which we were driving and once when we stopped to consult the map and take compass bearings we could hear a herd breaking down trees nearby. Bill kept reassuring me that we would not meet elephants on the track, that the piles of dung were old and cold and that we would soon reach the river and be able to camp. He told me months later, in the safety of our flat in Salisbury with the field season completed, that some of the dung was still steaming and he had expected to collide with a pachyderm around each bend.

It was after dark when at last we came to, of all things, a brush fence, and had arrived at the district officer's rest camp on the banks of the river. The rocky pile of the lone hill was silhouetted against a starry sky and the night noises of frogs and crickets, and the damp smell of the African night met us when we stepped out of the rattling ute into the quiet darkness. Recalling the moment, I feel again the magic and mystery that is the Africa-in-my-blood as though it was yesterday.

The rest camp was a thatched hut with mosquito screening on two sides and a cooking hut, open-sided, with a stone fire-place close by, enclosed in a brush fence (to keep lions out). The deep-pit toilet was away in the scrub, and we found it only next day — which was as well because it harboured a large snake, spiders and heaven knows what creepy crawlies, and a lovely little black bat hanging among the thatch. We needed water urgently and were aware that crocodiles were found in the river, so we explored with torches and located a deep pool among the riverbank ridges. We sent the boys to fetch water, confident that it would be safer to wade in to fill buckets there than in the main river. We were to discover later that that was the one pool in the district that contained a permanently-resident very large croc.

First light revealed the beauty of this first camp—a swiftly-running river, dense riverine forest, the rock-pile hill whose resident fish eagles soared above their territory, and the dawn chorus of innumerable birds. For a few days we stayed there, using the top of the koppie to survey the area and put fixed points onto the map so that the geology could be fitted in later, and mapping of the immediate vicinity. Thereafter we moved camp as each area was completed.

One camp on the banks of the Sabi was particularly pleasant. Our tent was under a tree whose blue pea-flowers carpeted the ground. The trees formed a grove on a grassy, open area with only bamboos fringing the river banks and separating us from the water. In a remaining deep pool, at this time when the river was low and consisted of a number of threads braided across the pebbly river bed, a company of hippos had taken up residence. There were fourteen in all, from small, shiny, tight-in-their-skins babies to enormous adults. We gave them all H names, from Henry and Henrietta to Horace and Hyphene. They restricted our night-time activities because hippos hate fire and charge and stamp out cooking and camp fires. We had to eat early and have our fires out before it was really dark because the thought of a charging hippo with little regard for things like tents in his line of attack was not very reassuring. The loaded gun that lay between our camp beds was to be used to fire into the air and try to frighten away any hippo heard charging towards us in the night. I was more afraid of the loaded rifle than of the possibility of a hippo visit, guns and killing having been totally abhorrent to me for as long as I can remember.

It was in that camp that we ran out of petrol and hence out of food and were reduced to eating bamboo shoots. There, too, we had seven baby cobras crawling in our tent one day. They had gone under the mat that covered the ground inside the tent, having been born alive to a passing mother snake that was not of the egg-laying kind. They seemed too small to kill, even in Africa where the only snake considered to be good is a dead snake, so we caught them in a jar, and after thinking of pickling them in whiskey, let them go far away from the tent.

One evening at that camp we were going down through the ridges and bush fringing the river to walk about in the cool near the water when a thin grey snake swung out across my way at head level and spat on the back of the hand I had raised to fend it off. I stood dead still, Bill ran back to the tent for the shotgun and returned to blow the snake's head to bits. I had felt the spray on the back of my hand, and although it was washed off promptly I later developed a radiating pattern of small wart-like growths that disappeared only years later.

Bill's work was strenuous and often exhausting. From each camp he walked out on traverses, averaging about twelve miles a day. Sometimes he drove out when the country was open, or the area had a rudimentary track going in the required direction and did his traverse from wherever he left the vehicle. Then, at the end of his mapping he would tell the African field assistant to lead him back to the ute, and without hesitation the boy would set off, making a beeline for that spot in the wilderness, emerging within yards of the target after presumably operating on a mental map and noticing landmarks invisible to "civilised" eyes. The homing instinct shown by tribal Africans in this way was phenomenal.

Although it was winter, days were hot, and we rose before dawn so Bill could set out and complete the walking in the cooler part of the day. When he got back to camp, dehydrated and footsore, he drank gallons of Roses Lime juice with water-bag boiled water and rested in the cool of the tent. Then hours were spent in plotting and recording the day's information. I learnt to help with the plotting of the traverses on the map, specialising in stream traverses that he had mapped by recording numbers of strides on each compass bearing, and which then had to be wiggled in between the known fixed distances. I seldom accompanied Bill on long traverses, though sometimes when the day was cooler than usual, with a guti mist[26] at dawn, or after rain, I went along.

When I stayed in camp I was free to wander out into the veldt from the tent, to collect botanical specimens, identify plants, bird-watch, and to observe the game. I remember wonderful days when buck leapt over the wash line strung between the tent and a tree; when a kudu and calf wandered into our clearing and stood sniffing the air; when a new-born hippo calf stood triumphant on his mother's back with his umbilical cord still attached and the hippo family were inspecting their new addi-

---

[26]   Persistent drizzle, thin shower, wet mist

tion; and nights of dappled moonlight and owls hooting and the nightjars screaming like lost souls. I do not remember ever feeling menaced by the world of wild things outside our tent's walls; only the feeling of being privileged to hear a lion grunt and a hyena laugh and to be part of their wonderful world.

In one camp, in a remote area near the Portuguese[27] border, however, I knew primeval fear — of fire. We were camped in savannah far from any river, where a few waterholes in an almost dry stream enabled the local Africans to survive. Our water was fetched in 44-gallon drums a couple of times a week. We had a similar drum of petrol in our camp as we were too far from any depot to replenish our supply, and it and the vehicle had to be protected. It was late in the season and the country was tinder dry. Huge wildfires were burning in Mozambique and with the strong prevailing winds of that season were approaching our area. Fires in those dry grasslands, as in Australia, travel at amazing speed, burning out vast areas. Bill returned from his day's traverse early, having seen smoke on a wide front coming in our general direction. We had no real option but to stay where we were and protect our camp as best we could by burning firebreaks around our "island". With just four people, no water and the necessity to control the back-burn, burning the wide break we needed for safety and not letting the fire get away and destroy areas that might perhaps not get burnt if our worst fears and the fire did not eventuate, it was awful work. Beating with wet sacks and a torn-up blanket, breathing the smoke and heat and frantically trying to win a race against time and the approaching wall of flames and billowing smoke, I remember thinking that if I died in the fire at least I had known perfect happiness in the last few months.

By the time the fire reached us the wind had dropped somewhat, the flames ringed our island and went on relentlessly across the grassy plain, into the woods, and towards the river. We were red-eyed, exhausted, hair singed, black and somewhat hysterical. The only remaining problem was one that we had not antici-

---

27 Portuguese Mozambique or Portuguese East Africa—now the Republic of Mozambique

pated. We found we were sharing our small brown island in a sea of blackened grass with everything living that could fly, creep, crawl, slither, run or limp into its sanctuary. In the common bond that links survivors after a holocaust we shared our space and even our beds with all comers. Like the sheep that lies down with the wolf, we flopped as we were and slept — and all around us predators and prey rested side by side through a moonlit night. Pugmarks of a lion in the mud next to the water drum, hoofmarks of buck; snakes and birds sharing perches on the few singed trees, and birds singing a dawn song of hope and life with the first rosy tinge of dawn. And everywhere a green and brown swarming of insects — in one's hair, down one's neck, slippery underfoot.

We had stayed in that camp for longer than in most others as the open savannah made it possible to drive in trackless country and cover more territory. I had brought my new Singer sewing machine with me and many dress lengths of fabric, and as there was not the same botanical collecting and exploring to do as the river camps had offered, I made myself a new summer wardrobe. The "New Look" was all the rage, and I remember two very special, very feminine dresses that I made in that camp and wore with pleasure for several years afterwards. The local piccaninnies, who used to creep close to the tent in the long grass to watch what the alien people were doing, were absolutely fascinated by the sewing machine and I would look up to see shining black faces peering at me. If I moved to the other side of the tent out of sight they rustled through the grass and reappeared where they were able to see.

The only frustrating thing that I remember of that year's field work was not being able to enjoy the rivers when one was hot and dusty. Bilharzia (Schistosomiasis) was so prevalent that even fast running water was out of bounds. Washing water was heated for long periods or had permanganate added, drinking water was boiled, and if for some reason one had come in contact with untreated river water, one promptly washed off in Dettol solution.

Tintintabulating frogs talk to the busy stream
Which chuckles, gurgling, among the reeds
And round-rolled pebbles.

# SABI BUSH HOSPITALITY AND THE MASHABA FIELD SEASON

The only social occasion during the four months' stay in the Sabi-Chiredzi wilderness was a weekend visit to the Hippo mine close to the Portuguese border. The mine manager, who was the sole surviving employee and caretaker of the mine, passed through one of our camps and invited us for a weekend. We set out one Saturday on the rudimentary track that ran to the mine and before long were wishing we had not embarked on the trip. The track was atrocious. Rocky ridges with huge loose stones were difficult to cross and the ever-present risk of holing the sump or breaking a brake cable made it a risky process. Those were days before 4 WDs were in general use. It was terribly hot and when we arrived at the mine the real endurance test started.

Our host was so pleased to have company that he had set his young native cook to work for days before and full-time while we were there. In that heat and after that shaking up in the ute, we were immediately sat down to a five-course lunch. Fish from the Sabi River, guineafowl, kudu steaks, homegrown vegetables, paw-paws and oranges, cheeses and cream cakes. Because all the other staff houses on the mine were now empty, our host Clem was making use of eleven fridges and had them all stuffed with food and drink. And stuffed was the theme of the visit. We lay in a heat and food induced torpor in hammocks on the veranda during the sweltering afternoon. Towards evening we were offered baths – a luxury after months of basin-bathing – and we had to wait for the water to cool to a bearable temperature after the bath was run. The water pipes bringing the water from the river lay on top of the ground and the water became so hot and the pipes retained so much heat that cold water did not exist.

Then in the good Rhodesian tradition of sundowners at sunset, we were plied with drinks and savories, followed by a repeat performance of a five-course meal whose elaborate menu was amazing when one knew the primitive kitchen conditions and open charcoal fire from which it emanated. The food was delicious, perfectly served on fine china with silver and glassware and fine table linen — but the abundance was totally defeating.

We did our best, exhorted by our overbearing host to try just one more bit of this or that, and when at last the ordeal was over we staggered to our net-shrouded beds in the sleeping porch part of the verandah. As an afterthought when we were just about asleep Clem came in with a large cellophane bag of chocolate gingers and set it on the bedside table, just in case we felt peckish in the night. The ridgeback dog knocked it off the table in the small hours, making a loud explosive noise, and I leapt up saying "my god, Bill's burst".

We only just survived a full cooked breakfast — porridge, bacon, eggs, sausage, coffee and fruit and then had the quite awful prospect of the return trip. And we left laden with presents of, would you believe, food.

♠♠

On our return to Salisbury we moved into a bachelor flat in Clewer Mansions, a high-rise block of flats opposite the Anglican Church and also next to a car sales firm glorying in the name of Puzey and Diss. They were the agents for MGs so we acquired a bright red TC MG called Susan and made do with the two camp beds and other camping issue because the 450 Pounds Sterling she cost was more than a years' salary. Within about a month Bill had rubbed through the duco by his non-stop polishing, and had had the engine in pieces in order to "polish" the ports or whatever it is that is done to give high performance. From then onwards there was frequently a cylinder head on the table or bits and pieces under the beds, a state of affairs that was to continue in the field in the following year when we were mapping in the Mashaba district near Fort Victoria.

That year Bill drove our ute (and me) to the first camp site, hitched a ride back and fetched Susan, who could not possibly be left behind, and who complicated every move thereafter. I had only the most basic driving skills, having had a few lessons with one of my brothers in Pretoria, so when we moved camp I had to drive the ute, laden with camp and servants, at a very slow pace, following the MG driven by guess who. Some of the trips, I realise in retrospect, were plain dangerous. At the end of the season I stayed in camp, he drove Susan back to Salisbury, organized a lift back, and we all went home in the ute. And I did not see that there was anything strange about the arrangements or expectations!

During the few months that we spent in our flat between field seasons we made several trips to Pretoria, for long weekends and for Christmas, traveling the thousand plus miles in one hit. Roads in Rhodesia in those days were still "strips" — two tarred strips with a median section of gravel and the rest of the road graded by a bulldozer. When a car was approaching another coming towards it, each moved over, keeping one wheel on a strip and the other on the unsealed verge. Maintenance was not the best and pot-holes in the tar, eroded edges of the strips and very rough verges (or mud after rain) made travel an adventure. We left after work on these trips and drove through the night, reaching Beit Bridge on the border with what was then the Union of South Africa at about dawn. The Customs post opened early in the morning and one had to be cleared there and at Messina on the other side of the border. Roads in the Union were unsealed but used to be well maintained and the corrugations could be defeated by traveling at fairly high speed.

From reading letters to my mother about these early days in Salisbury and the trips to Pretoria, I was reminded that petrol short-ages were acute and only a small monthly allowance was made to each customer so we had to save up enough coupons to get us to the unlicensed supplies in Beit Bridge. And Bill was looking into the possibility of converting the car to run on "Bengal" that was presumably diesel or another oil-based fuel like people are trying out today – half a century ago!

Those journeys were special as only events can be at that untrammeled stage of one's life — so much a part of carefree youth and spontaneity. I remember so clearly the baobabs, like upside-down trees with roots in the air; night stops for a picnic dinner on the Lundi River with the damp fragrance of the river and the night chorus of frogs and insects; wandering into the Beit Bridge Hotel annex in the pitch dark before dawn to freshen up in a bathroom and stepping over travellers who were sleeping on the floor and waiting, like us, for Customs to open. We used to arrive at my family's home at about lunchtime, spend that half day and the next, and then repeat the travel process.

♠♠

The Mashaba field season was rather different from those in the Sabi. The area was not as remote, it had roads and small towns and mines, and there was little game — and none of the big game that had been so exciting to be living among. The atmosphere was also slightly different because Bill was increasingly disenchanted with the set-up at the Survey and felt he would be a field geologist forever, waiting for dead men's shoes with the way it was organized, and he was beginning negotiations with Anglo American with a view to moving. I was beginning to see that he was either all enthusiasm or all depression, that being his nature — and I was learning to deal with that because I loved him and accepted him as he was.

At our first camp, on a small reedy stream that burbled engagingly as it ran past in the open woodland, I made a garden round the tent by bringing in rocks and planting aloes and other succulents that I had dug up in the surrounding veldt. We made a brief visit to Bulawayo one weekend and met up with the man who had been the love of my life during the war, and with friends at the Museum. That break was our only social one in all those months because the local residents in our mapping area were neither friendly nor unfriendly — they just left us to ourselves.

One local man I remember because he was a monster who used to beat his small children with a sjambok (usually reserved by Europeans for beating natives). And we had some contact (as little as could tactfully be managed) with one very off-putting woman who owned and ran a local mine. We had been warned that she was a nymphomaniac, though in my innocence then I did not know what that meant, and she told us with pride how she had instructed her much younger brother in what to do in bed by taking him into hers. The locals told us in hushed tones how she used to line up all her native mineworkers for a medical check, make them strip, and examine them for STDs. As for the young brother, he was to prove a worry during the last few days of our stay, when he arrived home after being incarcerated for several years in a juvenile detention centre for rape and armed robbery. He wandered into our camp one day when I was alone and because I had heard about him I was apprehensive. But he behaved like any polite visitor on that occasion and on following visits, which he made in spite of my lack of enthusiasm and his being warned off by Bill. I think he was lonely and needed to talk to someone of his own age.

The field assistant and cook who were our "issue" this year were townified Africans, not very happy with living in a tent in the middle of nowhere. Our cook, in particular, was drawn irresistibly to any surrounding kraal where kaffir[28] beer parties were in progress. He was seldom in camp, never sober and always surly, so we made a trip to Fort Victoria and put him on the train to Salisbury. Then through a friend in the Native Affairs office in the town we were introduced to Nehemiah, a young man who had just emerged from a mission school. He was the happiest, most ingenuous person one could hope to meet and an enthusiastic

---

[28]   kaffir – an insulting term for a black Africas

helper and learner. He wrote and spoke good English, much influenced by the mission teacher, bringing Lord Jesus into the conversation at every possible and impossible opportunity, and his cheerful presence gave us much pleasure. At night, when we sat at our campfire and the boys at theirs a short distance away, we heard Nehemiah trying to teach the field assistant good English and practicing new phrases that he had picked up by listening to us. One day, on a visit to town I had bought an illustrated book of bible stories for him, knowing how he would love the pictures of a gentle bearded Jesus holding a lamb or performing miracles. When I gave him the present he was completely overcome, suddenly shy and unable to say anything. He grabbed the book and fled to his tent. Later across the darkness that separated the two fires we heard him carefully rehearsing what he should have said — "For the bible book very many thanks", "many thanks sir and madam for the holy bible book". ` We camped for the last six weeks of that field season in a rondavel on an abandoned gold mine, which was luxury compared with a tent and cool with its high thatched roof. We had to be careful moving about in the compound because of open mine shafts, snakes under sheets of rusting iron, and tangles of wire and bits of machinery hidden in the grass waiting to be tripped over. Shortly after we had settled in our classy accommodation I had an unfortunate encounter with a scorpion.

Bill had left camp in the ute at dawn, and would not be back until about noon at the earliest. Nehemiah, our camp "boy" had gone along with him to be dropped off at a farm to collect milk and vegetables. I was alone and set about tidying up the hut. I was folding clothes and turning a garment right-way-out when a small black scorpion that had been inside it stung me on the back of my left hand. The pain was instant and excruciating and I knew that blue-black scorpions could cause blindness and dramatic symptoms in some cases. I reckoned that because the back of a hand is just skin and gristle not a lot of poison could have been injected. I debated with myself whether to get a razor blade and slice the bite, like we were advised to do with snakebite in those days, but I could not face that. So I decided that it was a small scorpion, I would be more likely to die from panic than from the amount of poison I could have received, and I had better calm down and think of something practical to do. First things first — I found the scorpion where it was scuttling off across the floor, killed it (but kept the remains as an exhibit) and planned my day.

The only way I could blot out my anxiety about the possibility of having a severe reaction before Bill and help returned was to get absorbed in some activity — and there was not much choice offering. So I lit the camp fire, made a vast pile of good red charcoal and began baking in the heavy iron camp-oven. When Bill eventually arrived he was met with sponge cakes, rock cakes, scones, biscuits and even fresh hot bread. The flour stocks were exhausted, and so was I — but I felt all right and the pain in my hand and arm was steadily abating. We did not know that there might be more to come and in retrospect should have headed for town and a hospital for safety's sake. In the early hours of the night I was suddenly so ill, with rigors that resulted in my camp stretcher dancing across the mud floor of the rondavel, and with symptoms like arsenical poisoning — but it was too late to do anything. By dawn the crisis was over and I slept, oblivious, for a day and a night while Bill went through agonies of worry. After a few days I was fully recovered, so I was lucky.

♠♠

When we returned to Salisbury in December I found I was pregnant. We were over the moon and involved not only in planning for our first child, but also in looking forward to the move to join Anglo American and work on the Witwatersrand mines in South Africa in the following June.

I did not see Salisbury, the Geological Survey and the life we had started to build there — among friends and the much-loved familiar places in which I had grown up — as the dead end which it had become for Bill, and for me the move was not as necessary. I was learning that being a geologist's wife would be full of challenges, and living with someone who was the first person I had ever known who could switch from seeing things as all rosy to all negative almost overnight was going to require lots of adjustment by me. Strangely enough, though I remember recognising all this so early, I did not ever see that I had any alternative but to accept the situation and fit in with it. Nor did I ever want to escape from the often difficult emotional situation. I loved him, he needed me and I believed he would always do what was best for me and the children, so my role was always clear — and I now know that that is a recipe for happiness — mine at least.

Crickets chirrup;
A lonely night-bird's weird and wavering cry
Comes from afar.


# ANGLO AMERICAN MINES, SOUTH AFRICA

In June 1950 I flew, very pregnant, to Pretoria to be with my family while Bill packed up in Rhodesia and moved to the town of Springs on the Witwatersrand, not far from Johannesburg. He was to receive preliminary training there, after which he would be sent to his allocated mine somewhere within the Anglo-American empire.

We rented a new flat over a new block of shops in a Springs suburb and our few bits of furniture from the bachelor flat in Salisbury filled one corner, because it was an open-plan place, more like a shop or office apart from its minute kitchen and a bathroom. But it was clean and new at least. The Head Office people in Johannesburg were friendly and concerned for my welfare so, though the Rand [29] mining areas were depressing places with mine dumps, African "locations" and lots of heavy industry, everything was ready for our baby's arrival. The young Afrikaans doctor was friendly, and, I later found, terrified, because I was his first obstetric patient since he had joined the practice of an ancient doctor after leaving university only weeks before). Anglo American pulled strings and guaranteed me a bed in the local maternity home, where bookings usually had to be made almost nine months before.

I chose a bad time to go into labour — a Sunday when doctors were off duty, followed by, worse still, the August bank holiday when golf tournaments engaged them fully. But everything came all right in the end when late on Monday the seventh (my lucky

---

[29] Rand - the Reef—a 56 km scarp containing large quantities of gold

number) the old doctor at least was found and was able to deliver the baby with forceps. These days no one would be allowed to go on for as long in second stage labour as I had done, but I did not know that then. Husbands were banned from the whole proceeding, from the time that one entered the maternity home until after the baby was born, and mine took a deep chloroform-flavoured breath when he was at last let in and promptly passed out, just like new fathers do in comedies in films. By then Mom and Dad were there too, anxiously waiting.

I spent seven days recuperating from the birth in the Kimberley Maternity Home, as was normal practice those days. The baby was kept in the nursery, only brought for brief feeding visits, and he was so tightly wrapped up that I saw only his face and hands and there was minimal instruction on routines or management in preparation for taking him home.

When David was about a month old we were posted to Klerksdorp, a small mining town on the Western Reef. There was no accommodation there apart from a few mine houses that were all already occupied — so we lived for a couple of months in the local hotel. It was a fairly new building and quite reasonably comfortable and there was another young couple there with a very young child, so I had company when washing nappies in a rooftop laundry and hanging them up on the flat roof to dry.

The Vaal River ran through the flat and rather uninteresting countryside nearby and Bill bought an ancient sailing dinghy and used to spend weekends sailing it laboriously with endless tacking up the narrow river channel, then flying down in a couple of minutes. The wind always blew straight down the river, and sailing was only possible in one direction because a weir and rapids lay just below the launching place. I used to take the baby in his basket-ware crib and sit on the river bank under the trees, and it was a break from the hotel and the dreary little town. Sometimes I was homesick for Rhodesia, and often I was homesick for the Cape, and it was hard to see how being a mine geologist working in quite appalling conditions in the bowels of the earth could ever have looked good compared with the fresh air and freedoms of fieldwork in my beloved Rhodesia.

Needless to say, it was not long before Bill saw that job as entirely joyless, the man whom he worked under as an incompetent idiot, and the prospects as bleak as they had been rosy only months before. The mine shafts were so deep that rock at the depth of the tunnels was too hot to touch, and the air supply was unsatisfactory. The humidity was such that Bill used to take off his clothes to wring them out periodically. A day's work entailed walking five or six miles underground in those conditions, visiting the ends of tunnels where the mining was proceeding, and mapping the geology there. It was small wonder that just after we had moved into a flat above the greengrocer's shop he became ill. It was probably a complete upset in mineral balance from all the sweating as much as anything, but he was very weak with no sensation in his legs and with all sorts of other symptoms that came and went. The local doctor, also a young and new Afrikaans-speaking one, had no idea what was wrong. There was polio about among the native population and it was even suggested that Bill might have a low-grade form of it.

The flat we were living in was sweltering, facing west and getting the full afternoon sun on its windows and low tin roof, and he lay about, red-eyed, miserable and frustrated. I phoned my mom and told her all about it and asked what I could do when the baby did nothing but cry at night with heat rash and teething and Bill seemed determined not to try to do anything to get better. She told me that there was nothing I could do — "just battle through, it's like that with babies and life in general, and when one set of worries goes it is always replaced by another." After a couple of weeks the Company sent Bill to a private hospital in Johannesburg for extensive investigation — and even then no one was any the wiser, but the break helped and he recovered enough to go back to work. I had had a few days with my family and they enjoyed their grandson.

By then I was pregnant again and I had worked out a routine to escape the afternoon heat. I took my little boy in his stroller into vacant land behind the shops where a few trees made a shady island. I amused him there or read while he slept. The area was little better than a garbage dump, but there were a few birds and sometimes a breeze. There was no park and there were no street trees — and houses with gardens were quite far away, and I did not know anyone there to visit. Escaping the heat helped with one problem that our housing presented. The other was unsolvable. The greengrocer's shop below was cockroach-infested, as was the back yard where rotting produce lay among broken crates and junk. In the evening, swarms of the creatures rustled in under the doors, through cracks in windows, even up the drains. If you turned on the kitchen light in the night you found the whole floor moving.

Imagine our delight when at last a mine house was offered to us. Its owner, blinded in a mine accident, was going away to stay with a relative and we could move in at once. We started taking the portable things over that evening and slept on a mattress on the floor, and I could not believe our luck—a cool house in a pleasant garden with a green lawn! But we were not out of the woods yet. Next morning there was a cable from Belfast saying that Bill's brother Derek had been killed in a motorbike accident. By lunch time Bill had left for Pretoria by car, and by next morning he had flown off to the U.K. He felt he had to go, knowing what a terrible blow it would be to his mother. He had lost the key of the flat before he left and most of our stuff was still there. I was without transport, very close to being without money because air tickets to Britain were expensive then, and I needed to get into the flat to get at what possessions remained there.

Fortunately, there was a young geologist at the office (who was the only one who knew that Bill had rushed off), and he came with a pickup vehicle and broke a pane of glass in the door and got the furniture out, and he dealt with an irate landlord who did not like having his window broken. Next day my brother Bob and a friend arrived from Pretoria to take me back home until the crisis was over. We had a pleasant ride in the lovely old Rolls Royce and the family made room for us when we arrived at the Waterkloof house for an indefinite stay. The place was extra crowded because a sister and brother of my dad's were on their first and only visit to see Dad. They had not seen him for about thirty-five years and a great fuss was being made for their visit. It was a restless household where dogs fought each other under the dining room table, strangers were forever coming and going and the servants were flapping about, trying to carry out Ouma's muddled and ceaseless commands. It was all too much for a young child, coming on top of all the upheaval and the disappearance of his dad, and David started having night terrors.

As it turned out we were to stay in Pretoria for nearly a month, by which time I was seven months pregnant, because there was an airline strike and Bill could not get back. He was lucky not to lose his job. The powers that be were not very happy about him disappearing without a word and I had to deal with all sorts of questions and remarks. Eventually the planes flew again, Bill came back, and we all drove home and unpacked in the new house and started making ready for the arrival of baby number two. I knew she would be a girl and had decided to call her Helen but in a light-hearted conversation Bill said that with the impending size of his family he would now never be able to swap the MG for the BMW he had always craved. So, I decided that our daughter would be Barbara Mary, giving her the initials and him the BMW he would never otherwise get.

We had graduated to having a native houseboy in the mine house — our first servant (excluding the field assistant and cook that were essential in the camping in Rhodesia) and in time for the baby's arrival we had also acquired a European nurse. She had travelled out to South Africa on the same ship that Bill had when he was returning to Rhodesia, and she had agreed to come for a couple of weeks to help me. She was a dissatisfied woman of about forty who felt from the start that she was wasting her precious time hanging about waiting for the birth to begin, and she disapproved of everything, being used to hospital precision in which every bed in her wards was made up exactly alike to within a fraction of an inch, each corner perfect, each locker with glass and bell placed exactly the same. She knew nothing about children, found that a fourteen month one did not respond to barked orders and inflexible rules — and she was the last thing that I needed. I was made to feel that it was just my inefficiency that allowed the birth to be late. It was a relief when the baby started to arrive. I walked down the road to the local midwife's house, leaving the dissatisfied dragon in charge, and next day our new daughter arrived as the mine whistle blew at 7 a.m. That afternoon Bill and the now big-brother came to fetch me home. I carried heavy David because he would not let me go after what had been a traumatic twenty-four hours for him, and Bill carried newborn baby Barbara — and we went home.

Two days later the nurse decided she had done her duty and departed. Mom fortunately came to the rescue and took a week's leave and came to help me. A fourteen- month-old son who was difficult and often screamed a lot at night, a new baby, severe sciatica from a literally back-breaking labour, and a husband who did his best but was down the mine at all hours of the day and night, had me frazzled.

ZoZo calmed everything down, loved the children and let me rest — and after that I remember only the joy of being with an enchanting child in the garden while the particularly good baby just slept or smiled and gurgled, and I was supremely happy.

When the children were twenty months and six months old, Bill was transferred to the Orange Free State sector of the Company. Welkom mine had been operating for some years and now the new mines of Lorraine and Jeanette were having their shafts sunk. We went to the new township of Allanridge that was being developed to service those mines. We were allocated a tiny cottage at first but when the Chief Geologist visited from head office in Johannesburg he had us transferred overnight to an executive style house on the other side of the township where houses had gardens and the mine managers, shift bosses and others in the hierarchy lived. We had a native servant girl who had been, and probably still was, a prostitute. She had active VD and kidney disease and was mostly sick and not much help.

It was in this house that I discovered Barbara one morning, just able to stand up, gripping the bars of her cot with one hand and the back-end of a very large cockroach that had probably just emerged from the sewers, in the other hand. Green guts and legs were smeared all over her face and around her mouth. I felt instantly sick and panicky, imagining the diseases it carried and unable to decide if I should stick my fingers down her throat or wash her mouth out with Lysol.

After I had flapped around and worked myself up into a lather, I just cleaned her up and got on with things. She didn't suffer any effects and it probably did wonders for her immune system.

We were to learn there about the mining town mentality — the hierarchy and the nonsense where people on one salary level associated only with others on the same level; of the antipathy of the almost exclusively Afrikaans work force to English-speaking people; of the ruthless exploitation of the Africans by the bullying white shift bosses and others; of the lack of companionship with people of like mind and interests. We had had an introduction to all that at Klerksdorp but somehow hoped it would be better when Bill had his own office on his allotted mines.

The work on those shaft-sinking mines was extremely dangerous. It also had to be done in the face of prejudice from the ignorant shift-bosses whose bonuses depended on the footage sunk each day and who therefore would not hold up proceedings for an unnecessary geologist to look at the walls and floor and record progress as the shaft went down. The sinking went on round the clock and the geologist went down at the end of each shift sitting on the dynamite that would blast before the next shift came to clear out and set the next blast.

The conditions under which the Africans worked in the bottom of the shaft were appalling and they were no better for Bill, though his stay was as brief as possible. It was incredibly hot, incredibly noisy, and for Bill it was shattering to find that the boys who made a mistake or did not work fast enough, or had the temerity to answer back, were kicked and hit and verbally abused. The typical shift boss was a mindless Afrikaner with the body of a prize-fighter, a foul mouth and heavy boots. (See my racist attitude showing — against fellow whites too!) There were many awful accidents. If they did not involve injury or death of whites they went unreported. The siren used to wail and everyone in the mine township would hold their breath waiting to hear if anyone close to them had been killed—and things would go back to normal instantly when it was known it was only Africans.

One morning, I was in the butcher shop waiting to be served. That morning, in an exceptionally bad accident, the bucket had free-fallen down the shaft killing all in it and many below it. The butcher was joking with a customer; "Plenty bleddy meat in Number One shaft today, hey?"

"Bleddy kaffirs, man, bastards should of got out of the way..." — and they laughed.

I unwisely said, "For God's sake, they are people aren't they — how can you talk like that!" and I was instantly in hostile territory with everyone in the shop silent and shutting me out. I left without any meat and walked home, pushing my pram and fuming and weeping inside.

By then Bill had had enough and had applied to join the Colonial Service, hoping to go to Northern Rhodesia. That application was unsuccessful as the Survey there was about to close and had kept junior staff to finish the business. As an experienced senior geologist, Bill was advised to apply for a post in British Somaliland.

# SOMALILAND 1953

Camp in giant Euphorbias;

Barbara and Widdy

# SOMALILAND STORY

Faintly I hear lilting, liquid music
Plucked on a Jew's harp by an African musician
Away in outer darkness.

## SOMALILAND 1953

Letter from Camp, 8 miles from Boramo, 14th May 1953

We are camped in a grove of giant euphorbias and are all very happy to be back in our tent. It feels almost as though we have never been out of it. The only difference this time is that we have two additions to the family — a cocker spaniel pup called Widdy Wowo and a baby tortoise. We all wonder how we ever existed without Widdy.

On Monday morning a neighbour phoned and asked if we would like a puppy as a present as the man who had booked him had not taken him. Widdy is adorable as all spaniel puppies are. He is black and silver like the ones in pictures of King Charles and he is pedigreed. I have never known a puppy who is less trouble. He is house trained, didn't cry for his mother, and takes trekking in his stride. He sleeps under my legs in the car and on the end of my bed at night and we can't let him wander out of the tent because of jackals etc. around. The children adore him. Barbara needed a dog as she wept every time a tortoise in the garden went away. David proudly tells everyone that he is learning to carry Widdy, and the poor puppy is tightly held against a fat tummy and loved to bits. It is the first dog Bill has ever had of his own (!!) and he carries it about in his bush-shirt pocket. We've let the little tortoise go away as it would not eat, and we did not want it to die. He was only two inches long with a perfect tortoise-shell back and the sweetest legs with big feet with claws.

The country is beautiful after the rain. Boramo is supposed to be the best station in the country as it is at 5000 feet with good rainfall among big hills with comparatively dense vegetation. Here where we are on a watershed between tugs there is no grass cover, but the thorn trees are very green and there are lots of flowers. The upland country from Hargeisa to Boramo is rather like high veldt, especially in parts where there are granite koppies. Boramo is almost on the Ethiopian border and the views of the Highlands are glorious. There are sloping grasslands leading to them and there is supposed to be lots of game.

In the camp we have good shade from the euphorbias. We have a couple of camels which we will send for water if it's easier than sending the truck. We have had visitors already. Colin E. a locust officer is constantly dropping in as he goes by in his jeep. He has just found 200 square miles of locust hoppers, so there will be a rush on, putting down poison bait. They use gammexane in bran and scatter it on the ground. The areas where the hoppers are this time are very remote and it will take quite a lot of organisation to deal with them.

Letter from Hargeisa. 25th May 1953


We have been told that we can have the rest-house there during field seasons, so when Bill has to go on camel treks alone we can go there and see him at weekends. It rained like fury that morning. We drove through sheets of water and the whole country was a lake as 99.5% of the rainwater is run-off. We had to stop at one stage for a while as the road was a river and we couldn't be sure how deep. When it abated a bit we went on and I paddled ahead over the big tug to see if it was all right — a most enjoyable paddle. An hour later, on the way back the road was quite dry, so you see how it is in this land of contrasts.

On Monday we were to move camp and there were thunder clouds all around and I wondered just how wet we would all be before we were re-established. Bill went out at 5 am as usual and while he was away I packed up, leaving only the children's beds so they could have their rest. The men took their tent down and just when everything was outside ready to be loaded it poured. Bill came back dripping. We had an early lunch and packed up and went about 6 miles further along the road. We found a perfect spot where the tent could open onto a euphorbia tree where there was deep shade and a lawn under foot. That part of the country was lovely — green grass full of flowers and lots of shade. We were near real Rhodesian-like koppies.

We got the tent up, stuff dumped in, and the men had to race to get theirs up before the deluge. We were just in time and the rain was unbelievable. We were on a slight slope and with the hill nearby it was a tug—a river-bed area. There had been no time to dig a trench round the tent and this we had to do from the inside with the children's spades and we made dykes with tent pegs embedded. It was glorious in the cold and seeing all that water. The children watched from a stretcher all wrapped up and we two worked like slaves for an hour or more. At one stage the water outside was about three inches higher than the floor level and we were determined to keep it out and not live in dampness ever after. The rain stopped just in time and when it was over the men appeared from their tent and dug a ditch and we made permanent mud barricades so as not to have to worry again. All the time it was pouring Bill was making trips outside to collect water in basins under the tent flaps. We collected a bath full, two buckets and a baramel so we are able to go an extra day without fetching water in Boramo.

We got the tent straight and were organising the children to bed when Colin E. of the locusts came to call to see our new site. He was in daily after that as he liked the cake always in abundance. It was very useful having him passing regularly as he brought fresh vegetables from the magala and would have brought post had any come through. We did a lot of botanical collecting in that camp. The koppies were perfect. There were pink aloes in flower on the hills, yellow on the flats; orchids, hibiscus etc.

In the tent with the front under the big euphorbia it was greeny-gloomy and cool. We sat outside under the tree all day and it was cold in the shade with a fresh rain wind. We did not want to leave at all. On the Sunday when we went in to Boramo to the Petahs there was a child present who had the typical Somali flu with high temperature at night for three nights and no symptoms and temperature normal all day — just like David had had at Christmas. And David picked it up again and that night had a high fever. He was all right next morning, but the next night it was up again. The work was to have been finished by the week's end, but Barbara looked as though she was in for the flu too, so we decided to come home early. We were met by drought, of course, in Hargeisa. No rain since we left, and after the greenness of Boramo it was a disappointment. But the garden is all right and there are four-foot-high marigolds in a blaze of flowers at the front of the house.

We had a simply mammoth storm last Thursday and the big tug which is divided and banked to accommodate our house was in full spate in half-light in the evening. It was exciting and the garden was a lake. Now there are big areas of river sand with ripple marks and the children dig delightedly. Stan Elliot got the front wheel of his Morris in a hole only a foot wide but a yard deep on the road. A waterfall had made it in half an hour, and it was invisible under all the water.

The Coronation party for the children on the 2nd was a great success. They looked very sweet and excited, and you have never seen little things eat as much. Each child was given a coronation mug with sweets and a souvenir hankie. They staggered to the car and straight to bed.

When J.A.H. goes on leave Bill will be in charge. J.A.H. has turned out to be a sex maniac and more than a little mad in other respects too. It was disillusioning and disappointing to find out

166

that he is far from nice. He has even been sent to a psychiatrist in London from here after a nasty incident when he flogged a small Somali nearly to death. He is well known by all — in fact notorious for being round the bend after 28 years of loving and living with Somalis and the Governor hasn't a good word for him. He was made "Geologist in Charge" not Director of the Survey, simply to get him out of Administration and into something less "dangerous". The Somali Colonial Service is apparently a dumping ground for misfits and incompetents. Not very nice for anyone working for him but it helps having allies all around who know him for what he is. Dr Shaw from London saw how it was here and told Bill and John Seymour that he could see what the difficulties were. The Seymour family left because they refused to take any more of J.A.H. and when they went to the Colonial Office with the whole story the man who interviewed them grinned and said, "quite, quite," and suggested a posting to West Africa. But the work is interesting, and we are happy. I am desperately sorry for Marjorie who is starting to find out after three years of marriage just what J.A.H. is like, and for Judy who is treated one moment like a stranger, and an unwelcome one at that, and the next as an adored child. She is nervy and far from robust as a result.

Letter from Hargeisa. 14th June 1953

Today is "Eid", the Mohammedan Christmas which marks the end of Ramadan. During the last month, until they spotted the new moon last night, they have been fasting all day and eating only at night. Now there is revelry and indigestion, and of course no servants. During last night someone broke the padlock on the pantry door and stole the ironing blanket, a table cloth, serviettes, four soup plates and two dinner plates. We were lucky because none of the stuff was valuable, and they left all the other crockery and things which they could easily have removed. So, we have had police in again and made reports. There is no chance of getting anything back as it all goes straight over the Ethiopian border where things are in great demand. There is not a Somali that I trust. It is always possible that it is an inside job, which is not a nice feeling. We will replace locks and leave security lights on as well. Don't get the idea that this is the Mau Mau or that there is danger. They are just petty thieves and there have been no murders or violence.

We went to the Government House Ball for the Queen's birthday on Thursday night. We left the children with Liban the office interpreter, who is headman on trek and who the children know and like. We only stayed till 11.30, when I was just beginning to feel I would like to stay but did not want to leave the children any longer on this first experiment. At Government house there were four marquees on the terrace and dancing was in the dining room. A new Government House is being built as this one is a bit small and homey.

Letter from Hargeisa, 19th July 1953

It rained gently all last night and today there was a low guti mist till 10am. The children and I climbed the reservoir hill after breakfast. We go to the water tank on top of the hill and sit there with our legs dangling over the side and survey our realm. You can see the whole valley, very like the Xanadu valley, to the conical hills out Berbera way and in the other direction to the hills we go through to Boramo.

This afternoon we all went in the car to collect flakes. We found a lovely place with a wide river bed winding in big trees. The tug was down yesterday so there were new stretches of white sand. While Bill went off with his geological hammer to look at the rocks and outcrops the children made sand castles and dug, and with the fresh cool wind we could have been at the sea. Bill persuaded Widdy to go with him and said that Widdy cried all the time and tried to make him come back to us, even pulling him by the pants, impeding his legs and generally being impossible so Bill had to come back much sooner than he would otherwise have done. On their way back Widdy galloped along without hesitation— and the fuss he made of Dave! Widdy is nearly grown up and is a lovely dog. He is so faithful to the children, takes endless punishment from them and never complains.

I have been having a baking session for David's birthday party. I think Dave is doing well for a three-year-old. He informed Bill he is going to be a botanist and not a geo-lodger because there are skorpies under stones but flowers are nice.

♠♠

Bill was away at Sheik for four days. What a welcome he got from the children when he returned. Before he left David asked him to bring back a baby tortoise or "even a locust". Bill saw endless swarms of locusts while he was away and he met a swarm at Sheik and duly collected a specimen and brought it all the way in a tin — to find that the swarm was eighty miles across and stretched 200 miles, moving like a giant lawnmower—and had eaten every leaf here as well. You have never seen such locusts. They sat so thick on the ground that the new ones arriving had to circle and circle to find an inch to sit on. The ground was reddy-brown and yellow like a carpet and they have a strange smell which is almost pleasant. They ate every vegetable so that there are only stalks— if those. The carrot patch has nothing above ground. We had no boy that day, so I only kept them off the flowers by banging. Each child had a tin and a spoon and loved it of course. When Bill came back and presented his locust the feeding swarms had gone and there were only stragglers, but the present was received with jubilation.

There was a 16-foot tug on Wednesday night, the largest for some years. The immense concrete causeway over the river was broken at one end because the wild water came so high. Complete trees on the original bank are gone. There is a new donga[30] system with gullies up to fifteen feet deep and 100 yards back from the stream bed, and there is mud and debris everywhere. Houses near the tug nearly had to be evacuated.

---

[30] Donga—'a dry gully formed by the eroding action of running water

We heard the roaring all night and our private tug was chattering through the garden. This has been a good year for rain with some most days, and sometimes soft soaking rain at night. The country will need it after the locusts!

The following night a couple of our friends were returning from a rather drunken party when they drove slap into the tug and were lucky not to be drowned. They said they were going dead slow, and the brakes failed etc. The car got stuck in a deep hole but was not destroyed and they got out through the windows and when the water was gone the car was pulled out. The Governor had John Stewart in to ask what had happened and John was rather hurt because the Governor laughed like hell at his story.

Letter from Camp 18 miles from Boramo. 16th August 1953

We are in a perfect area among the hills, and it is as good as a holiday. Everything is green after all the rain. So far there is no excessive Karif wind, and we are all so glad to be back in camp. We are at between 5500 and 6000 feet, so it is bracing. We would like to stay longer in this camp but are moving on tomorrow into limestone country. Our journey here was most pleasant. David sat in the back of the car with Widdy for the first time, so I did not have both children on top of me. Parts of the roads were quite impassable with mud, and we had to do miles in the bushes alongside the road to avoid getting stuck forever.

Bill visited one of the famous ruined cities yesterday — an old Arab trading post in a valley near here. He was not very impressed as it is so recent, but he brought back pottery. There is a cave up in the hills above here and we are not going to try to dig it out as apparently a lot of Italians were popped in there instead of being buried during the war — which is a gruesome thought. The whole area is a mass of foxholes, slit trenches and gun emplacements as there was a big campaign here. The driver of our lorry was in the fight when a group of Somalis were dug in on top of this limestone mountain, so he knows all the details. I wish he didn't as I find it all very depressing.

Letter from Camp 3 Boramo District. 26th August 1953

We moved to this new map area yesterday and are now under a large thorn tree on a sort of shelf about 200 feet wide with erosion gullies with tug beds in them on either side. In the tugs there is white sand, and it is a lovely place for the children. The veldt around us is full of red and yellow aloes and quite pretty, though not as nice as the last camps which were on granite. This is a very beautiful part of Somaliland. We've had one shower of rain and one storm with the biggest bang of thunder I've ever heard. Both children screamed and we rushed to them, and the dog was outside and sure he had been shot and tore clean through the tent and was out of the laced-up end before he could stop. He was so funny that the shock of the bang was soon forgotten.

We have had several visits from Bert Payne, a locust officer, and he has been very kind, sending us special drinking water which his lorries fetch at Gogti in Ethiopia. Last night we had a visit from the Lands Officer who came on the ten miles beyond Bawn after coming all the way from Hargeisa, to give us some mail. He will get his lorries to call and find out if we want anything from Boramo, so we are well off here. We are due to return to Hargeisa in eleven days and will be there for five or six weeks before the next big trek. J.A.H. is due back in a few weeks and we hope he will get lost before then.

Our move yesterday took quite a long time considering we only came ten miles, as the road is bad, and we had to construct several tug crossings and we had to make a few new bits of road. The limestone is terribly stony and bare of soil on the ridges and there is no road maintenance whatever. We were in no hurry and at each hold-up Bill and the men tackled the obstruction with spades. The children, dog and I sat in the shade, and I knitted.

# MIDWIFE

Somali men

Camels,                          A partially made gurghi;

A gurghi

The melody is endlessly repeated
Till it becomes the very heart-beat of the night

# MIDWIFE

It was while we were camped in this bare and stony limestone country somewhere in the Bawn district near Boramo that I had an unexpected and quite incredible experience. The day had started as usual with Bill leaving the camp at first light and the children and me playing in the tug while it was cool. We had come back to the tent and both children had fallen asleep on their beds. It was hot out of the wind even at this quite early hour and I was drowsy myself and wondered idly what was going on outside where there was loud talking, more like arguing, from the camp watchman and interpreter who were in their part of the camp nearby.

Liban, the interpreter, came to the tent eventually, coughed politely before looking in, and I went out to talk to him where we would not wake the children. He said that a family of Somalis were camped just a little way away from us on the tug and could I please help because the young wife had bad trouble and there was no woman to help her. He did not like to say what the trouble was, only that it was bad, very bad, and only women dealt with these things. I gathered in a round-about way that a birth was not going right, and I knew from what I had heard that only unclean people—women—were able to be involved in such matters.

There was no one to turn to, no transport to get help, and I was not at all sure that I was qualified to deal with the problem, but in the circumstances I had little option. I thought that if I could at least find out what the problem was. Bill would be back soon and able to do something. With Liban on guard I could leave the sleeping children and go and see what was going on. I thought of all the films were people boiled water and got clean towels, and tore up rags in civilised houses when babies were arriving.

Apart from that they never showed one anything the least bit useful. I had the presence of mind to arm myself with scissors and string because I knew at least how to tie off a cord if we got that far, and I gathered a couple of towels and some Dettol, a face washer and a bottle of water. I was flapping already and had to tell myself to slow down, take a deep breath and remain calm. I set off with a very old man leading the way, me in the middle and the camp guard following at a safe distance.

There were two thin camels, a few scraggy goats grazing in the bushes and a gurghi (half-sphere house made from camel blankets covering curved sticks) when we reached our destination. A young Somali with frizzy red hair was leaning against a tree among the goats, seemingly uninterested, and he did not move. The old man pointed to the gurghi, dismissed me with a gesture and went to join the young man in the shade. The camp watchman squatted down on his heels well away from the danger zone and there I was, no Florence Nightingale, never before anywhere near a gurghi, and I would have turned and fled if I could have. I remember thinking it was ridiculous to be creeping up to a gurghi as though it was going to bite me, and that raised my spirits and I bent down into the crouching position required to enter, determined not to be such an idiot.

It was dark inside the gurghi. After the harsh brightness of the desert there was a period of blindness. Crouched in the entrance, assailed by darkness, fear and stench in equal proportions, I knew how an animal feels when it enters a strange lair. I had to fight down a moment's unreasoning panic.

Eyes accustomed to the gloom, I could see the girl huddled on the thick camel blanket. A few bundles and native cooking vessels were the only furnishings. The girl looked like an emaciated child. The enveloping haud cloth shroud concealed even her condition. I felt hopelessly inadequate without a common language, without the knowledge to help her, and robbed by heat, smell and nerves of the ability to think at all. Then to my aid came the realisation that she was absolutely petrified of me — a terror as stark as that seen in a cowering animal in a trap. In the face of such elemental fear, there was no room for lesser fears. I soothed her as one would soothe the wild, trapped creature she had become, talking and crooning, then stroking and cradling her head in my lap. And she turned convulsively towards me and wept her heart out, and I held her like a child.

Whether it was the relief of tension or the terror which had preceded it that worked the magic there is no knowing, but suddenly we were both very busy. There was hardly time to manoeuvre a towel into position to prevent the infant making his landfall on the filthy camel blanket. He was as slippery as an eel and as surprised at his sudden debut as we were. There was a long moment's silence and then a thin, wailing cry — and the warmth of the miracle of birth flooded in and overwhelmed us — tears everywhere, mine and hers and his — and excited voices outside as tiny lungs told the big, unfriendly world that this was his moment. I wrapped the tiny child and gave him to his mother, and cleaned up as best I could. What do midwives in gurghis do with afterbirths? In the end I wrapped it in a rag and left the parcel at the edge of the hut, hoping that a passing hyena would remove it in the night.

When the girl was sleeping peacefully and seemed to be all right, I took the child and crawled out into the white glare and handed him to the old man. His lined face was wreathed in smiles, and he passed the baby to the young man and together they inspected it minutely — obviously delighted that it was a boy. My assurances that the mother was all right met with little interest — after all it was natural that she should be, after three blistering days of labour under those conditions. After all what are women for?

My woman's job done I was equally uninteresting, so I left and walked on shaking legs down the track towards our camp, exhausted, angry, elated — as close to being defeated by the harsh and unforgiving land and its people as I was ever to be. And I was harshly criticised by Bill for going into such a situation on my own, and the camp guards should have known better than to involve me! It chilled me later when I thought about it and realised that had something gone wrong, or had the child been a girl rather than a valued male, I might have been in real trouble. Women, and especially European women, had such low status then in Somali culture, I could have been blamed and punished, even killed.

Mother and baby survived. The children and I saw them leaving next day to walk to wherever they had been heading when an inconvenient labour had interrupted their journey. Worldly possessions piled high on a camel, the curved gurghi frames sticking out at awkward angles, the childlike mother trotted behind while the old man and his son led the procession, driving the goats before them, and setting the pace. They did not look up to smile or wave or even to acknowledge our presence.

The dry grass rustles and a tiny mouse
Scampers into the fire lit circle,
Picks up a crumb and darts away again,
Breaking the spell

# LETTERS FROM HARGEISA AND CAMP

Letter from Hargeisa. September 1953

Our return from camp went well. We went as far as Boramo on Friday and camped on the airstrip. We had to make up about a dozen tug crossings before we could get the Vauxhall through on the way in, not because of mud but because after all the rain the small tugs were deep-cut like trenches, or because all the soil had gone, and the rocks were a menace. It was all fun and easily accomplished and we were in Boramo by 10am and had a very makeshift camp up shortly afterwards. We went to see the Petah family and, in the afternoon went out to Amud where there are Arab ruins, but there was a storm coming and a wide tug likely to flow and cut us off, so we turned back before getting anywhere.

We did not even light the lamp that night —we went to bed with the sun to be ready for an early start. The road home was fairly good, and it was a pleasant trip with lots of dik-dik to see, jackals and masses of flowers, though the veldt got drier and drier as we approached Hargeisa.

J.A.H. is due back on Friday by air and I am still praying that he will fall out of the bomb hatch or something. Bill has managed all the office work and yet been out in the field, which J.A.H. never accomplishes, and there has been no flap. The Secretariat have said how nice it has been without the 'old woman'. Marjorie is not coming back. J.A.H. finds that a wife and family are a hindrance, and he can live cheaper alone because no one stops him from eating jowari (millet) and mutton as the Somalis do. His home in England has to be run for his other children and first wife, and for

Marjorie's other children, so at least they will all be together there (made to manage on an impossibly small allowance, I'm sure) and I think happier than with him. He is so incredibly mean you would not believe it, and that on a simply vast salary and on top of all his other awful characteristics. However, we will be happy in spite of him.

We have been playing more tennis and enjoying it. We have a new geologist called Joe Mason who came back with J.A.H. (who is the same as usual and we wish he wasn't), but Joe is very nice indeed and he and Bill will be going off on a camel trek for a month in about a fortnight and will fetch us for a short while in the middle of November.

We have had Mr Watson the agriculture director in to supper and he is extraordinarily nice. Elizabeth is with us a lot while Jimmy is on trek. I am helping regularly with the Elliot's new twins, as Robbie cannot manage the double bathing and feeding alone, and I am the regular Friday help. (All of us girls are "rostered" till she can cope.)

♠♠

By this time I was expecting again. My mother ZoZo had had some kind of breakdown and illness and she was such a worrier that she was not told —no one in South Africa was. The fact that I was RH negative, and the baby would need specialist treatment at birth, on top of the rough living in Somaliland, would have been too much of a worry and would have set ZoZo back. So, these letters to my parents say nothing about me being pregnant.

Letter from Hargeisa, October 1953

Bill has gone off alone on his camel trek and we are adjusting ourselves and I try to fit in something special in the way of an outing each day to compensate the children. They are very good, but we all miss Bill and if possible, we will be joining him before

Christmas. Winter has almost come, and the nights and early mornings are getting cold, and dew drips from the eaves again.

This Survey closes down in 1956 and Bill has had a long letter from Mr F. of the Geological Survey, Salisbury, saying that he thinks the chances of us arranging a transfer to Northern Rhodesia under the Federal Government would be good. So, we are going to start working on that and hope it comes off as it would be just right in many ways.

Bill's work is going well, and he has had Joe with him a bit. He is now involved in such complex geology that his mind is fully occupied. I've been making curtains and a bedspread for John Lawrie. I'm always a sucker. He has a new house and I always feel that I must offer because I have an electric sewing machine. The sewing was quick but sewing on 108 rings by hand was not. I have spent a lot of time at the Herbarium and am busy on the card index. The children love going there and play on the lawn or stoep. We had a flood yesterday. The water is only on for two hours in the morning and two after lunch. The boy had left the tap on and gone away and when I went to the pantry it had about two inches of water in it, seeping out of a very small crack. When I opened the door there was a tidal wave which delighted the children. They played in the mud and puddles for hours.

October—November 1953

Bill was away most of October and November. Several letters from him during this long trek, sent by runner to the nearest road and then by trade truck assured me he was well and happy and working hard and getting good results. It was hot on the edge of the Guban where he was, but getting cooler by the day, and by the time we were to join him at Abdal Qadr (which was higher too), it would be pleasant enough. Probably because our life was all divided up into segments of trek and town and planning ahead, time flew by. It was nearly a year since we had arrived, and what a happy year it had been.

Bill had said he'd be home on the 19th, but I was so sure that he would be early that I had a chicken roasting, a lemon meringue pie ready and the house spring cleaned. He and Joe arrived at 5.30 pm after two days of double marches as J.A.H was being difficult, trying to slow down the work and was restricting the use of vehicles. Bill had walked 350 miles in the month and that was with Sundays and most Saturdays in camp. He was brown and fit and so happy to be back and quite overwhelmed by the children who wouldn't leave him for a minute. They just hugged and hugged him and talked so fast to tell him everything.

Bill's stay in town was brief and we left with him for the next trek of about three weeks and planned to have a week's local leave at the sea at Zeila. Zeila in winter was perfect and we could nip over into Djibouti[31] from there to get some apples and duty-free wine and things for Christmas.

Letter from Camp 30 miles W of Bawn, Zeila Road.
26th November 1953

At the end of his last trek Bill had walked to the next camp site and dumped his tents and gear there before he and Joe walked back to Hargeisa. The camp took quite a bit of finding as it was well off the road in thick alluvium bush, and he had only seen it so briefly for the one night, and then not from the road. When we got there at about 2pm we found everything all right but the headman down with fever. Joe followed in a pickup and got to the camp shortly after we did, and we all had a welcome picnic lunch. Then Joe left to continue with the camels to the next camp. A field man we had brought with us had fever too — the change from the heat of the Guban to the cold mists and winds of the plateau had brought it on as there had been no mosquitoes during the trek so far. We had to send the headman into Boramo when the lorry came back next day as he had had fever rather too long and was weak. As he was old we did not like the worry and

---

[31] Djibouti was the capital of French Somaliland until 1967. It is now the Republic of Djibouti.

responsibility. We spent a day in the camp because of the lorry taking the headman to Boramo then moved on to Abdal Qadr and fairly far out into the Guban. We were in a vast valley which came up behind the escarpment from the sea and it was a wind funnel up to the plateau. It blew a gale from about 10 am till well after dark. It was not too unpleasant, but it tended to make me a bit irritable as everything flapped all the time. It was warmer here though the wind was chilly, and the nights were cold. It was very open country with stony clear ground and lovely mountains all round and little else. We were on the bank of a dry tug and its bed was full of grey, yellow and pale green bushes, white pebbles and sand. With the blue hills beyond and the strong southeaster blowing it could have been in one of the desert-encroached areas in South Africa.

Getting there was an adventure, as always in this country. There were endless tugs to cross and we got stuck in two feet of sand in one for over an hour. The lorry was loading and due to follow us so we knew there would be help eventually but we had nearly dug the car out by the time they arrived. Then there were several more where we had to be pushed through parts or made new ways on more solid sand. We saw quite a lot of game — gerenuk, dik-diks, deer and warthog. It took four hours to cover the twenty miles. We chose a camping site a few miles back from here, but one of the men persuaded us to go on a bit because he said there was a wonderful place he knew of with trees etc. We drove on and ended up at a disused locust camp on a track, miles from the Zeila road where there was one tree, an old thorn zariba and all the dirt that there is round an abandoned camp. So, we were very rude to the man and went on farther to this place which was far less desirable than the first we'd chosen. We swore we'd never listen to a Somali again. We were in that camp for a few days and then had two more camps nearer Abdal Qadr and sent our mail with passing cars on the main road nearby. We then moved about seventy miles down the valley to Zeila and the sea.

Letter from Hargeisa, 17th December

It was such a joy getting a letter written by you, Mom, showing such a change for the better. I knew when I heard you were going to Joan's farm to recuperate that you would soon be better.

We came home yesterday — I can't believe it was only then as it seems ages ago! I wrote to you from Zeila and once after that in camp and I do hope that the letters reached you. (Apparently, they didn't so the details of our visit to Djibouti etc. are lost). I always doubt the trade truck drivers. We enjoyed our last few days in camp and on the Sunday had a most interesting day excavating a cave in the limestone where we only found Wilton[32] flakes. We moved on Tuesday morning and went to camp near Bawn in a beautiful spot in the hills where there is grass and trees. After the Guban that was luxury.

We expected to have a day to wait for Joe, but he appeared, walking out of the blue, while the tents were going up — and his camp followed on camels shortly afterwards, so we had the largest tea of the remains of Djibouti cheese on toast as we had all had an early start, and then an equally substantial lunch. Then I set to, to bake bread and biscuits, and to make fudge, as we had decided to go back to Hargeisa next day, a day earlier than planned.

A large number of elders from Bawn and other villages came to pay respects. Bill was well liked and respected now, and we had none of the rudeness or lack of cooperation others encountered in the bush. The elders brought beautiful camelhair rugs in soft colours to sit on and the palaver with Bill was conducted on very correct lines (via interpreter). It transpired that they wanted to give us a present of a sheep. Bill did not want to accept, being an officer of the government, and tried suggesting that they took it back and feasted on his sheep. But the elders would have none of that and the sheep became a present for the children which he had to accept. So, when our heavy baggage comes tomor-

---

[32] Widespread stone tools of the southern African Holocene Later Stone Age. I was unable to find out if Wilton flakes could be found in Somalia.

row the sheep comes too. The elders then said they wanted to give a dance for us and so we duly got smartened up and sat in front of the tent and about 50 local men did a violent dance with spears and clubs — a most stirring affair. I must admit that my blood ran cold in spite of knowing that they were well intentioned. Poor old Dingaan's[33] victims have my full, if belated, sympathy.

After the dancers had stamped and sung and laughed themselves to a standstill the elders had a further discussion with Bill and begged to be allowed to send a petition to the Governor asking for Bill to be appointed permanently to this area so that any riches which he might find would bring them wealth. All very amusing and the whole affair a new experience. The children were enthralled, and the dog was apoplectic. He was tied up to the tent pole and kept lunging at the nearest dancers, every hair on end and snarling, swinging round on the end of his line like a struggling fish.

Then we packed essentials into the truck and all of us into the Vauxhall and left the tents and most of the heavy stuff to be collected by lorry the next day. We were in Boramo early and back in Hargeisa a few hours later. Bill and Joe went out at dawn with guns and Bill got two yellow neck partridges. Joe stayed with us last night and may do so again tonight. He is no trouble. All the food parcels ordered from Aden have come and also Christmas decorations, so we are all set for Christmas. The parcels of books you sent have come and will be opened on the day. Thank you very much, darlings. We are going to have a very desert-type Christmas tree — a thorn tree suitably decorated. Joe is going to stay with us, and a few other friends will have dinner with us in the middle of the day. Joe's mother sent him a vast Christmas cake which he has given to me to ice.

---

[33] Dingaan the Vulture—a Zulu Chief - was one of Darkest Africa's crudest black despots. He became King of the Zulu Kingdom after murdering his brother. Initially friendly to Europeans, missionaries and the Voortrekkers, he treacherously killed their leader Piet Retief and his followers. He then attacked a White settlement near what is now Durban. He was defeated and fled to Swaziland where he was assassinated in 1843.

High white clouds scudding past,
A night breeze faintly stirring
Bringing wisps of smoky fragrance
From fires that are stoked all night

# SECURITY ON TREK AND A MURDER

Although most of the trekking in Somaliland was rough, through difficult and usually waterless country, there was no active menace from the people or the wildlife. We had had our camels threatened with poisoning in a camp on the Guban where the locals resented the intrusion of a different tribe of camel men, but a little diplomacy and presents of tobacco had solved that problem. Everywhere the local Somali on the whole were aloof and tended to ignore us. The harshness of the land and the struggle for survival seemed to me to have made them lean, hungry and potentially dangerous — and when one knew the country it was no surprise.

The large team of men that accompanied us on treks, with guards on duty night and day and the "official" presence so clearly displayed no doubt was necessary and contributed to our safety. The locust officers who operated alone in jeeps with perhaps one servant, and as mobile units in remote areas, had no such protection and their work was dangerous and several of them were murdered during our stay in Somaliland.

♠♠

Re-reading diaries that I kept in Somaliland has reminded me of a different sort of threat, details of which I never mentioned to my family in letters. We were warned that low-flying light aircraft from neighbouring hostile nations occasionally had a bit of "sport" involving peppering the camps, or houses, or anything moving with bullets, and we were told to take cover if we heard a small plane approaching. Ten camels had been killed in one such raid, and a few tribal Somali up to that time — "nothing serious!" In the strange way that memory works, now, more than half a century later, I am instantly transported back to Hargeisa when one very small private plane with that same engine noise flies over my peaceful green valley here below Middle Brother Mountain in Australia. For a moment I can visualise the desert and the hill with its water tank, and I feel anxious about the children—are they somewhere safe? When this first happened shortly after my move to this property, I hastily thought about other things and had no time for such mental tricks. Now I enjoy the moments that still happen when not swamped by work or too much going on and let them bring other good memories from that very special family time.

♠♠

One exception to the rule that the locals were no threat occurred on a visit into an area on the Ethiopian border in late 1953, and there was also a trek on which I witnessed a strange and disturbing incident that may have been a murder.

The children and I were in camp with Bill in the western sector operating from the Zeila road which ran from the coast up to the Ethiopian border. This was an eventful trek because we had also interrupted the camping to travel across salt marshes to Zeila to stay in the rest-house there while Bill talked to the Administrative Council.

Traversing the salt marshes was hazardous and getting badly stuck would have been serious because some of the patches were more like quicksand than slimy mud and few vehicles ever used the tracks. The pickup which accompanied us was more at risk of foundering than we were, and we would have had no chance of pulling it out with our car. However, we made the journey safely.

We all enjoyed the swimming in the lagoon at Zeila and the break from tents in a fabulous rest-house with enormous rooms that opened out on to wide balconies overlooking the sea. Bill made a quick trip to Djibouti in French Somaliland and stocked up with apples, cheese, ham and wine—none of which were available in Hargeisa. Our camp after that interruption was in the wide crater of an extinct volcano, now a hill-ringed depression with a spring in its centre, where tamarisk was in bloom. In the crater rim we excavated a large cave which had been occupied by early humans in this area and dug out a series of layers with different age stone implements, ostrich egg fragments and bones.

♠♠

It was in the next camp when we were near Bawn, in a desolate part of the country, that I was witness to what I think was murder. The children and I were playing in the sandy tug near our tent, and I could see the office pickup, which was on its way to Boramo, stopped not very far away on the track. Our interpreter and several of our camp men were engaged in lively conversation and much shouting with a group of local Somali. Some of the young men, dressed in haud cloth shroud-like garments and with the customary wild and woolly hairdos, carried the long spears which hunting parties usually did. Our people seemed to be mediating in some sort of dispute and the aggressive stance of the antagonists was unmistakable, while the shouting and tone of voice of all concerned conveyed the tenseness of the situation. I watched fascinated, wondering what was going on. Suddenly one young man sprang forward and stabbed one of the main protagonists in the back of the neck. I saw it clearly; there was no doubt about it. The man fell, out of my view between others in the small crowd, and I saw the spear being stuck into the ground, presumably to clean it.

There was total silence... After all the shouting it was heavy and tangible. With a feeling of complete unreality and as if in slow motion, I saw two of our men and two of the strangers pick the stabbed man up. He was stiff as a board, with arched back and they raised him to shoulder height between them and slid him onto the tray of the pickup. Then everyone climbed into or on the back of the vehicle and it drove off slowly towards Bawn. I had to shake myself to see if it had all really happened, and to this day I have a photographic memory of the scene, every detail etched on my mind.

When Bill came back and I told him all about it he did not know what to make of it all. When the men and the pickup came back eventually from their errand and were asked about the matter they were evasive and dismissed the whole thing. According to them they had given a few Somali a lift, but it was obvious that they were embarrassed and we were left with a very unsatisfactory feeling. Later there were rumours that the D.C. had heard about a pay-back killing, and the Administration did not pursue the matter because a sort of Somali legal system operated side by side with the European one in the wilder parts of the Territory.

I was not very happy in that camp and the added worry of a probably rabid dog seen hanging about on the fringes of the camp did little to reassure me. I had Widdy tied up in the tent and the children close at heel. When we moved on it was with some relief.

♠♠

Shortly after this camp we had the encounter with the Esa which began this story and very nearly ended it. It had all rather shaken my confidence and as we had finished our first tour of duty we were due for our Home Leave — three months leave in the UK, all travel paid. The prospect of this leave had been dangling in front of us for so long and it couldn't have come at a better time, not only because of the recent dramas, but because Bill was fed up with J.A.H.'s behaviour in trying to slow the work down and drag things out until his retirement, making everything very difficult and unpleasant for the geologists and other staff. I felt that Bill was about to explode with what would be disastrous consequences if he had one more run in with the man. He (J.A.H.) was really quite unhinged.

# MARY E. WHITE AND BARBARA ECKERSLEY

Letter from Hargeisa, 9th April 1953

Last week Bill went with John Lawrie to Ghan Libah, the escarpment mountains with cedar forest in the mist belt about eighty miles away. They started a very promising excavation in a cave. They got bone fragments and a series of implements, so we will have a fortnight there next tour as local leave and do it properly — and who knows? A Somali ape man may be simply waiting to show his grinning skull. They left on Saturday morning and came back home for lunch on Monday after being in thick mist during their entire stay in the forest. Bill said it was glorious and quite incredible in this country.

I've been helping our young geologist friend Joe prepare for his wedding which is going to be a big affair at the club as they have had to ask the whole Protectorate. We spent the morning putting the almond paste on the three tiers of the wedding cake. Joe's bride and mother-in-law came on the plane last Saturday morning. They are most charming. Lady Touche is a no-nonsense lady, and it was she who washed the floors and did the dirty work when they moved into Joe's new house on Tuesday. She is a refreshing conversationalist — funny how the really well bred who can take it for granted can put to shame all the social climbers (and the Colonial Service is full of those). She reminds me of you, Mom, in looks and in energy. Penelope is exceptionally nice. She and Joe are starting out with absolutely everything from carpets to Royal Doulton because there's masses of family money, and a stately home, in the background. But there is no ostentation. We are so glad that Joe has done so well for himself. So often one feels that cash is wasted on nasty people, and it is nice when one of one's own sort comes in for a bit of it.

Elizabeth is back from leave. Her baby is sweet but she ickle-diddilums it until I am nearly sick and so does Jimmy. I was always a trifle nauseated when she did it to the dogs before the baby came, and I thought the baby would cure her. By the look of things it is going to be hard to avoid squirming in their presence. They are the worst case I have encountered!

Barby is talking now. The other night when there was lightning flashing she told me she thought she had better come to my bed — which she did with the Princess Anne doll under one arm and her pillow under the other. David's high-falutin accent would either amuse or horrify you. Lady T. says she has never heard better enunciation and it is like an elocution lesson. He is going through a phase where he is very conscious of words and has a vast vocabulary and tries each word until it is right. Why his accent should be Oxford when the examples he has at home are Cape Town and Belfast is a mystery.

What with helping with the wedding, helping another family move into their house, seeing lots of friends and packing up there has not been much spare time lately. It has been well over 90 degrees F for a while. However, we are all fit and it has not been too tiring. It will be nice to be in the Club for the last four days for the finishing off and to adjust the children to meals in public dining rooms etc.

# HOME LEAVE

Bill, Granny White, Mary, Barbara and David

# RETURN TO AFRICA

The family back in Hargeisa

I hear again the haunting native music
Played by dark-skinned Rhodesians who believe
Their ancient tunes will keep at bay
The fearsome spirits of their night

# HOME LEAVE

We flew to Aden and had to wait a couple of days and nights in a most basic room in the awful government rest-house — in the middle of the Native Quarter. It was occupied by a number of permanently drunken Locust Officers and their yelling and brawling all night, the sharing of bathrooms and other facilities with them and the visiting native "ladies of the night", was not easy. Me very pregnant; wooden bed frames and hard sleeping mats of dubious cleanliness; no sheets, just a grubby blanket each; trying to protect the children from germs in all the filth in the accommodation and in the incredibly crowded and dirty town; heat and high humidity... but we survived!

Our voyage on the *Arcadia* was almost too luxurious after all that and the spartan living conditions in Hargeisa and in camps. The ship's doctor turned out to be a University of Cape Town graduate I had met when I was there, and he was very nervous when he saw my condition. The shipping line had regulations and no one more than seven months pregnant was allowed to board— but the Colonial Service was a law unto itself, and I was only going to get to my destination in time, with very little to spare. At the slightest sign of imminent rough weather, as in the Bay of Biscay, he drugged me so that I slept and did not hasten the baby's arrival with my seasickness. That was fortunate as an early birth and no blood exchange available would have had serious, maybe fatal, consequences for my baby.

We were met when we reached Tilbury docks and taken by Colonial Service officers to overnight accommodation in a hotel by taxi even though it was thirty miles away. It took me some time to adjust to the thought of a place the size of London. Uncle Tom and Aunt Nin, my dad's relatives, came to welcome us at the hotel and next day we flew to Belfast and made the short journey to Bill's parents in Bangor. The spoiling of the children on a grand scale started immediately—both Ma and Pa made the most of their time with their grandchildren. I was treated with the greatest kindness and affection, and it was my fault, not theirs, that I never felt at home in Northern Ireland. I had come from desert landscapes and wide-open spaces. What I saw of countryside was "pathologically green" as I described it to my mother, and the Ulster background of all the people I met was just so different from my African one. I know that Bill also felt the differences in attitudes and interests after only his short emancipation in that continent.

When my baby arrived, officially two weeks late, in the old Poor House building in Belfast that had become the Maternity Hospital with the specialist services we needed, the professional attention was all that could have been asked for. I remember the cobbled floors in passageways, where metal trolley wheels made an amazing noise, and the "mill girls" who were the other maternity patients, and my enormous feelings of relief that my beautiful child had arrived safely. Above all, I felt such deep gratitude to the doctors who had transfused her, and to the unknown donors who had provided the right blood. The mill girls used to come to the door of my tiny cubicle and look in and giggle shyly and rush away. The sister said they were so interested because they called me "the little girl from Africa" and I was white, not black, and my baby was a bit yellow after the treatment.

After a few days we were allowed to go back home to Bangor, to a great welcome from grandparents and their friends and I could announce to my parents in South Africa that they had a new grandchild—to their great delight. Dad was so grateful that we had kept the pregnancy a secret as he knew that ZoZo would have worried and her return to health would have been jeopardised.

In Bangor, everyone, particularly Ma and Pa, was lovingly supportive, sharing Bill's and my joy and wonderment. So I have thought long and hard before deciding to mention Pa's immedi-ate reaction to his new grandchild when I handed him the pre-cious bundle on arrival at his door. I know his heart was full of love when he held her—but his Ulster, Low Church indoctrination was so deeply imprinted that his welcoming words were, "I can only hope that they did not give her any Mick[34] blood!". And I had the immediate return of the feeling of being a person from a different planet, let alone a different continent, even though I already loved my in-laws. My in-laws also objected to the name Zoe, saying that no child of theirs would be called by such a 'heathen' name and that they'd be calling her by her mid-dle name. So Zoe was Margaret while in Northern Ireland and Bill's nicknames derived from that stuck for many years—Mag, Maggot, Pag and Paggot.

Four days later Dad died of a heart attack in South Africa. I was shattered and terribly worried about my mother. But I was determined that my grief would not spoil the very special, short time that Ma and Pa were sharing with their grandchildren. The new baby was unbelievably healthy and happy—sleeping, feed-ing, gurgling with delight and just about never crying. The only private time I had for grieving was while I was feeding her, alone upstairs and she was wet with my tears but, I hoped, not trauma-tised. Throughout her babyhood she was the easiest, most con-tented and confident child, so that was probably the case.

It was midsummer during our visit and the early sunrise was like what we had in Somalia, so while the others slept in until at least 9am, my little family and I used to steal out of the shuttered house at about 5am and go for a walk and play on the jetties and park down the road. I loaded the pram with baby and the mak-ings of the kids' breakfast, and we had a special time together, without the over-stimulation of grandparents' attentions. Another "deep-down Ulster response" resulted from this activity. Pa asked me please not to leave the house like that so early in the morning because "the neighbours would think I was not being properly

---

[34] Mick - Slang: disparaging and offensive- a contemptuous term for a person of Irish birth or descent; in this case Roman Catholic Irish

treated at home". But I continued, explaining that no one was awake then to think anything and I had been getting up a five every day of my life, and so had the kids.

The only other person regularly enjoying the early sunshine was a retired businessman, dressed for the part to show his retired respectability in immaculate dark suit, white shirt, tie, folded white hankie in top pocket, walking a tiny poodle. He did not even look at us (he had not been introduced, and I was a lady on my own!) One day, when the poodle messed on the pathway, not on the lawn as required, he took the immaculate handkerchief from his top pocket, picked up the specimen and folded it up, and placed it in his trouser pocket. We watched, entranced, and he continued with his parade along the walkway as though nothing untoward had happened and as though we were invisible.

Towards the end of August 1954, we left Bangor and went to London, where we stayed in Aunt Nin's house for a few days, waiting for the *SS Himalaya* to arrive, and Bill went to Australia House to apply for a geological job in the Bureau of Mineral Resources.

Being with Aunt Nin, one of Dad's sisters, was like coming home—her friendly house completely free of tension. Aunt Nin was the most wonderful person and an inspiration. Although she was almost crippled with arthritis she did nearly everything herself, even the laundry, and she still found time for church affairs and committees. She was adored by her neighbours, friends and relations. She and Ruby (a cousin) were away when we arrived, and another aunt had come up from the country to see us in. She was a darling too and gave us a great welcome. There were little notes all over cupboards saying where things were, a bath ready for the baby, a special tin of biscuits next to my bed so that I could keep my strength up while feeding my baby in the night, etc. Uncle Tom and some other relatives of my dad came to tea. It was nice being in the house by ourselves when they all left.

The following day Uncle Tom took us to London Zoo. The children were in the process of adjusting after all the upheaval, missing the extra attention etc. Zoe was wonderful as usual. David was happily attached to Ruby, and she got no peace in consequence. Poor Barby had had a couple of tantrums which baffled and exhausted me. I knew she'd settle down, but it was shattering while it lasted. Bill had a lot of business to attend to in London.

The days we spent in London were glorious. I came away strangely comforted about Dad, having dreaded the visit because I thought it would be very upsetting. Aunt Nin was such a completely amazing person, and her house was a real home where one was enfolded in kindness without fuss or strain. Her garden was lovely, and the weather was wonderful. There was an atmosphere about it all and what we saw of London was far better than expected. It all felt reassuringly right in some way. Never in the days that we were there did I manage to do any family ironing, which had been rather a tiring bind every day in Bangor. Someone — Ruby or one of the aunts, did it quietly with obvious enjoyment. The kitchen was a large and comfortable room, and all the jobs were done to the accompaniment of family chatter.

> I seem to hear again the peaceful breathing
> Of sleeping family around me.
> I feel secure, and privileged to be alive

# RETURN TO AFRICA AND PLANS TO LEAVE

We boarded the SS *Himalaya*—another lovely ship, if not as special as the *Arcadia*— around the 1st of September 1954 and sailed down the Thames to the sea, looking forward to an enjoyable and restful voyage. We had two comfortable deck cabins on A deck. The children were happy and good, and we all enjoyed baby Zoe. David and Barbara were more at home on the ship than they ever were in Bangor. I think the endless attention with many people amusing them was bewildering, and Barby felt the strain because she was so little and had to keep up with David. Her tantrums disappeared and she was confident and happy. Though we enjoyed very much being with the family in Bangor and London it did feel good to be on our own again and I looked forward to having my own house again –we were to have the big stone house that used to be Marjorie and J.A.H.'s in Hargeisa, so we would be very comfortable.

The second day on board I was rather seasick but didn't want to take anything because of feeding Zoe. It was very rough in the Bay of Biscay, and I only just managed to do what I had to with the children. Once we were in the Mediterranean it was calm and beautiful.

Letter from Aden. 12th September 1954

We are here in the Crescent Hotel in Aden, and what a different story from the last time. We left the ship yesterday evening and we fly to Hargeisa tomorrow. The voyage was wonderful to Port Said, then we met quite incredible heat as we had a following wind through the Suez Canal and Red Sea. Never have we

196

known such heat. Port Sudan is supposed to be the hottest place on earth and "Hells Gates", at the entrance to the Gulf of Aden, no better. On your birthday it must have been 110 degrees F in the cabin and hardly a breath of wind on deck. David ran a temperature of 104 all day — just the heat. The doctor says it is quite usual for small children on this route and half the children on board were affected. Next day Barby had her turn and David was better. Zoe was all right. I propped her up in the washbasin on a towel and she lay wet and bare all day, gurgling and delighted. Yesterday was still very hot but not as bad and we managed to pack up. It was pleasantly cool by the time we left the ship.

I look forward to seeing all our friends and Widdy in Hargeisa and showing them Zoe. We are in a luxury suite at the Crescent — probably occupied up to now by an Ethiopian dignitary, and have a truly immense room with mosaic floor, very high ceiling and archway onto a covered porch. Private bathroom, shower room and lav. There are enormous fans going all the time and we will stay indoors and keep cool.

On the day before leaving Aden I went down with heat stroke like the children had had — a raging temperature for twelve hours. It was so hot that the cold bath water was 99 degrees F in the middle of the night and the room under the fans over 90 degrees F. I don't know what the highest temperature was, but it was too much anyway. The morning we were to fly from Aden to Hargeisa I had a temperature of 101 so Bill packed up and arranged to have our seats reserved on the plane so that we could go at the last minute. The airways were helpful and kind, but the Hargeisa plane was withdrawn at the last moment as unserviceable and we had to wait over an hour until there was another. It was not too bad as by then I was feeling better. Once in the plane and high up in the cool I was all right. Barbara slept all the way to Berbera, Bill and David talked and Zoe was angelic. I retired behind a purdah curtain and fed her on the way. We had to land at Berbera, which was hot and glary. We sat in the shade of the plane and ate ice which we had brought in a Thermos and we buried Zoe's disposable nappy in the desert sand on the runway for luck. Then on to Hargeisa—the bumpiest trip we have had. I was sick repeatedly, David and Zoe slept and Barby just survived, green to the gills.

♠♠

We were met by Joe Mason and old J.A.H. Joe took the children and me straight to the Club while Bill saw to Customs. We had that night at the Club, and I went to bed early and was all right next day. We had a wonderful welcome with constant visitors from the time we arrived, and it has gone on ever since.

We moved immediately into our house and unpacked around ourselves. The crates of new things came from Berbera with everything intact. With new pictures up, bright embroidered cushions, leather pouffes etc bought in Aden it all looked nice. Barbara was very overwrought at first. I refused all invitations that first week and stayed at home so that a routine could be established. It was quite a bit of a juggle managing the three children at bed time with supper, feeds and baths, but with Bill going away again soon I had to manage. I liked having my children to myself again. When they were being spoilt and taken over by others all the time it reached a stage where I only did the dirty work and the correcting, and all the pleasure was had by the others.

I had an adequate servant who really helped a lot. He did all the cleaning, the washing apart from Zoe's, and all the ironing. My new little electric stove was a blessing. We retrieved Widdy and time after time we had to go and collect him again, as he was so happy at the Douch's house while we were away that he did not know where he belonged.

While we were away from Africa we'd had a chance to think seriously about the situation in Africa in general and South Africa in particular. We were increasingly disturbed by the injustices, inequalities and horrendous racism that was rife in South Africa. Apartheid, a legally sanctioned system of racial segregation which began officially in 1948 was now firmly entrenched and with each new law enacted the lives of non-whites was being made intolerable. The Population Registration Act of 1950 classified all South Africans as either Whites, Coloureds, Asians or Blacks. The Group Areas Act established residential and business sections in urban areas for each race and members of other races were barred from living, operating businesses or owning land in them, leading to thousands of non-Whites being removed from areas classified for white occupation. More than 80% of South Africa's land was set aside for the White minority! Blacks were moved into segregated neighbourhoods and were stripped of their South African citizenship.

Not surprisingly there was huge unrest, with civil disobedience protests and riots and blacks were killed and injured by police. Bill and I were very distressed by the situation and could see it only getting worse. There was no way we wanted to raise our family in a country like this and we had been weighing up our options for some time.

Letter from Hargeisa September 1954

Lately we have been giving much thought to our next move. The Survey here is due to close in 1956 and is proving quite unproductive. We want to settle near schools and amenities for the children and do not want to be permanently in England or Ireland. Transfer in the Colonial Service now would mean the Gold Coast or Nigeria and some other unsuitable places for children. And we do not want to live in South Africa permanently. So we think that we will head for Australia with a view to becoming Australian permanently and bringing the children up as such. I am telling you this because Bill has been offered what looks like a really good job and is biding his time to find out what else is available. You may feel that Australia is very far, but we will not go there if the salary is not large enough to manage leave with you.

When in London Bill met the Australian geological representatives and they were all for signing him up there and then. Aunt Nin says "if the way opens" we will go, and we feel rather that way ourselves. Don't panic at the idea, darling, we will give you lots of warning if it comes — only I did not want to keep you in the dark. I think Bill is going to do very well in his geology. With all the wide experience he has had he would be valuable to the Australian government with its new exploration programs. I will go anywhere at all on earth as long as it is healthy and suitable for the children, but I can't face boarding schools for them and endless separations. We want to buy a bit of land and build a hut or something one day, so who knows, we may yet have tame koalas and kangaroos and that quite awful Australian accent!

I've been homesick since we came back to Hargeisa and so empty without Dad... Knowing that you are all right is a help and we all think you have been wonderful.

We are settled in our new house and Bill will be in town till after Barby's birthday if possible. I will not go out on trek with him till after Christmas as I do not want to expose Zoe to heat and glare too soon. J.A.H. is still as usual — if possible more revolting and hateful after being away from him. When we leave Somaliland I will be so glad to have seen the last of him. What a creature!— and he got an OBE in the last honours list, such is the Colonial Service!

Bill has sent off a batch of his maps and reports in lieu of an interview at Australia House. They seem really keen to have him and he is applying for a supervising geologist post in the Bureau of Mineral Resources (there are other posts to be filled as well). I am all for Australia, but I am torn between going and being nearer home. Life seems so full of conflict when one grows up, but you will understand that and we have to think of the children and their future. We will let you know what happens; if anything. We have no idea when we'd go, or how. If it's at all possible we'll come via South Africa, but that seems a faint hope. Next best we'll see to it that in two years we were in a position to send for you to come to us.

Letter from Hargeisa, Thursday 14th October 1954

Today Bill went off on trek and he will be away for two long months. But we have to get used to separations again as it goes with being a geologist. I may have a bit of trouble with Barby this time. She is at a stage where she takes any emotional upset hard. David is on the best of terms with me these days and Zoe continues too good to be true.

Joe and Penelope are back from trek. Joe goes again tomorrow but P. will stay as her baby is due in February. He has been camel trekking all over the Guban, walking miles each day to defeat J.A.H. who this time has refused transport to anyone at all. Bill at this moment is camel trekking for four days along the main road because J.A.H. refused to move his camp by lorry to the new area, although the lorry was there delivering rations and the camel men were in the process of being changed. He is quite abnormal, that man — and is at the moment doing all that he can to hold back the work, as he wants an extension of the survey until 1960 on the grounds that it will be inconclusive in 1956. So no work is allowed to be done properly at all. Very frustrating for all the geologists. But J.A.H. can retire on maximum pension if the thing goes on till 1960, such is the Colonial Service. The Somali say that he bought his house in England with what he fiddled from General Services which he conducted before he took on geology. A nice specimen, but his days of getting away with anything are over.

Letter from Hargeisa, 10th November 1954

In a few days we should know what our plans for the future are. Bill has had an offer of a Senior Geologist job with the Australian Commonwealth survey with prospects of rapid promotion depending on merit. He has to find out here about length of notice required, repayment of passage money when a tour is incomplete etc. but he is going to accept the job. I hope we will have your blessing in this darling. I know that Dad would have been wholehearted in his approval if that is any comfort. We are so keen to get established now with school coming up for David and wanting to put down roots. South Africa does not appeal at all apart from being near you, as we have no desire to bring the children up with all its problems and hatreds. We feel so strongly that we must go to Australia, and now is the time.

When Bill's letter about the job came on Tuesday last week Bill was in one of the least accessible areas of the Colony with camels. I had to send a police wireless message to Boramo with instructions that a runner should go from there, and then send a runner to Boramo by trade truck with a copy of the letter. I hoped that the police message would halt Bill, but it missed him and he went progressively further from the runner, who finally caught up with him on Friday night. The runner said he had had a terrifying journey as he was all alone going through the "Dibrawein" which is very wild, no people and lots of lions. Bill walked on a crows-fly line cross country to Boramo — forty miles through extraordinarily rough and mountainous country in three marches, getting there at 11.30 am on Sunday and getting a lift to home at once, most providentially. He arrived here at 4.30 sunburnt and fit and happy and it is glorious having him back.

Bill saw the Chief Secretary of the Survey and gave the required three months' notice, and a passage was booked to Australia in March. I was fairly overwhelmed by the packing up again and had some deep regrets about leaving very good friends (and our dog Widdy) but I loved Bill and would follow him to the end of the Earth (as I had already done) and I knew that was the right thing to do.

Bill went back to Boramo after six days with us and we slipped back into our routine. I sometimes viewed, almost with dismay, the prospect of starting off in an unknown continent without family or friends. Even the names of the main cities were unfamiliar, but to balance that there was all the excitement and interest. We found it easy to make friends in Somaliland so no doubt we would soon feel at home in Australia.

I read Australian papers to get an idea of things and to try and get my head around what to take and what to leave. I was sure that such a vast country would have so much to offer in every way—like Africa but without its racial problems. I looked forward to having a new flora to get to know.

I had no illusions about how much work would be entailed in bringing up a family in a country where there were no servants, and where I would be often alone, but I knew I had the physical strength to cope with all that, the foundations being already well laid. I liked work of all sorts, and when it was for those I love it was no hardship. I had no doubt that in Australia I would thrive because I would buy labour-saving devices and I would wean Zoe and have more energy.

Letter from Hargeisa, Tuesday, 30th November 1954

Your first letter since you had our Australia news came yesterday and I can see that you have mixed feelings about it. I am not at all surprised. As for me, there has been and will continue to be, considerable heart-rending about it all. I hate above all to give you worry or disappointment. It must seem heartless to go on about our own business as if nothing has changed at home. I wish we could come via Durban, but it is impossible. The Bureau wants Bill now and even the three months notice is a lot for them... Believe me, I don't want to go off without seeing you first. Your happiness means a tremendous lot to me, and your present loneliness and sorrow are constantly in my mind. Apart from sorrow about Dad and wishing I could be a real help to you at this time I am happy, so don't you worry about me. Bill has realised my need for extra comfort and reassurance lately and has been wonderful. He is at home now and is not going out on trek again. He will be busy getting his reports and maps finished. J.A.H. was not pleased about his leaving but he has had support and help from the Chief Secretary.

♠♠

In retrospect, the British Colonial Service and Somaliland Protectorate was an amazing experience. A man-made desert populated by poverty-stricken hordes hostile to the unwanted white managers, yet the European community continued to live with all the pomp and ceremony of an outpost of the British Empire! But it was very interesting geologically. I was so happy with my young family, so interested in everything, that hardships and the very real dangers that we faced when in the field did not count. What I learned about man-made deserts, floodplain landscapes, and so much more proved, much later, useful in understanding such things in Australia and I made a Herbarium for the Government during the three year stay.

To know the lovely night and be a part
Of all creation

# LEAVING AFRICA

Somewhere around the middle of March 1955 we flew out of
Hargeisa and met the SS *Strathmore* in Aden. Our heavy luggage had preceded us via truck and dhow to Aden and was
much reduced because we had sold or given away most of our
replaceable possessions. I was to regret this later, but at the time
the problems and uncertainties of transport made it seem the
way to go. We would have to start again from scratch, accumu-
lating the basic domestic things like pots and pans, and as we
had left all our initial furniture in South Africa we had to start again
there too because it was not feasible to get it sent all the way to
Australia.

The voyage, calling at Bombay and probably other ports
which I cannot recall, took about three weeks to Fremantle, and
we arrived in Melbourne on 8th April, presumably in Sydney a few
days later, and after a night there went by train to Canberra. I
remember that while we were in Fremantle dock we hired a
car and drove around in Perth and its vicinity and I was struck
by the great similarity between the Southwestern Cape where I
had spent some of the happiest days of my life, and that part of
Western Australia. It was my first awakening to the evidence for
and omnipresence of Gondwana.

I had not realised that underneath the excitement of coming
to a new land there was so much tension and so many regrets at
severing all ties with Africa until I had a strange emotional experience a few years ago. Then, on a visit to Perth I was taken up
to Kings Park where we had gone briefly during our 1955 call at
Fremantle. There is a wonderful avenue of blue gums on an ele-
vated road from which one can view the city spread out below.
We had been there sightseeing and I recognised the avenue as

the place in my recurrent nightmares over the years since. I was overwhelmed without warning, there in the middle of a beautiful day among friends and amidst all the happiness of a very pleasant social occasion, by a black cloud containing all the emotions of those nightmares. Those dreams that haunted me during times of worry or unhappiness were filled with unreasoning fear and despair and frantic hunting for lost children; or with trying to find my mother who is sick and has wandered off in the darkness of that long avenue where everything is strange, and I have no one to help me to find her before she has gone forever. Strange what tricks the mind plays, and since that upwelling of something that was buried so deep I have not had those "strange dark forest full of horrors" dreams. Having recognised where they came from I have also come to see that I was not guilty of causing my mother's worries and uncertainties and did not "abandon" my parents in their latter years when I could have been there for them. Nor did I abandon Africa, the land whose essence is in my blood. I just moved on and life's river took me like flotsam into another realm. There has never been the slightest doubt that coming to Australia, becoming totally Australian and raising an Australian family was the best thing to do, and I have no regrets, only gratitude for what this country has given me.

♠♠

We found the transition from Africa to Australia easy. Both were Colonial in those days, people were the same, friendly small-town people typical of far-flung bits of the British Empire (how the Republicans would hate me for saying that!) Australia then, was without the feeling of personal guilt and the problems that had afflicted the Africa we knew, with its black-white and Afrikaans-English conflicts; there was unbounded opportunity for geologists and botanists, and for me an untouched field as a Gondwanan environmentalist or whatever I have been able to become. And in this field my African beginnings have been fundamental. That we were alone, a truly nuclear family, without extensions, and had no one to turn to for help or moral support or advice in those early years was a sacrifice that went with the territory, and even today I miss my mother's letters which kept me in touch while she was alive.

When in 1983 I made a once-in-a-lifetime visit to Africa after an absence of nearly thirty years it was a trip into nostalgia, revisiting the places I loved, shutting my eyes and mind to the political problems that had been the reason behind our migration to Australia so long ago, and spending time with family and friends. I was just a tourist because my parents, and therefore my roots, had gone and my belonging was now where my children were, in another land. And towards the end of my time in Africa I could not wait to get home to Australia and was counting the days! The African chapter of my life story was neatly packaged. The wide brown land that colours my thinking and draws me into its far places, Australia, is where I belong.

# PART II

---

# MARY'S AUSTRALIAN STORY

# PREFACE

When Mary died her account of her life in Africa up until 1955 was fairly complete and she had left a rough time-line of events for 1955—1980. I (her daughter), have put together her life in Australia from her letters, Dad's letters and various pieces of writing she did in her lifetime. I have also dealt with her eventual deterioration and death. The aftermath of her death, Part III, is a separate story —mine, not hers.

My relationship with Mary (I'll call her Mary as I've always been uncomfortable with "Mom" in this country, where mothers are Mum and Mummy) was always close and loving. She said she knew me before I was born, knew I was female (long before sex determination was possible), knew who I'd be, and bonded strongly with me *in utero*. There was an instant two-way bonding when I was born and we shared something very special through-out life. We had the same values, appreciated the same things and what mattered most in life. She loved my husband Richard and connected strongly with my children. She said it was like a rebirth of her own children and in return, my children thought her a magical grandmother, a grandmother who absolutely adored them, lived on a beach and had a house full of interesting curiosities such as fossils, rocks, animal skulls, gemstones and dinosaur models.

The Mary I knew was a complex human being, with a huge amount of charm and charisma that people responded to, and which made people instantly feel that they were very special to her. But like most of us, she had another side—her share of human failings, insensitivities and feelings of superiority. She was loyal and caring to a fault, and snobbish, as was Dad. Our relationship was not perfect—she was a very strong-minded person, opinionated and often judgemental and could be, at times, somewhat over-bearing—although there was always a beguiling, disarming charm about her frankness. But she was my mother and had always been thus, and I loved her and never questioned or judged her harshly for it, though I was often irritated by her pronouncements and lack of tolerance for all sorts of things. She had been shaped by the country and times in which she was born and raised, and the intolerances and prejudices were ingrained in her and became more pronounced as she aged.

Mary died on 5 August 2018.

So, who was this Mary E. White who became a highly acclaimed Australian scientist, scholar, environmentalist, writer, educator and powerful role model and whose death caused so much drama and quite a bit of excitement in the media?

Mary was a surprising woman who, in 1986, rocked the sci-entific world by writing **The Greening of Gondwana**— a major publication that seemed to have come out of the blue. Mary had, for the first time, combined all the scientific disciplines and theories from plate tectonics, geology, botany and the evolution of plants with her powerful visionary insight into life to create this major opus. It was an extraordinary book that stunned Sir David Attenborough and renowned neurologist, naturalist and science historian Oliver Sacks who wrote personal letters to Mary to this effect. Many luminaries of the scientific world congratulated her and praised her highly for a beautiful and scientifically very important book.

How did a north shore Sydney housewife, mother to a large family and a totally devoted and subservient wife, achieve such a feat? Mary was an Australian paleobotanist, yet first and foremost she was a wife and mother. She always put Dad and the family first. Mary was not a submissive personality—far from it—but she had very strong, old-fashioned views on the role of a wife and mother (and so did Dad).

Despite this, Mary managed to find a little time each day, being careful that it didn't impact on the family in any way, to develop a deep understanding of the evolution of Australia's flora through her work with fossils and her interests in the theory of continental drift. Then a few years after Dad's death, in the mid-1980s, with the help of Jim Frazier, an extraordinary photographer who brought her drab old fossils to life, an extremely talented editor/book design team, Helen and Bruno Grasswill, and brave publisher Bill Templeman, she produced *The Greening of Gondwana*.

If Dad had lived she would never have written *The Greening* or any other books—she would have been sailing in the Pacific with him, living *his* dream. He would have scoffed at her and asked, "what makes you think you could write a book when you're not an expert on the subject?" She said he would have meant it in the kindest way, to shield her from rejection and failure. But after his death when she was in her early fifties, she realised that she *could* write the book that she had needed all her working life—a book that explained Australia's unique flora in terms of Australia-in-Gondwana i.e. its geological history!

Mary engaged a professional cartographer for her first four books, but in a lovely and loving collaboration, I taught myself to use the relevant software and produced the maps and diagrams for her subsequent books. She was very organised, knew exactly what she wanted and supplied me with mock-ups, which I converted to digital, print-ready files. We worked well together and enjoyed each other's company and the sense of achievement and excitement about the projects.

Until recently, I'd never really thought of my mother as extraordinary or that she had had an extraordinary life. She was my mother, always there for us, loving, solid, practical, positive and more than capable. She was in fact, quite extraordinary, achieved much and really lived a very full life.

Mary compensated for Dad's depression and moodiness, acting as if everything was completely normal because she adored him and knew that he adored her and had a deep need for her. This, and my close bond with her, probably saved me from being too damaged by Dad's black moods and remote parenting.

Like Mary, Bill was highly intelligent and complex. On one hand, he knew everything—we didn't have conversations or discussions with him—what he said was right and that was the end of it. Between them there was little room for our opinions or interesting discussions about anything much at all. On the other hand, I suspect Dad had his own demons, insecurities and doubts that he masked by being outwardly confident and self-assured, when not completely consumed by his depression. And, I need to say, that despite all this, Dad was a decent and loving father and I loved him.

Mary described her early years in Australia as a very "domesticated", very happy and fulfilling period of her life, mainly about looking after children, surviving the daily problems, and coping alone when her geologist husband was away for up to seven months of the year. Apart from showing Mary's ability to cope with things that would have defeated most of us while maintaining a positivity and cheerful optimism, the details are not of great interest to readers. However, during these years she did manage to establish a part-time profession as a palaeobotanist (palaeobotany being the study of fossil plants) where she built up her knowledge of co-evolution of the flora, fauna and physical environments of the Australian continent through geological time.

My special bond with my mother, for which I ultimately was to pay a very high price, lasted until the last few years of her life when with advancing dementia she became someone else. She lost her essential self and I floundered to relate to the stranger she became. They were a hard few years for all of us, but particularly for Mary, who was well aware of her brain's demise and her rapid advance toward oblivion.

I'm sure Mary would have had many more personal memories and experiences to enrich her story, but they have been lost with her. Many, many times while writing this I have wished I had asked her about various people, places and happenings that crop up in her story. Consequently, much is based on my memories which may not be the same as hers, or those of my siblings, but such is memory.

# NORTHERN TERRITORY FIELD SEASON 1955

NT camp

Mary and kids at the billabong

The kids digging in a dry river bed

# NORTHERN TERRITORY FIELD SEASON

Mary wrote:

In early 1955 we left by ship from Aden, the nearest port on the Red Sea, heading for Australia where Bill had accepted a Senior Geologist post with what was then the Bureau of Mineral Resources in Canberra.

A four day wait in Fremantle, while the ship unloaded, re-introduced me to Gondwana. We hired a car and drove about through the sand-plain floras, and I could not believe that thousands of miles of ocean separated me from the Cape of Good Hope. I saw and recognised the same plant families, the same sort of ecosystems. It all told of common ancestry—a Gondwanan connection — confirming my complete acceptance of continents drifting although the scientific community was not to accept the ideas fully until the late 1960s.

♠♠

A couple of days later we docked in Melbourne and boarded a train to Canberra where we were put up for a week in the house of a Mrs Kennett in Turner who took in new arrivals until accommodation could be arranged. We were all then flown to Darwin for the geological field season, during winter when temperatures were bearable, and before the wet season set in. For four glorious months we camped on the Mary and Alligator Rivers with another geologist and his family. Dad was in charge of the Goodparla Party –so called as the South Alligator River was on Goodparla Station land. The landscape, so iconically Australian, yet so African in many ways—dry, rugged open savanna—sparse, stunted eucalypt woodland over grassland, and rocky outcrops under spectacular skies. Ancient landscapes that have been deeply weathered over millennia, thin infertile soils of red and yellow dirt, then surprisingly rich and luxuriant vegetation around billabongs—beautiful and tranquil and supporting an abundance of wildlife. We found it all comfortingly familiar as well as excitingly different.

Life in camp was very like that in Somaliland—Dad leaving camp early in the day and we children playing in the sandy, dry river bed and resting during the heat of the day. For my parents, the absence of large dangerous game must have been a huge relief. We all swam in a large billabong—once again to discover at the end of our stay that it belonged to a large crocodile. Mary collected plants and delighted in the abundant birds—the swirling clouds of budgerigars— and the small marsupial hopping mice that scuttled around the campsite at night— and we were all thrilled by sightings of kangaroos.

The grass between our camp and the billabong was very tall and I'm told that I was often met by a large goanna, rearing up on its front legs to its full height—and I was apoplectic, my screams bringing everyone running. "Bill the cook" was so upset by my screams that on one occasion he shot the goanna as it eyeballed me, which I found far more distressing than the encounters. I quickly learnt not to lead the charge to the billabong and let someone else deal with 'locals'.

At the end of the field season we drove a five-ton lorry back to Canberra, heavily loaded with all the geological specimens, camping gear etc. "*Elephantina Jiggelbonnet*" was uncomfortable but apparently it was a good three weeks and interesting for Dad visiting mines on the way and was, no doubt, a great introduction to Australia. David and I sat on empty dynamite boxes between the front seats and Zoe sat on Mary's lap. Mary used to wash the nappies before we got underway in the mornings, tie them to a rope and dry them out the window as we drove. At night we pulled off the road under some trees where possi-

218

ble, and camped beside the truck, sleeping under the stars every night except for one occasion when bad weather forced us to stay in a hotel. I have a clear memory of bathing in our zinc bath-tub while kookaburras laughed at us. "What's so funny?" David demanded standing up and shaking his small body at the birds and we got the giggles which went on and on.

Mary wrote:

**Crossing the Barkly Tableland we camped where there were a few trees in the vast expanse of grass and there was a bird which sang the theme notes of Dvorak's New World Symphony—I felt strangely welcomed and accepted in this 'our new world'.**

The Canberra house 1960; the 4 children Derek, David, Barbara and Zoe

Barbara and Janey          Dad, Mary and Derek in the car Dad built

Moving the car to Sydney

# CANBERRA

After that first field season David and I had to start school so there were no more family geological camps. Dad was away every year for three to six months and I think his mental health suffered from the long periods of separation and isolation. He became more withdrawn, moody and, as Mary put it, difficult. Coming home each year to suburban Canberra and a family who had moved on, grown and become used to his absences, must have been really difficult. And just when he was adjusting to suburban, family life he was off again.

Dad hated Canberra—the artificiality of the place—it was young and laid out like a scar on the landscape. He hated its soullesness, its stratified society. He felt very keenly that geologists were looked down upon by the diplomats, public servants and doctors. He hated the climate and that it was inland and so far from the sea, on appalling roads. There was no lake until after we left; not that it would have changed his mind about the place, but at least he could have puddled around in small boats — an activity he loved.

We lived in a house in Deakin whose diplomat owners were on an overseas posting. It was right on the outer edge of Canberra with paddocks and sheep at the end of our street. Houses were depressingly uninspired brick or monocrete construction with small yards and just about no trees or gardens.

We acquired a (tiny) Fiat 1100 and a golden cocker spaniel to make up for leaving my beloved Widdy in Somaliland. My misery at leaving Widdy apparently ran deep and my resentment for some time was directed at Mary. I'm told I gave her the odd sharp kick in the shins to vent my frustration. Ginger Janey was never a very robust dog and the damage that had been done to her heart by distemper she'd had as a puppy in the pound, was to kill her six years later when we moved to Sydney and she got a tick.

Canberra winters were extremely cold and the little government house we lived in had no insulation and no heating except for an open fireplace and a wood stove in the kitchen. Mary suffered badly from chilblains. Her letters to ZoZo talked a lot about them, how crippling they were, the chilblain cream she found that helped and the fur-lined boots she had to buy to survive. In one letter to her mother in the very early months of our first Canberra she wrote:

**I was nearly going mad. I have never known such irritation. I couldn't sleep at all one night and there have been odd spells of a few hours where I was nearly in tears of rage and frustration at the itching...The bedrooms are so cold my leg bones ache when I go into the children at night and even during the day.**

Other letters, particularly those to Dad, were about punctures, flat batteries and slipping clutch plates when they weren't about tonsils, middle ears and trips to the dentist. A young geologist from the BMR used to come out occasionally to chop wood for us. We children were oblivious to the cold but as our immune systems had developed to deal with a totally different set of viruses and diseases we were constantly sick each winter. David got tonsillitis, I had bronchitis repeatedly and Zoe had recurrent middle ear problems. There were weeks during winter when Mary couldn't get out of the house because one or other of us was sick. When David had his tonsils removed and his health improved, I wanted to have my bronchioles removed.

When we were not sick we had lovely picnics out at the Cotter or Murrumbidgee Rivers. Mary obviously missed camping and was always keen to cook chops and boil a billy for tea on a campfire. When Dad was at home we rarely went on picnics as he had had his fill of campfires, flies and sand.

Mary did lots of sewing, knitting and carpet making in those Canberra years. I remember long sessions of being read to by the fire at night, delaying our retreat to the freezing bedroom; the yeasty smell of homemade ginger beer when the bottles exploded, and the South African staple—rusks—that Mary made regularly and were so crisp they had to be dipped in tea before they could be eaten. Mary tuned in daily to *Blue Hills*, an ABC radio serial—a very early Aussie soap. She said that she felt she became personal friends with all the characters, and it made her life less lonely. When I hear the music that introduced the series, it takes me straight back to my childhood in Canberra. We kids listened religiously to the *Children's Hour*. David and I became Argonauts, contributing drawings, letters and stories to that wonderful, educational program.

After every field season, 44-gallon drums of fossils would be delivered to our front door. Mary would work her way through the drums, unpacking specimens packed in cotton wool in small fossil boxes. I still remember their peculiar smell and I was allowed to have a couple of boxes to put my collections in—little found treasures like smooth, round rocks, shells, bleached bird bones etc. I'm still a collector of 'treasures' as is one of my granddaughters, so it must be a genetic trait or a Lamarckian inheritance—or something.

I recall clearly Mary's excitement as she unpacked the drums, holding up a piece of rock and exclaiming "Beautiful Glossopteris!" or "Lovely Gangamopteris!" By identifying the plants she was able to tell the Bureau of Mineral Resources what age the rocks were; Permian, Upper Permian, Cretaceous etc. She built up her knowledge by examining, identifying and reporting on all plant fossils collected by the field parties mapping the geological basins in search of coal, oil and gas and other mineral deposits.

Fairly early on Dad was promoted to Supervising Geologist over another senior geologist who appealed, lost and thereafter became very difficult to work with. Dad's customary descent into disillusionment and dissatisfaction with the job began. He was supervising work and in charge of mapping in a huge area from Tennant Creek in the Northern Territory to Chillagoe near Cairns in Queensland as well as work in Papua and New Guinea, Woodlark and Misima Islands in the Louisiade Archipelago off New Guinea.

As his disenchantment with fieldwork grew Dad considered taking an academic post at the Australian National University where he wanted to work on his island arc theories[35], which now fit into accepted Plate Tectonics, but were ahead of their time then. Why this did not eventuate, we were not told.

In November 1957 Mary's mother ZoZo arrived for her one and only visit. What should have been a very happy reunion and stay was marred by Dad's depression, moodiness and the move into our allotted government house, which was incredibly dirty. Dad fell down the back steps and broke his ankle which didn't help his mood—but he did save the milk bottles he was putting out on the step! A ten day stay at Mossy Point before all the drama was the highlight for us, and Mary and ZoZo probably managed some quality time together, if such a thing existed in those days. Mary, in her typically loyal-to-Dad way, only commented that her mom's visit had been far from relaxed.

When ZoZo left at the end of January 1958 Mary went to Sydney with her and they stayed overnight in the Metropole Hotel. The parting must have been heart-wrenching as they both knew they would not see each other again, but as kids we were oblivious to all of this.

Dad was involved in a Phosphate Survey of the South West Pacific, Solomon Islands and New Guinea and was away much of that year, arriving home two days before child number four, Derek, was born. David had just broken his arm having the ignominious honour of being pushed out of a tree by the little girl next door, and the house full of squabbling children, a newborn and a neurotic dog must have been very hard to adapt to.

---

[35] Island arcs are chains of islands formed by volcanoes located along the subduction zone, which is anywhere that two of Earth's tectonic plates collide and one slips underneath the other.

In his months at home Dad escaped the family chaos by retreating to the garage, where he was building a sports car, a Repco KM 300. It had a fibreglass body and modified Holden chassis and engine.

♠♠

The Phosphate Survey continued during 1959, expanding to include Fiji, Gilbert and Ellice Islands (now Kiribati and Tuvalu), Ocean Islands and Nauru. Over Christmas Dad got hepatitis and nearly died, with 90% of his liver out of action. When he was partly recovered we went camping in the sand dunes at Shoalhaven Heads where Zoe and I nearly drowned. I remember being awake in the night with Dad, sobbing and reliving the horrors of that near-disastrous event until the early hours of the morning.

The liver damage following the hepatitis undoubtedly con-tributed to Dad's depression which became a constant and major illness from here on—one that he would not acknowledge or seek treatment for. As the years passed he became a black glowering thing, hunched in his chair in the living room, not inter-acting; reading or listening to his classical music. It was never dis-cussed, and we tiptoed around him. I constantly blamed myself for his black moods—they must have been because of something I'd done or failed to do, or he was disappointed in me, and so on. I was often angry with him for the way he behaved and wished he'd snap out of it and get on with life. Mary tried to shield us by being upbeat, positive and happy and didn't let his moods affect her. I realise now that depression is complex and difficult, that it is an illness and Dad's upbringing made it difficult for him to admit that he was ill and needed medical help.

In 1960 Dad did his usual field season trips to north Queensland and then went off on a Scripps Institute ship, the *Argo*, from Mauritius to Perth and was away for much of that year, including over Christmas. *Argo* was a research vessel involved in an interna-tional effort to explore the Indian Ocean, its currents and to map its seafloor. My impression of Dad during the phosphate survey trips, the *Argo* trip and the following year when he went on an OTC ship *Recorder*, surveying the route for an under-sea cable from Australia to Japan, was that he was happiest when at sea and his hankering for a life sailing the Pacific began at this time.

After trips to Rum Jungle in the Northern Territory (the site of a uranium deposit discovered in 1949), Dad left the BMR and joined Ampol Exploration in 1962 as their exploration manager. He made a trip to Sydney on his own, went house hunting and settled on a tiny house in Ferry Street, Hunters Hill. He then went north again for six weeks while we packed up in Canberra. Dad returned for a couple of days for the actual move, then went back to the field.

Mary wrote:

**We stayed in Canberra until 1962 while Bill was doing geological mapping of remote parts of Australia and also New Guinea so that he was away from home for up to seven months each year. Child number four arrived and I was very busy with family. I was lucky in that I was able to work for the Bureau of Mineral Resources as a palaeobotanist, very part time and at home, because there was no one else available—and plant fossils that had waited for millions of years to be identified could wait patiently while I was busy with kids. Fossils don't wither and die. Having a scientific interest and escape, I am sure, kept me sane during those years. So I built up my knowledge by examining, identifying and reporting on all plant fossils collected by field parties mapping the major geological basins in search for coal, oil and gas from 1956 to 1986.**

**When Bill changed jobs and we moved to Sydney, the BMR collections followed me—44-gallon drums of fossils delivered to my door. Child number five completed the family in 1965 and when at last they all were going to school and I could escape for a few hours, I started working, also very part time, for the Australian Museum, curating their massive plant fossil collections and turning them into a fully documented scientific collection of 12,000 good specimens.**

Hunters Hill house     Sabot with Gladesville Bridge under construction

David and Barbara sailing a Gwen 12         Veronique

# LIFE IN SYDNEY

Dad wrote to Mary about his impressions of Hunters Hill (I don't think it was meant to sound so elitist or racist):

**I wish you could have seen the place tonight. It was lovely… the whole place felt just right—a sort of quiet dignity—just our sort of place with an atmosphere a bit like Waterkloof without any Africans.**

There were serious money issues—the BMR super fund wouldn't refund 100% of Dad's contributions and paid no interest, and the bank would only loan them part of the money needed leaving them 200 pounds short. Dad wrote of having to rely on his pay going into the bank on time, of juggling tax refunds and agonising over whether a cheque of Mary's would be cleared in time, even suggesting, heaven forbid, that she ask a friend for a loan if necessary.

After the Hunters Hill house was paid for Mary wrote:

**…there was no money left in the account, I was very harassed about money and sold the shares I had in the Manuka Co-op in order to survive the month without any cash. I used up all sorts of unlikely stores in kitchen cupboards to feed the family…**

I remember little of the whole move to Sydney in 1962 apart from being sad about leaving my friends—and a night spent in a motel in Gladesville before we could move into our house. The motel had a no animal policy and we knew that Janey would howl all night if left in the car, so after dark she was smuggled up some back stairs and settled in the room with Mary and the two youngest children. She then set to snoring like a trooper all night—the whole room reverberating—and Mary started her years in Sydney with the reputation of being the most incredible snorer!

Our new house at 7 Ferry Street was a beautifully hand-crafted weatherboard house, the owner-builder being a skilled carpenter. It had a lovely, lush garden compared to the barren Canberra gardens, with bandicoots living in it (and therefore, a great number of paralysis ticks). It had a magnificent view of the Parramatta River and the Gladesville Bridge which was under construction at the time. Until the bridge was finished the coal boats that came up the harbour at night would hoot loudly for the old bridge to open and let them through. In the still of the night, the fog horns echoing, the lights and the moonlight reflecting on the water were magical and it was a great disappointment when the bridge was completed and they no longer had to signal their presence. Boats with names such as *Hexam Bank* and *Mortlake Bank* brought coal from the northern coalfields. They were loaded at Hexam on the Hunter River and other coal sites in the Newcastle region and shipped to coal wharves up the Parramatta River, such as Mortlake and Blackwattle Bay.

In that house we also delighted in the small prawn and fishing trawlers that came up the harbour at night, their lights casting long reflections in the black water, voices and sometimes singing and the strumming of a guitar, drifting through the still night air. Living by that harbour was special for us and we appreciated its beauty and how alive it made us feel.

But the house was tiny—two small bedrooms for six people, one small bathroom/toilet and a small laundry fitted out as a sewing room with a foldout sewing table, shelves, drawers and racks for cottons reels, all beautifully made. Dad agonised over how we could fit into it in letters to Mary from the field before we moved to Sydney, trying to reassure himself that we could make it work—we could convert the laundry into a bedroom and move the washing machine under the house, we could excavate the big lump of sandstone the house sat on and put a room underneath, and there were already plans drawn up by the previous owners to extend the house—if only we had money to do anything to it!

So, we squashed in. Derek, aged four, shared the main bedroom with Mary and Dad, David had the laundry, the laundry tub being removed to make room for his narrow bed. Zoe and I fitted with great difficulty into the second bedroom—Zoe was incredibly difficult to share anything with, she seemed to like to cause disharmony and fight about everything—and I was probably no better, although I was more easily pushed around and always gave in to her. This was, I think the beginning our lifelong rift, never having any personal space or privacy, two totally different personalities forced to live right on top of each other.

The primary school where I was in Year 5 was in a magnificent old sandstone building with a yard shaded by huge Morton Bay figs. There was a large brass bell in the playground that was rung by hand—an oddity after the sophisticated electric bell at Forrest Primary in Canberra. Mary was invited to give a talk about dinosaurs to the school, but I was too embarrassed and pretended I was unwell and stayed at home that day.

♠♠

Late that year, ZoZo and Ouma became ill with pneumonia and Ouma died. There wasn't the money for Mary to fly to Africa and too many children to leave behind with Dad away so much. I can't imagine Mary's grief at being so far away and unable to see her grandmother before she died or comfort her mother and grieve with her. She put on a brave face and life continued as normal. All her life she hid her deep sadnesses and worries from us all which I find incredibly sad as they were lost opportunities for us to get to know our parents and grow emotionally.

Granny and Grandpa White came out to Australia from Northern Ireland for a visit that November and stayed with us until after Christmas. I have no idea where Zoe and I slept as they had our bedroom, but I remember long agonising waits for the bathroom as Grandpa spent ages in there, doing what, no one knew or dared to ask!

After our dog Janey's death Mary got a kitten for Zoe's birthday. We called her Bertha. She came from the author Kylie Tennant who was living in Hunters Hill at that time. There was an ulterior motive to Bertha's acquisition—she was to be our sex education! Mary figured we could learn about mating and birth from this lovely little cat. The plan, however, failed dismally as we hated the yowling, fighting male cats that descended on us when Bertha came into heat, and we spent our time trying to chase away the horrible males who were hurting our little cat. (Cats are induced-ovulators and painful intercourse is required to stimulate ovulation). The pregnancy that resulted anyway was followed by birth by caesarean section at the vet surgery as the first kitten got hopelessly stuck and we came home to a basket of kittens that may as well have been brought by the stork!

Shortly after Bertha, David won a cat in a raffle at a school fete. We called this one Pombey for some strange reason, and Mary's love affair with cats began in earnest. I then added an abandoned week-old kitten to the mix. I've always thought that I'd raised little Tiger-bogue (bogus tiger) but in fairness, Mary did most of the hard work, carrying her around in her skirt pocket and feeding her two-hourly while I was at school. All our cats, except Pombey who just disappeared, lived for over twenty years so Mary had a succession of overlapping cats right up to her last few years of life.

We children allowed our cats to sleep in our beds at night something Dad disapproved of totally. Pombey even used to suck David's pyjamas. When he raised the subject one too many times Mary said, "Stuff and Nonsense! It's quite all right, the cats haven't caught anything yet!" He had no answer to this and fumed off. Stuff and Nonsense! was a common response of Mary's to any whinge or complaint. It was not that she was unsympathetic, but she simply didn't have time for what she perceived as unimportant, and we were usually dismissed with, "Buck up and get on with it!"

Eventually the sandstone under the house was excavated—a long and noisy job using jackhammers. The sandstone turned out to be a much more massive lump than it looked, and the job went way over budget and there was the usual stress about lack of money. Eventually a room that was accessed through a hatch in the floor in the corner of the dining room was built. It was never really successful as, even though it was sealed and waterproofed, there was a constant seepage of water from the sandstone it was cut into. Gutters were dug around the base of the walls to channel the water to the outside, but the room was always damp and musty. David didn't seem to mind and lived down there (Derek shared the room for a while) and liked the novelty of a ship's hatch and ladder and lots of space. I moved into the laundry and built a little ladder of my own that allowed my cat to come and go via the high window.

♠♠

Life in Sydney soon revolved around the harbour, sailing, messing around in boats, fishing from the Ferry Street wharf and clambering about on the green algae covered rocks on the Parramatta River foreshore. As soon as we got to Sydney Dad decided to give up smoking to save money, and to sell the nearly completed sports car and buy a boat! And so *Nimanoa*, a 7-metre Bluebird with two very cramped bunks and a head (toilet) which required us all to vacate the cabin as it was housed under the bunks, became the first of a string of always bigger and better yachts that joined the White family.

The boats gave us wonderful access to all the celebrations of the city from the most beautiful harbour in the world. We watched the firework displays, the starts of the Sydney–Hobart yacht races, the opening of the Opera House, Tall Ship festivals and the wonderful weekly spectacle of the 18-foot skiff races etc. We felt a special involvement and ownership of the harbour and its white sailed boats, colourful spinnakers and the sense of excitement of being amongst it all.

Whenever Dad was at home we would sail up the harbour and overnight at Store Beach or Quarantine Beach just inside North Head. The first trip (of many we made to Broken Bay) included the very tiny kitten I was raising and bottle feeding every few hours. Most of us got very seasick and did not enjoy the sea travel but weekends and holidays on Broken Bay were glorious. There were always major dramas when engines broke down, propellers got snagged in ropes, water got into the engine oil etc. Dad always expected everything to go wrong, and it usually did.

One trip up the harbour that involved picking Granny and Grandpa White up at Manly wharf for a lovely picnic in a nearby bay was cut short when a massive storm hit. Three of us kids and our grandparents were hastily unloaded at Manly to get a ferry home as the storm approached and Mary, Dad and David lowered all the sails and stood well offshore as the gale force wind and torrential rain battered and drenched them. The storm lasted only fifteen minutes or so—a typical Sydney southerly buster—and then utter calm followed—not a breath of wind on the water. The boat was low on petrol but they motored as far as the Harbour Bridge before the petrol ran out. Then as night fell they just drifted with the tide, eating rusks, singing and laughing despite being soaked to the skin.

Eventually they were given a tow by a small passing fishing trawler filled with inebriated fishermen who fought vociferously all the way. Mary wrote that the trip home on the breathtakingly beautiful night-time harbour would remain one of her best memories and that it had all been a most stimulating experience.

David and I were given a Sabot (a small single-sailed dinghy) that we raced at the local sailing club until we grew too large for it, and we graduated to a Manly Junior. Eventually we sailed a Gwen 12 together—we were a good team, anticipating each other's moves—Dave skippering and me sailing for'ard-hand and hanging out on the trapeze wire. Dave and I still have a close, loving bond to this day.

When Derek, the youngest at that stage, started school in 1963 Mary wrote:

**I am free all day and I find it Bliss! I expected to be desolate after 13 years with a small child at heel... It's a nice feeling to be on my own and to get the chores done rapidly and then do what one likes without reference to anyone at all until school comes out.**

She talked of being able to take a ferry into town to shop, to paint pictures, garden or do nothing, although the latter was not something I could imagine her doing.

There was never any money and Mary suggested she get a part time job with CSIRO or the Australian Museum to help out financially. But Dad with his very old-fashioned views on the role of women and mothers particularly squashed this idea very quickly. He wrote from out in the field:

**... you sound very enthusiastic and keen, and I don't want to pour cold water on it, but frankly I'm not too enthusiastic. A really part time job, say a few hours on one or two days a week would be fine, but I wouldn't be happy with anything more. And I can visualise the obligations of a part time job expanding and taking up more and more time... It seems to me that too many houses in which mothers have a part time job cease to be "homes" and I don't want ours to be like that, not at least while the kids are still kids, even if they are at school all day... I won't be stubborn or obstinate about it ... It is just that I don't want you to get too excited and arrange something only to find out that I'm not happy about it...**

At this time, Dad's work took him on exploratory trips to North Queensland around Proserpine, presumably searching for oil. There was also a trip on a beautiful yacht called *Moonbi*. What they were doing, I'm not sure, but it may have involved prospecting on the inner reef and looking at beach sands. I wonder if Dad ever thought about the effect that mining, drilling etc. would have on places like the Great Barrier Reef and other island paradises he made prospecting trips to. The *Moonbi* trip made him very restless and want an even bigger and more seaworthy yacht.

The work with Ampol, which had been so wonderful, his bosses such fabulous people etc. etc. started to go the way of all his jobs. He became disillusioned, dissatisfied and unhappy (un and dis with everything, Mary called it) and he joined Kennecott Exploration from Utah, USA. A dark green-black Rambler station wagon was supplied as a company car—a real Yank Tank! At least we could all fit into it but it looked and felt like a hearse. In the years after the Fiat 1100 we had had a Mark 7 Jaguar and a Riley Pathfinder. I learnt to drive on an old Morris Major Elite—Dad changed his cars as often as he was to change boats and had a thing about European and British cars. When I bought my first car in the late '70s Dad was horrified when I chose a Honda Civic— Japanese trash! I think he was surprised when it turned out to be a great little car that served me well for years.

♠♠

We always ate together at a fully set table (even breakfast) and meals were supposed to be genteel affairs. We didn't have to dress for dinner, but almost. Mary's way of teaching us table manners was to "donkey bite" us under the table. The offender would be quietly eating (or not so quietly and definitely not using his/her best manners—elbows on the table or talking with his mouth full!) when she'd bite—a very sharp, firm squeeze to the thigh just above the knee usually resulting in a jump and a loud squeal from the offender. I shudder to imagine what Mary would think of the lack of table manners of most people today as no one is being taught to eat nicely in case, one day, they have to dine with the Queen!

In 1964 Granny and Grandpa White emigrated to Australia and bought a flat nearby, making a huge move and dislocation from lifetime friends and family at the age of 70-something. No one thought they'd make the adjustment, but Dad was their only surviving child and we were their only grandchildren. As we'd never had grandparents in our lives, (or cousins, aunts or uncles), we were underwhelmed by them and didn't really enjoy our weekly Sunday night dinners with them although they had a TV which we did not, and that was a drawcard!

Dad was away for months at a time as usual, exploring the New Guinea highlands and a two-month trip to the USA in 1965 to acquaint himself with all the Kennecott staff, mines and ore bodies. During this trip he got what he thought was an insect bite on the neck when at a mine, and he still had a gland up in his neck when he returned. At this time Mary was pregnant with her fifth child. She had been advised to terminate the pregnancy as the RH negative problems made the prospect of a live child just about nil. She refused and was told not to even think of it as a pregnancy but as an illness she had to get through. And due to problems with very high blood pressure she had to spend the last three months in bed. I remember doing the cooking under her instruction and taking over a lot of the household chores. But she was totally confident that the baby would be all right and it was.

In June 1965 she broke the news to her mother in a letter, saying:

**Can you think of anything more divine!? When I think I'll have a tiny nuzzling, velvety-headed new one all of my own again I can't believe it could be true. We are all so excited you'd think it was our first baby and not our fifth!**

I suspect Dad was not as thrilled initially— another child to raise and educate would put off his plans to retire to the Pacific even further!

The baby was induced a month early and a healthy but tiny (three pound) baby boy, Peter, was born at the end of August 1965. Dad had to deal with Derek's tonsillectomy during this time. Mary came home, but Peter was kept in a humidicrib at the Royal Women's Hospital for over a month. David and I used to take bottles of expressed breast milk in to the hospital by ferry and buses every few days. I think she fed all the babies in the neonatal care unit for months if not years.

Peter's first taste of sailing on the tiny, overcrowded Bluebird yacht complete with my bottle-fed kitten, was before he was three months old and he learnt to brace himself against the side of his bassinette when the boat healed over. His nappies were washed under waterfalls in the bays we anchored in at night and dried hanging from the rigging like surrender flags. Mary slept with his bottle containing boiled water against her body so that it was at body temperature when he woke for a feed in the night, and she could simply add the milk formula powder and not have to disturb everyone by having to heat it up.

♠♠

When Peter was a few days old Dad had a biopsy on the gland in his neck.

Mary wrote in her piece on 'What it's like to be Eighty':

**... days after Pete's birth, the phone rang and the incredibly insensitive doctor who had done a biopsy on the lump in Bill's neck that had started as an insect bite informed me that it was advanced lymphatic disease and we would be lucky if he was alive in six months. While I was literally trying to get my breath back to answer he told me to take Bill to the North Shore Hospital on Monday for the Cobalt Bomb treatment that he had just booked for us. No kind words for me or attempt to soften the blow, though he knew that we had just had all the baby worries, and he added, "as he will be a bit groggy after the anaesthetic when he gets home, don't tell him the bad news so that he can have a pleasant weekend"—and that was the end of the conversation—but not the end of doctors' incompetence. The microscope slides that were made were damaged and not conclusive. The specimen from which they had been made was accidentally trashed, a leading oncologist who was consulted said the diagnosis was probably right but because of the bad preparation of**

**slides no one could be 100% sure, and the cobalt bomb treatment
had been so fierce that it had killed any remaining evidence (and
who knows what else).**

But life went on—with a newborn and four other kids from
seven to fifteen there was no choice. Dad's prognosis was not discussed with us. Nor was his illness. Dad sold *Nimanoa* and bought
*Veronique*, a lovely old boat that was described by an old local
yachtie as, "As round as an apple and as lovely as a lily!"—bigger,
beamier and with a head in a separate, though tiny, compartment. What more could we want! Looking back I find it surprising that after his diagnosis Dad went ahead and bought another
boat but that was how he handled it. By not acknowledging his
illness and continuing as normal, the problem didn't exist. Dad
always ignored things and even people that he didn't like, including some of my boyfriends!

I doubt that Mary was very happy about another bank loan
when the prognosis was so grim, but she wouldn't have deprived
him of the one thing that would make him happy.

Shortly after this they sold the Hunters Hill house and bought
a house on Forty Baskets Beach in Balgowlah with three bedrooms
and a study and a second loo! I still had to share a bedroom with
Zoe though. This move was not motivated by the investment
potential of a waterfront property in Sydney but simply that Dad
wanted to have his boat moored where he could see it and not
have to lug dinghies and heavy sail bags up a steep hill. Although
the house, in one of the most beautiful locations in Sydney was
not hugely expensive in 1966 it involved another massive bank
loan. Obviously, the banks knew nothing of his cancer diagnosis.

In 'What it's like to be Eighty', Mary wrote:

**So there I was, a brand new baby, 4 others from 7 to 15, my
world in tatters. And I did a deal with the Almighty, whatever that
might be, that if Bill could just have 12 years until my youngest
was in high school and I could get a job, I would never complain
again no matter what life threw at me. We lived under the shadow**

first of 3, then 6, monthly check-ups, then annual and at 12 years almost to the day the cancer was diagnosed as back again and widely distributed—with another sentence of 6 months. During the 3½ years of chemo, radiation and surgical treatments with short almost healthy spells between, the aim was to keep everything as normal as possible. That's how Bill wanted it, and how I, hopefully, managed to keep things. I wanted Peter, who was still at home and between ages of 13 and 16 while this was going on, to be spared the misery of waiting for the end to come and knowing the hopelessness. There was never any promise of a cure in all the treatments, only of delaying the inevitable.

## FORTY BASKETS BEACH 1966

Forty Baskets beach and our house    Dawn from Mary's writing desk

Sylvena

# FORTY BASKETS BEACH

Forty Baskets Beach is one of the most beautiful places on Sydney Harbour. In 1966, 34 Beatty Street was the only house built on the edge of the beach with a garden behind the house that scrambled up to road level via dozens of irregular sandstone and crazy-paving steps, or cascaded over a large sandstone outcrop down to the house depending on your trajectory. It certainly kept us all fit. Tree ferns and luxuriantly growing sub-tropical plants including strelitzias (birds of paradise), banana and paw-paw trees and very large orb web spiders that nightly built their webs at face level across the path made coming or going an adventure. All the other houses in the street were built at road level with manicured front gardens and civilised paths leading down to the beach but none had the charm and magical, secluded feel of our little piece of paradise, which had its own microclimate, and was only forty minutes from the CBD by Manly ferry.

The front of our house opened onto a garden under a huge jacaranda tree. Beyond this was a row of Norfolk Island pines on a green lawn which ran down to the perfect white beach with its jetty and enclosed harbour swimming pool. We kids were in heaven, the luckiest children on Earth. We never tired of puddling around in the rock pools, exploring the bush between Forty Baskets and the deserted, absolutely pristine Reef Beach, swimming and playing on the sand. Peter was nearly one when we moved there, and I spent all my free time minding him on the beach as it gave me an excuse for being where I could check out all the teenage boys that came to the beach. Looking back on it years later, I wondered if the neighbours thought Peter was my baby and we had moved there so no one would know. However, as I was a late maturer and very much a kid at fifteen, maybe not.

Mary had a passion for gardening, or maybe it was just that Mary now had a large wild garden and she had to garden hard and often. We were often woken by the crackle and smell of smoke of Mary's burning-off fire or were brought a cup of tea and a rusk in bed—her way of making us get up early in the hope that we might attack the garden with her.

Something I only realised later when reading Mary's part of this biography, was that like her, the move gave me a chance to change from the shy, quiet, frightened-to–change-anything-in-case-anyone-noticed-me girl into someone more confident and relatively outgoing. I literally let my hair down. I had worn it in a single plait for years, never wearing it out because someone might have commented. This change was helped, too, by the girls in my science class on my first day at Mackellar Girls High in Manly. They greeted me with an invitation to join their table "if I liked boys"! Of course I said I did, even though I'd never given them a thought in that way. So, I found I had new friends who found me interesting, something I had never been before!

David's bedroom was at the back of the house and was accessed by a beautiful old wrought iron spiral staircase. One day when he came home from university he found a strange man asleep in his bed. We didn't believe him when he reappeared asking who was in his bed and we crept up to see what he was on about. Mary immediately flew into a panic imagining that he was a dangerous fugitive or lunatic, so we closed the door on him and called the police. The poor guy had a rude awakening when the police bundled him out of bed and questioned him none too gently. He looked startled and confused and we felt very sorry for him. It turned out that he had wandered out of a low security mental health facility, somehow found his way to our house and up the stairs where he found a comfortable bed and had fallen asleep. I don't remember us becoming more security conscious after this and doors were still left open and unlocked.

Mary's mother ZoZo died after a long battle with leukaemia in 1967 and once again we were sheltered from the misery of her illness and Mary's inability to go to her. I'm sure Mary resented all the money spent on boats, which were bottomless pits, as if it weren't for them she may have been able to afford a trip home before ZoZo died, but she never said anything. Dad sold *Veronique* and bought a newer, bigger, better boat called *Sylvena*.

♠♠

Living on a beautiful old boat in North Harbour (adjacent to Forty Baskets Beach) was a delightful old salt, Harry Newton–Scott (known lovingly to us all as Scotty) and his wife, Oceana. They became great friends with Mary, Bill, David and me and Mary used to regularly take them freshly baked scones and ginger-bread. We'd sit in the sun in their cockpit and listen to their tales of their cruising which fuelled Dad's burning desire to go cruising in the Pacific. They were both in their eighties. Scotty particularly was a great character and an absolute darling—gentle, wise and loving. I have vivid memories of being met as we climbed aboard, by an incredible smell of strong pipe tobacco (Oce was the heavier pipe smoker of the two) and over-proof rum, mixed with the smell of bilges, engine oil and smoke-impregnated belong-ings. The main cabin was decorated with bits and pieces from all over the world and with cartoons, drawn by famous artists, of Scotty in a ridiculously tiny dinghy or playing the goat in a hula skirt complete with Sherlock Holmes-type pipe. I still treasure a large shark's tooth that Scotty ferreted around in the boat's lockers to find to give me.

Their boat, *New Silver Gull*, was designed and built by Scotty during WW2 at Yowie Bay south of Sydney, using a lot of tim-ber that he found floating in Port Hacking as materials were dif-ficult to get due to the war. It was launched in 1939. Scotty was an accomplished yachtsman, but Oce would get seasick on a

Manly ferry. In spite of this and being in their late sixties they set off in 1946 to Chicago via New Zealand, Fiji, Hawaii, British Columbia, San Francisco, the Caribbean and East Coast USA and Nova Scotia to the Great Lakes. After twelve years, they headed back to Australia via the West Indies, Panama and Galapagos Islands, cruised through the Pacific Islands including French Polynesia, the Marquesas, Cook and Society Islands, Fiji and Vanuatu arriving in Sydney after something like twenty years away—all without modern navigation aids—just charts, a sextant, compass and trailing log!

Scotty took a great interest in the local sailing club and all of us who sailed Gwens and 14-foot skiffs. He was my greatest fan as I was the only female sailing—on trapeze with my plait skimming the water and expertly (some of the time anyway) setting spinnakers etc.

♠♠

Dad was still working in New Guinea and much of their getting around in the remote NG highlands was done by helicopter in very dangerous terrain and weather conditions. In 1968 a helicopter crash killed the pilot and injured the geologist on board. Luckily for us Dad was not involved but he later talked of just how dangerous the work was in NG and how close he had come to disaster on many occasions. One such tale told of him narrowly escaping death at the hands (or spears) of some very menacing highland tribesmen who had sworn to kill the first white men they encountered. He managed to stay on the opposite side of a small river and was picked up by a helicopter in the nick of time.

In 1968 Kennecott, under Dad's direction of exploration, discovered the huge copper and gold ore bodies that were to become the Ok Tedi mine. Dad established and ran the camp, and the Kennecott Copper Corporation was formed and began exploratory drilling. Dad was also at this time involved in setting up a branch of Kennecott in New Zealand and Mary accompanied him on one trip to New Zealand in 1970. She was blown away by the alps in the South Island, the geology generally, and the plants, and years after Dad's death she made a trip to NZ by herself to revisit it all.

Always restless, despite what must have been very exciting work, Dad resigned from Kennecott in 1971. His father died suddenly of a heart attack around this time. Dad joined David S. Robertson and Associates, a consulting firm that was expanding from its Canadian base to other countries including Australia, exploring for uranium. He worked for them for several years and made a trip to Canada in 1972.

Dad was decent and caring but found it difficult to accept that I was old enough to go out on dates and stay out reasonably late. Every evening I had to run the gauntlet before going on a date—come down to the living room where he sat in his chair at the bottom of the stairs and hear his criticisms—my skirt was too short (mini-skirts were in), I had too much eye makeup on (black eyes were in), my hair was covering my face (long fringes were in) and he didn't think any of my boyfriends were good enough for me and let them know by barely grunting a greeting or acknowledging their presence sometimes.

David also suffered—his problem was his hair. Dad didn't like "long haired louts" and even though Dave's hair was not long, it was too long for Dad's liking. He made him have short back and sides haircuts which I remember being acutely miserable about for him, although Dave doesn't remember anything about this. It obviously affected me more than him. Anyway, the upshot for me was that after a couple of years of Dad's scrutiny and increasing tensions, Mary encouraged me to move out of home and I moved into a shared flat in McMahons Point, on public transport and closer to university.

♠♠

Mary was a magnet for orphaned and injured animals and one of her acquisitions was a galah which was unable to be returned to the wild after injury. She named him *Gulargambone*

*Jack* from Goonoo-Goonoo (pronounced Gunna-G'noo) and he presided over the outdoor table under the wisteria where morning tea was had, shouting for his bit of cake and having been rewarded for shouting, he shouted even more. As if one noisy, demanding bird was not enough she was then given a beautiful Major Mitchell cockatoo who had been raised in a local bottle shop. *Mitch* would go crazy when she saw a cardboard box and cry loudly until she was given it, whereupon she would demolish it totally, snipping it into tiny pieces. Apparently when boxes of beer and wine were delivered to the bottle shop she was always given a box as it kept her entertained for hours. *Mitch* sadly died while still a young bird at *Falls Forest Retreat* and Mary was heartbroken and wondered whether the accumulation of some toxin in the glue or cardboard could have caused her death. *Jack* was eventually replaced by an even more demanding, noisier galah called JoJo who moved with Mary to Bundanoon years later, where he escaped when she forgot to shut his cage door due to her deteriorating memory.

Mary always fed the local possums in Balgowlah, and she had a number who would let her handle them and even their piggy-backing babies. There was one very old male possum who she named *He-begat* as he was obviously the father of all the local possums. When he reached the stage of being almost hairless, just skin and bones and was being fought by all the other male possums, Mary spoke to a vet about putting him out of his misery. She was given a strong sedative which she crushed and fed to him in jam on his bread. As he ate it she said to me, "I hope that someone will do the same for me when I'm old and decrepit!" *He-begat* disappeared and Mary heaved a sigh of relief and then got a huge shock when, after about a week, he reappeared looking refreshed and wanting his evening handout. He'd obviously had a wonderful sleep and was ready to continue begetting.

Some years later, Mary's menagerie grew to include a duck—a beautiful shining white Pekin duck with real Donald-Duck-yellow bill and feet. He had originally been given to Richard and me and had been named *Bankstown* by his previous owner (after what he deemed a crappy suburb). True to his name he quickly wore out his welcome by crapping all over the paving and door-steps in our little house in Annandale, so he was dumped on Mary where, instead of appreciating his new home in paradise, he rapidly disgraced himself again and was banished to the washing line lawn on the first terrace up the back garden. *Banks* had a toe fetish and had us all dancing the highland fling while hanging the washing and he chased the small grandchildren squealing up the garden steps until he reached a step that he couldn't jump up due to its height. This step became known as the Bankstown step and the grandkids, who also had trouble scaling it, were safe if they could beat him to it and scramble up it. He also greeted visitors who came down the garden stairs and refused to let them pass until he had had a good go at their toes. One of my friends became hysterical and had to be rescued from the toe-eating duck. Eventually Mary decided she couldn't cope with a mad duck, and he was passed on to someone with a few acres and a big dam somewhere outside Sydney and was a very happy crapper thereafter by all accounts.

♠♠

Dad decided the only way he could afford a boat suitable for the extended cruising in the Pacific that he was determined to do, was to build one himself. He started building the boat to house his dreams in 1974. I presume he sold *Sylvena* to afford it, and *Pelagian*, a 42- foot Swanson design fibreglass sloop—the perfect cruising yacht—was launched in November 1976. Dad worked on fitting her out for the next couple of years, sailing her and test driving her as soon as her mast was stepped, and sails were made. It turns out that Dad and my three brothers all became very skilled, self-taught wood-workers and found great satisfaction in creating beautiful boats, furniture, homes etc.

# BILL'S ILLNESS AND DEATH

Bill

Pelagian

# BILL'S ILLNESS AND DEATH

In 1978 Dad had a consulting trip to the USA and when he returned he was given a diagnosis of Non-Hodgkin's lymphoma and had lumps removed from his temple and neck—it was independent consulting when he was well enough between treatments. Mary increased her work at the Australian Museum where she was curating/cataloguing their huge, chaotic fossil collection, to help pay the bills and keep her sane.

The following few years must have been hell. Dad still would not talk about his health or dying and demanded that life should go on as though nothing was wrong. Even when he was dying in the palliative care ward in Sydney Hospital he talked to me of getting back to Forty Baskets and *Pelagian*. In retrospect, we were denied an important part of life—being able to say our goodbyes, reassure him that we would look after Mary, that we would all be okay and know that he was resigned to his fate and accepting of death. Mary prevented Peter from visiting Dad to say goodbye as she thought it would be too hard for him. I know she meant well but…

Dad died on the 16th of June 1981. I had been visiting him with my 10-month-old baby Rachel, when he was given what was probably his last big dose of morphine. A couple of minutes after the injection he turned to me and said, "Ahhh—it's so warm," and his face relaxed and he floated away as the morphine did its thing. He died in his sleep later that night.

So ended a real love story. Mary never doubted Dad's love for her, and his letters endlessly expressed his love, his longing for her and how hard he found the long separations from her and us, his children. When asked in her interview for the National Library's Oral History in 1995 whether she loved Dad she replied:

**Absolutely, absolutely, and I managed to remain in much that state and attitude towards him for all the time we were together. I really loved that man. He was a very difficult person as he got older and not very well ... very difficult to live with, but I absolutely loved him, and he was the only man in my life. So it was not a problem... it also had to do with the fact that we were so different, that he really needed me... he was somebody who could always see a thousand problems and a thousand negatives in everything. Everything that happened he could see all the problems—I could see all the solutions. It's just the way I was brought up, I think. I've always been very practical and always very optimistic. I think that if he hadn't married someone like me he would have ended up a cot- case of some sort. Truly, because he suffered from the most awful depression, and I think it was war neurosis to some extent... as a young, very sensitive 16-and-17-year-old (he) was acting as a fire warden and hauling dead (bodies) out of buildings (during) the bombing of Britain and Northern Ireland...**

♠♠

Mary was so stoic after his death that I presumed it was such a relief that the hell was over, but I discovered later when she showed me the collection of poems she had written in the period after his death, that she was totally shattered, heartbroken, emotionally exhausted and destroyed. Once again, she kept it all from us, wouldn't let us in to share her grief, wept privately and put on a brave face so that our lives weren't shattered as well.

Mary wrote:

**The final six weeks in the ward for the dying at Sydney Hospital were hell on earth, though on the surface, where we all kept things as far as possible, all was bright and harmonious. I travelled back on the ferry each night, heartbroken at the beauty of the harbour**

252

that he would not see again, isolated from all the happy revellers but on the surface no one would have known. Looking back, I owe everyone an apology for the way the funeral was arranged. No eulogies, no music, no anything. But I was emotionally absolutely dead, and, recalling it all now (when before I had hardly dared to open up the dark cupboards in which it was all stored away) I am not surprised. And after the week of weeping when physically I came to some sort of acceptance I luckily had to return to the Museum to stage a big exhibition for an international botanical convention.

Some years after Dad's death, using poetry writing as a form of therapy, Mary wrote a eulogy for Bill.

FOR BILL

Darling, I wrote no Eulogy for you.
You were long gone when coma turned to death.
We had been severed bit by bit
Along the way, while you were dying.
The anguish and the age-long misery
Had left me numb and dead.
Watching your cruel destruction,
Powerless to help, was Hell so horrible
One walked a slender bridge above
An abyss of mind's Inferno.
If one had dared to look into the depths
One would have seen
Thoughts too dreadful to imagine.
And, balance lost, gone plummeting down
Into unfathomable despair.
Instead, one looked around at normal landscapes,
Feigned interest in the world of other people;
As isolated in one's shell of misery
As if one walked alone on this wide earth.
And others did not know a chasm gaped

Below the path one traversed with such care.
Nature is wise to dampen down the pain,
And turn off deep emotions at the source,
Allowing one to go on with each day,
And putting off the heartbreak and the knowing
Till Time has had its chance to heal the wounds.
And meanwhile you did not complain.
You would not think of Death,
Used waning strength to fight invading thoughts
Which, entering, might admit defeat
And let the conquering foe come in to claim you.
You quietly withdrew deeply inside
The labyrinths of your mind.
I stayed and held your hand, hoping you'd know
That I was there to love and comfort you.
Your laboured breathing cut and tore my heart.
I raged inside. Why not stand up and scream into the listening night
"Leave him alone, you cruel and heartless killers-
He's kind and good and gentle and we love him.
Why pick on him, the world is full of others
Unloving and unloved." If there was God
I'd hammer on his door, demanding intervention,
Cursing and blaspheming.

Peace followed rage.
I had a vision as clear and photographic
As a picture of the real world.
I saw you far away and small,
In a distant corner of an empty house,
And though you were a man, you were a child—
A new-born essence of the you I loved,
Ready to leave the earthly home
From which your mortal family had moved
Leaving you by virtue of their living.
The light was orange-brown, late afternoon—
The rooms were mellowed wood—

A friendly house, and you were small and brave,
A wind-borne seed ready to float away
To carry life into another place...
And I was comforted and went home to sleep.
When I had rested, you were gone.

# LIFE IN LIMBO

Mary describes the years following Dad's death as a time in limbo. She stuffed her grief and misery behind a firmly closed door and soldiered on, mounting a very successful exhibition. Peter was only fifteen but he refused to finish school and against Mary's better judgement and advice, left school. Mary arranged for him to get an informal traineeship as a museum preparator at the Australian Museum.

Within a few months of Dad dying Peter was involved in a very serious accident when the Land Rover they were travelling in on a museum specimen collection trip at night, left the road and rolled down a deep ravine in very remote country in the Warrumbungles in northern NSW. A couple of the occupants were seriously injured, Pete was almost scalped, and another youth was uninjured but knocked silly. Pete, weak and injured with a T-shirt wrapped around his head to hold his scalp on, and the physically strong but totally-confused-and-unable-to-think youth had to climb up out of the ravine to the track and try to get help. They ended up following the road and then bush-bashing until they came upon a rough little house early next morning. Pete collapsed in a wheelbarrow outside the house with a now very bloodied mess for a head and his mate tried to explain to the startled and horrified occupants what had happened and where help was urgently needed. Somehow, everyone was rescued and eventually recovered from the spinal and other nasty injuries and Pete had his scalp sewn back on, but that was the end of his stint at the Museum. Soon afterwards he headed up north and lived with brother Derek for some time, eventually getting odd jobs fixing boats among other things and developing his woodworking skills.

This drama and worry on top of everything else really shook Mary but as time passed she gradually turned again to life, writing poems that were her way of expressing her grief; taking an interest in her grandchildren and mapping out her future little by little. Dad's mother died in 1984 having outlived her husband and both her sons.

Mary expressed a huge spirituality in her love and reverence for life, but she was not at all religious in the conventional sense. She called herself a heathen. The following poem reveals her thinking about God and Life.

OH GOD

If ever I had known an orthodox God,
A father-figure, one who knew my thoughts and prayers,
A personal friend as Church would have you think,
Who loves and cares for one and all who seek him out,
Then would I have known disillusionment profound.
How then to reconcile innocent children
Bravely dying in a cancer ward, or new-born infants
Who die in sleep without a sign or reason
And leave their parents torn apart with grief
And feelings of a guilt they do not deserve.

When tragedy has touched my life and I have seen
One that I loved destroyed before my eyes
More cruelly than by torturers who kill
By inches, allowing the victim
Not even the luxury of hope—
Then had I known this God that others follow
I would have had someone to blame,
Someone to hate for his callous indifference.
And bitterness then might have destroyed
Much of my emotional palette
Leaving me a monochrome world in which to wander
Aimlessly, feeling lost and disinherited.

Mary wrote of her years 'in limbo':

It was two full years of operating on a sort of automatic pilot, seeking diversions, behaving like someone else, working almost full-time at the Museum, before I emerged from this limbo. One early morning when I was driving in to work (6.30 am to avoid traffic) I suddenly saw the beauty of the Harbour as I approached the Bridge and I felt the weight of sorrow and deadness rise off me like a heavy army blanket lifted from above—the analogy was how I saw it in that moment. And I thought what a beautiful morning, a new beginning, here I was for the first time in my life answerable to no one, not having to consider whether what I wanted to do today would fit in with all the plans of other people, able to decide what new way I was going to go—and I was going to write The Greening of Gondwana that had been gestating in my head for many years, and life was wonderful.

I had promised myself that I would go back to Africa to see my brothers and other family when I was human again, and I went via the UK so that I could research Northern Hemisphere fossil floras to see for myself the differences from the Gondwanan ones that had become my area of expertise.

I worked in the British Museum of Natural History, staying at the Imperial College nearby, then in Cardiff with an expert on earliest land plants, then in Glasgow and Edinburgh while staying with a retired professor who had been at university with Bill. Then I went on to South Africa, staying with my brothers in Pretoria and Durban and touring in a couple of game parks and to see some of the special places in the Cape where my university days had been spent. I was able to work at the Bernard Price Institute of Palaeobotany in Johannesburg and with people in Pretoria, seeing the same fossil plants there as were in my Australian collections in the Museum, confirming my concepts of Gondwana. A brief visit to Zimbabwe showed me how it had changed into a desertified land with awful political problems, and the simmering problems with apartheid and lawlessness in South Africa made me realise how lucky I was to be an Australian and to have been able to raise my family here.

Coming home to Forty Baskets after the trip was like slipping back into my comfort zone but with new energy and interests and the feeling that I was going to try to fulfil that part of my destiny that had always been waiting for the right time—to become a writer like several of my ancestors had been and use the scientific mind that I had inherited from my dad.

# WRITING AND RECOGNITION

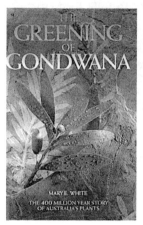 

*The Greening of Gondwana*    Mary with her publisher, Bill Templeman

Mary and photographer, Jim Frazier    Receiving her Doctorate from QUT

Mary receiving her Doctorate from Macquarie University with Barbara

# WRITING AND RECOGNITION

So she sat down and started writing **The Greening of Gondwana.** She'd get up at four in the morning in that heavenly place on Forty Baskets Beach, with a cup of tea and her working desk facing the harbour where the sun rose, painting her early morning in soft colours, and for a few hours the pages would pour out of her. Then she'd wander out onto the beach, often have a swim in the semi-dark and breakfast under the wisteria or on her stoep. The rest of the day she'd spend collecting the information from her research material and digesting it so that the following morning at 4am it had reorganised itself in her mind and was ready to pour out onto paper. She was incredibly focused and hard-working, and she did not have the tools we take for granted these days – the Internet, email and other electronic advances that now make research and writing so easy. She contacted scientists personally, by phone or snail-mail, had them send her scientific papers or advice on who she should talk to – all very time consuming. She was overwhelmed by the generosity, enthusiasm and support she received from just about all with whom she worked. Mary wrote:

When I wrote it, (*The Greening*) I had no idea of how the publishing world worked, or of how other writers worked either. I had assembled most of the information and had access to most of the literature over the years, and I drew the diagrams that I wanted, obtained maps or remade maps that would later be made presentable by a cartographer, and I was fortunate enough to have Jim Frazier, with whom I had worked at the Australian Museum, to do the fossil photography that was required. His great skills undoubtedly contributed to my launch as a writer. Because I had worked on so many fossil collections, including from Mining Museums and some private ones, I knew where to get the best fossils to photograph.

I worked on an old electric typewriter, too afraid of computers and anyway unable to afford one. When the whole job was done, and I had packed it up in a box so as to clear my office before a family invasion at Christmas, I thought for the first time seriously about a publisher!

Early in the new year Mary approached a number of publishers with her mock-up of the book under her arm. She was knocked back by them all. A close friend of hers then approached Bruno Grasswill who he knew was in the book publishing business. Despite the complexity of the manuscript Bruno understood the importance of the project. A lot of serendipity and extremely hard work followed.

Bruno wrote:

**"I could sense the despair of a woman who had dedicated a lifetime to raising a family, had lost her husband and had written her main scientific opus to let the world know what planet Earth was all about. Her main despair was about publishers being ignorant about the worth of her work, but also about their lack of vision into the future of this world.**

**Helen and I had been through similar situations in the past and we had won the war with the publishers. Mary was desperate for help. Her enthusiasm about the subject of her book was so intense she had commissioned at her own expense, the brilliant cinematographer/ photographer Jim Frazier to take the pictures.**

**I could see how brilliant these pictures were. As if by magic, old fossils had come to life by the clever filtering, polarising and lighting by Jim whom we already knew from books we had done with Densey Clyne, his documentary partner.**

**So, I had to convince (my friend and colleague from Reed Books) Bill Templeman to invest in the publishing of a book which at the time I guess would have demanded no less than a $250,000**

investment — which for all I knew could have been far in excess of the annual Reed Books budget. I must have been convincing enough and Bill saw the importance of such a book. But how to get the cash? This is where I think my great relationship with my friend John Avakian came to the fore. I also helped convince John about parting with the cash with a bit of, "I know what I'm talking about", though in publishing no one can be sure of anything.

Next Helen came on board and convinced Bill who was still worried about the academic (mostly unreadable) format and that the book — in its then present convoluted form to make sure the scientific facts were not diluted — could be turned into a mass market project. Helen's own book, "Australia — A Timeless Grandeur" had been both popular and reviewed very well in the scientific world, so she had credibility — ...

Together, our enthusiasm and determination, which Bill had seen on many previous occasions had worked to create success-ful publications, led Bill to work out a contract with Mary White — and to contract Helen and me to the "producing". Helen would be doing the editing, the rewriting in consultation with Mary and I'd do the layouts to match the text. Altogether Bill never interfered with our work. Helen devised to introduce each chapter with a clever simplified resumé of the complexities that followed, which she wrote with Mary's approval. With many trips to Mary's house, on the popular Forty Basket Beach, North Harbour, Helen pains-takingly rewrote and restructured the body text to make it more readily digestible for a wider audience.

Strangely, there were no dramas. Everything fell into place. "The Greening of Gondwana" was born...We were amazed when Mary's following project, a smaller project, was near word per-fect. Mary was a great learner of skills — as well as having a great sharp mind that was able to combine most scientific disciplines from biology to geology. She was quite a brilliant unassuming woman — with, let's add, a strong mind of her own."

♠♠

Two more major fossil-based books followed. Halfway through the first one, Mary's old typewriter literally caught fire—an electrical short and clouds of smoke—and a Brother word processor introduced her to the wonders of being able to move text about and all the other advantages, and a computer followed soon after.

**"By then I was hooked on writing—the exciting process when one gets a good idea, starts to put something together, and it suddenly gets a life of its own and takes over—taking one along avenues that one did not even know existed. I remember, when I held the first copy of The Greening of Gondwana in my hands, not being able to believe that I had made it and having a strong feeling that it must have been my dad working through me! Perhaps, in a way, it was all genetic. I remember also feeling very exposed and vulnerable, expecting real professionals to find fault with my work—and also exposed personally because I had "lived" the book for all those years and it was part of me!—idiotic, but perhaps some of you understand.**

**The twenty years at Forty Baskets while I was writing my seven major books and the kids' books and other bits and pieces were wonderful years. My life was full of interesting people, ideas, new knowledge and incredibly hard work. The lovely surroundings, the house, my beloved cats and birds were all the safe, familiar things and full of all the good memories. The travel all over the continent that came with conducting eco-tours and giving lectures all over the place, was a marvellous bonus. A number of close friends were very important in my life, dropping in regularly, or occasionally, so that I felt I had enough company and the stimulation of people with common interests. My family loved the place and were happy to come on visits..."**

Mary received many, many awards, medals, accolades and four Honorary Doctorates (from QUT, Macquarie, La Trobe and Wollongong Universities) and an Order of Australia 'for services to botany as a researcher and through the promotion of increased understanding and awareness of the natural world'.

Mary tirelessly promoted her books, giving hundreds of talks and lectures and interviews. A good friend of mine told me how her friend attended one of Mary's lectures and when a little old white-haired lady in twin-set and pearls (actually she wore cardigans but never a twin-set and she never wore any jewellery apart from a narrow wedding ring) came up to the lectern and fumbled around with the microphone, her friend turned to her companion with a look of dismay. But as soon as Mary launched into her well prepared and stunningly illustrated slide show/lecture they were all transported and captivated and found it a rich, inspiring and educational experience.

Mary sent copies of her books to, and corresponded with, Sir David Attenborough. When he came to Australia in August 1987 when filming for one of his series and making a visit to family in Canberra, he took time out of his busy schedule and had dinner at Forty Baskets Beach with her. His letter thanking her expressed his appreciation of her little piece of paradise and said "it was a wonderful and refreshing break in the midst of all the media nonsense."

He was also full of praise for her beautiful and important books. When she sent Sir David a copy of *The Greening* he had just returned from a filming trip, and he said: **"…I found your magnificent book awaiting me. What a wonderful (and I meant that most literally) gift it is… At the moment I am so bedazzled by the pictures that I have not settled down to the text, but I can already see how fascinating, thorough and valuable it is. I certainly know of no other book that has so much scope. Australia is fortunate!"**

When he received a copy of *After the Greening* in 1994 he wrote saying **"I feel ashamed that British publishers…cannot do something comparable about Britain and Western Europe. Obviously doing such a thing requires both an imaginative and brave publisher, and an appreciative, educated and enquiring public; but it also needs fabulous photographs and an inspired author. I do congratulate you unreservedly."**

The Greening of Gondwana received rave reviews from many highly respected scientists including British botanist E. Charles Nelson - '**This book is a triumph, the telling of an ancient tale, a story book for inquisitive laypeople and scholars of every land. Palaeobotany is made lucid and luminous. .... Jim Frazier's photographs are outstandingly beautiful. ....this is an erudite book, the result of exemplary scholarship.**'

Professor of geology at Yale University, Brian J. Skinner wrote '**Mary White has created a gem.....The result is a stunning panoply, one photograph more striking than the next. .....It is hard to imagine that anyone will soon better the remarkable blend of words and image found in the Greening of Gondwana.**'

Australian wildlife ecologist and conservationist, Dr John Callaghan, wrote that Mary White '**had joined the ranks of that, unfortunately, diminishing species of scientist who can write for an informed popular audience without loss of depth or scientific accuracy. ....Jim Frazier's success in making two dimensional flat fossils stand out from their rock background is spectacular.**'

It was also described by Scientific American writer Philip Morrison as '**the best book on palaeobotany this writer has ever seen.**'

♠♠

In the 1990s, with one of her oldest friends and colleague from the early days in Canberra, geologist John Casey, Mary conducted numerous outback eco-tours. Mary helped plan these trips based on her books, taking people to, and giving them talks and information on the geologically and scientifically significant places. They were wonderful trips covering huge distances and unplanned experiences such as getting stuck in the Strzelecki desert after rain, having to make big detours due to closures of outback tracks and an occasion where Mary was furious with, and soundly ticked off, the bus driver for engaging an emu in a race. Mary spoke of her incredibly spiritual connection with the deserts and remote outback and how at home she felt in these places.

# TO KNOW THE LOVELY NIGHT

Mary's life was full, happy and satisfying yet on occasion, grief still brought her undone, as her poetry expressed so well.

AMBUSHED

Would you believe it... After all these years
Suddenly I found myself weeping because you are dead?
There was no space between deep happiness—
(Standing, enjoying the early sun,
Drinking in the beauty of this bay you knew and loved)—
And total desolation...
Tears everywhere and no handkerchief
I'd turned to go inside, and I had seen,
Out of the corner of my eye,
Someone dragging a dinghy down the beach—
Old navy shirt, old shorts, just like you used to look—
Absorbed in thoughts of boats and wind and sailing.
And there I was, bereft,
My lovely world in tatters round my feet.
Sorry, so sorry—how inadequate the words,
That Fate had picked on you
And after all the agony of mind and body
Denied you the time you should have had
To drag *your* dinghy down the beach
And sail the boat you'd built to house your dreams.

I felt I should ask you to forgive me
Living my life to the full when you are dead.
There was no justice in your dying,
Only inevitability, and no one knows,
Though hearts may be transplanted,
How to transplant life and let one share
One's own allotted span with one whose time's run out—
That he may live a while, enjoy the early sunlight
And feel the gentle breeze upon his face.

# MARY E. WHITE AND BARBARA ECKERSLEY

Mary, whose life had been remarkably relatively kind to her, was surprised numerous times by the immensity of the hole left in the fabric of her life by Bill's death. Years later she wrote another poem about grief gestating in her soul:

GESTATING GRIEF

When I reached out and came in close last night,
Needing to feel a living warmth and hear your sleeping breath,
You could not know that I had need to share
The weight of age-old grief which had become
A finite body needing to be born; and you slept on.

But it had been gestating all day long—
Its umbilical cord had fed on insubstantial things;
On shell-pink, misty morning
When wraiths had moved across the glassy water;
On sparkling blue, white sails and high clouds flying;
On eagles soaring overhead; and small brown gentle ducks
Which came in to be fed, and came again when it was dark
Back-pedalling with phosphorescent feet, to have a bed-time
    snack.

And all day long a deep resentment grew
That one I loved had been denied the time
To be a part of this, his world of water, wind and Nature,
Which he had loved and sought whenever he was able...
His time ran out; and always in my heart
I feel the seed of sorrow, which is also longing—
And every now and then it grows and swells and comes alive;
Then leaves me quiet—and shrinks into a corner
Which it shares, in some strange mystic way,
With happiness and with an understanding
That there are plans for Life much greater than our own,
And we are unimportant in the Whole.

While Mary's poetry was mainly written to help heal her soul, revealing a very private side of herself—her deep emotions and hidden sadnesses—it also reaffirms her enormous love and reverence for life as seen in the following poem:

DAWN

The world around me fills my soul with awe,
My heart with happiness, with reverence,
With wonderment and deep content.
I watch the birth of each new morn
Across the lovely bay.
The stars have gone.
The greys of night, with lights like shining crowns
Along the water's edge, reflecting in long rays,
Change—colourless yet—
To silver water, black silhouettes of houses, trees;
With shining pinpricks in the velvet black...
And sky above so pale it has no colour.
Then pearly mists suffuse the low horizon,
Stray clouds ignite, angelic pink,
They seem to rise out of the bowl of night
To float into the miracle of day.
The conflagration spreads.
Gold radiance, warming to the sight,
Turns fiery orange-red,
And in a moment, an incandescent ball
Of living energy, the sun is there—
Before one looks away, dazzled by his brilliance.
The harbour turns to watered silk,
Its ripples black on silvery pinks and greys,
And golden pathways leading to the sun.
A flock of rainbow lorikeets
Wheels chattering across the dawn.
Another day begins,
New-washed and full of promise.

# LEAVING SYDNEY

Mary wrote:

So why did I leave Forty Baskets and my comfort zone with all its obvious attractions? I had started to realise that my horizons were closing in. Advanced age does that, one thinks twice about driving at night; does less of the walking and swimming that the place offers; friends and family die or move away; the vulgar moneyed brigade pull down the old houses and build monstrosities all around; one is sitting on increasingly valuable real estate and has less and less cash when one is largely dependent on book royalties; major expenditure is required for an inclinator to enable one to get out of the place and the septic tank is dying and it is time to connect, at great expense, to the sewer... So a visit to the Bank solves most of the problems—twilight mortgaging will enable me to have access to a million dollars (at a nice interest rate for the bank, so they are happy). And I think "good, now I'll settle down and write that big book on Antarctica", and a quiet voice is saying "more of the same, no matter how good it has been, perhaps there should be other things to do and experience because one does not have unlimited time".

Within days of the bank telling me I need have no more money worries I had a moment of what can only be described as revelation (without any religious attachment) and I knew I had to do what I think everyone should do if they have the opportunity—take personal responsibility for something about which they are passionate—in my case protection of a bit of the natural world and its biodiversity. So I decided to spend a million dollars and buy a piece of Australia that is asking to be protected from the encroaching tide of people that is swamping the eastern margin of the continent. I had been preaching in my books about what needed to be done and now I had a chance to make a difference. I just knew it was the right decision and the way everything fell into place and all doors opened confirmed my intuition.

Falls Forest Retreat was everything I could have dreamed of, with the addition of potential for development as an environmental education centre so that the messages of conservation could reach more people. That my son Derek was available and happy to help me settle in for the first year, and organise and do all the things that were needed to bring the property up to scratch, was a bonus beyond price, and it was a special time for me having him living in the house. I am forever in his debt as he has enabled me to make this place home.

Everything was new and different, and wonderful and interesting, and I had a feeling of unreality, that all this could not possibly be permanent and I would find it was all a wonderful dream or a holiday that would come to an end. The feeling of "living inside someone else's head" and having a brain that was seeking out similar events in the past whenever anything it considered out of the ordinary happened was slightly disconcerting. Why, when Xanth (my big black cat) died suddenly, did I have to relive my dad's death, my mother's, Bill's with all its attached anxieties that were with me for so many years, and even every detail of each loved cat or dog or bird whose deaths I had witnessed? When simple things happened, like a pump breaking down and no water coming from a tap, why was I instantly in a house in Somalia and almost able to reach out and touch the things around me, smell the dusty fragrance of thorn trees and be listening for the small children who were somewhere in the background? When I asked my doctor if I was heading for dementia or something she laughed and told me that stress does that and big moves like selling family homes and changing lifestyle have strange effects on one's mental processes and things usually settle down in two years.

When I try to answer the question of why this change of direction in my life has needed such a mental sort-out I think I know the reasons. This has been the first time when I have stepped outside the comfort zone that others had helped to build and made a life-changing decision alone. I don't think it was entirely selfish because I knew I would be able to help my family financially and hopefully they would be as happy to come to visit here as at Forty Baskets. And I thought, in my ignorance, that there need be no interruption in my writing—one can write anywhere. I had started on a major work and had made preliminary contacts with polar scientists—proposing to investigate 300 million years of climate and environmental change on the Antarctic landmass—a book that would be useful in understanding more about global climate systems. But I soon realised that that sort of high-powered science for general readers takes complete focus for up to a year—which I had been able to achieve living alone in a beautiful, peaceful place like Forty Baskets Beach on Sydney Harbour all those productive years. There, I had easy contact with colleagues etc as well. So that book will never go anywhere, I'm sure—though someone ought to write it.

About this time Mary also wrote:

I acknowledge that I am greatly privileged to be alive. Were I to die tomorrow I should have no right to protest that I had not had time enough and had hoped for more. Life's tapestry, woven so generously for me by chance and destiny, has been rich and beautiful.

# FALLS FOREST RETREAT, JOHNS RIVER NSW

Mary's house nestled below Middle Brother
Mountain; some of the forests

*I have experienced a wonderful feeling*
*Of coming home and belonging*
*In my daily living situation*

# LIVING THE DREAM

Mary wrote a letter to explain her conservation efforts and plans for her property *Falls Forest Retreat*

While I was living in Sydney and writing my four major works on co-evolution of the Australian environment and its biota—*The Greening of Gondwana; After the Greening; Listen our Land is Crying; and Running Down: Water in a Changing Land*—I had become alarmed at the rapid loss of biodiversity in Australia. My research for the latest book Earth Alive only confirmed my concerns and widened them into a global awareness of large-scale vegetation loss, ecosystem destruction and extinctions that now threaten the Life-friendly nature of the biosphere on which we humans depend for our productive and satisfying existence. As a result of these concerns, I decided to sell the home in which I had lived for 37 years, and which had become moderately valuable real estate and use the proceeds to purchase a piece of Australia that was suitable for protection by virtue of its situation. It needed to be adjacent to National Park or reserve land, with rich diversity of forest cover and with a river that had an undisturbed catchment. By doing this I would be leaving a legacy to Australia and repaying my debts to the Nation for providing me and my large family with opportunities for happy and productive lives.

Fortunately, I found Falls Forest Retreat and it had all the right features. I bought the 88-hectare property in 2003 with the primary intention of covenanting the forests, which have Gondwanan rainforest remnants that date back as virtually unchanged ecosystems through 60 million years. (We know as a result of surveys that its biodiversity richness is even greater than originally thought, and we have rare, endangered plants, insects, frogs, bats, birds and quolls—and many plant species that are either further north or south of their normal range, making the area valuable at a time of climate instability. Major fresh water and insect surveys are planned and I'm sure additions will be made to the lists.) The significance of the whole property as part of a major corridor from the coast to the Brothers Mountains and through valuable forest remnants (some covenanted) and westwards to the Divide, was not understood until recently with the coming together of the Great Eastern Ranges Initiative—GERI.

The property comprises a completely private valley surrounded by forested hills to the S and SW, and steep rocky slopes going halfway up Middle Brother Mountain into National Park on the NE side. (I recently purchased the "paper road" that ran through the valley, ensuring the future privacy.) The valley floor that was cleared of rainforest in the early 1900s for dairy farming has the entry road and buildings with park-like gardens with introduced trees surrounded by grazing paddocks. A Joint Venture Forestry (JVA) Agreement was undertaken by a previous owner in 1986 and eucalypt forests were planted on the lower slopes of Middle Brother Mountain, at the head of the valley below the Cascades on Jerry's Creek and inside my boundary near the dramatic Yoorigan Falls that are just within the NP that curves around that end of the property. Some younger trees in actively regenerating areas were actually removed to make room for the JVA. The forests, creeks, Falls and Cascade waterholes are of high cultural significance to local Aboriginal elders.

The retreat accommodation business that comprises six townhouses and a Conference Centre was run down and barely functioning when I bought it but it would hopefully be built up over time to finance its ongoing running costs and the never-ending property maintenance on the rest of the property, including the professional bush regeneration of the covenanted parts and the work required in the JVA forests. (With the Global Financial Crisis, in which my modest investments suffered like everyone else's, business has been slow, particularly in the last year when all small businesses in the Mid North Coast area have suffered the same recession problems. I am a self-funded retiree, living very simply, happy with my choice of lifestyle in this last stage of my life.)

The property was rundown and neglected with heavy weed infestation of the fenced paddocks on the valley floor and of the river banks, with weed invasion starting into the fringes of the forests. A great deal of iron and heavy rubbish had been put into the river, out of sight, and scattered in bush and paddocks, and needed to be removed, and large rocks had to be dug out and stones had to be removed from paddocks to enable slashing and weed control. Firebreaks had to be opened up and made navigable around JVA and natural forests, involving great expense on labour and machinery. I received grants to cover part of this, but only part. Walking trails have also been made or improved, and a labelled Botanical Walkway next to the entrance driveway along the river has just been completed—the longest and most detailed plant identification walk in the country (final plant identification by Gwen Harden of Royal Botanic Gardens). Some plant labelling near the waterfall and a second botanical walk to the Dark Gully and Magic Tree for children are also useful teaching and learning aids.

Covenanting of the forests was done with the Department of Infrastructure, Planning and Natural Resources (DIPNR) in 2004 (52 hectares) and a further 55.7 hectares in 2008 with the Department of Environment, Climate Change and Water (DECCW), ensuring their protection. International covenanting as a Land for Wildlife Sanctuary with the Humane Society International Wildlife Land Trust in 2010 has added another dimension to the protection.

It has now become obvious that the JVA forests that were planted into the margins of the now-covenanted forests present a threat to their health and integrity if they are to be thinned and later harvested. Their establishment on steep, rocky slopes guarantees erosion problems when they are removed, and the valley floor below is a series of small floodplains that feed into Jerry's Creek that is a tributary of Stewarts River. This will adversely affect the health of the Creek and the River and add to siltation problems in the estuary. The devastation of the amenity of the whole property that will result if thinning starts soon, and the total write-off that would occur when harvesting was done later would negate all that I have done to protect and enhance this place as a wildlife and native forest refuge (not to mention its role as an environmental education centre where I am teaching about GAIA the Green Planet where all Life depends on photosynthesis, and of the active role of the Plant Kingdom in climate-balancing roles etc).

When the JVA was entered into, the problems of the over-populated world and knowledge of natural balancing mechanisms in climate control were not of much general interest or concern. There was no knowledge of the richness of the biodiversity in the adjacent natural forests or that a global situation was approaching where mankind's world-wide destruction of forests since settlement for agriculture 14,000 years ago (80% gone) would be threatening mass extinctions and dramatic climate change making Earth far less Life-friendly, etc. etc.

Now things are very different, and we know the value of standing forests in carbon sequestration and their eco-service value in climate control. The JVA forests with their eucalypt species compatible with the natural forests will gradually increase their biodiversity over time. The true value of the combined forest to the Nation as a carbon sink and of this whole property as a Nature Reserve with multiple refugia for the plants and animals of this Mid North Coast region (where even koalas are approaching threatened species status because of habitat destruction) is great. The value of the JVA forests as eco-service providers is far greater than its supposed eventual value as logs.

The conservation of every bit of forest globally is of vital importance.

It is my hope that I will be allowed to buy back the JVA forests at a nominal price and have them converted to natural forests. Through the much-appreciated help of Peter Besserling MP they have been offered to me at a reduced price of $50,000— which is beyond my financial reach. I am seeking support of all my colleagues and others involved in this quest of mine. Sir

**Michael Jeffery of Future Directions Int. and Outcomes Australia has offered to facilitate contacts at Ministerial and Government level and his interest and involvement is greatly appreciated.**

**The wildlife corridor that this property makes with forest remnants going westwards to the Great Divide and East via South Brother Mountain is something for the government to be proud of.**

**The Great Eastern Ranges Initiative now encompasses another of my plans for the future of my region—the protection of South Brother Mountain as a National Park or Reserve. North Brother and Middle Brother are both National Parks, but South Brother has been forgotten. It is mainly too steep and rocky to be used for any purpose. As a biodiversity sanctuary it is of enormous value.**

♠♠

It is little wonder Mary had so little time for writing with the day-to-day tasks of running the business (she had managers but was still very much involved), the covenanting, arranging biodiversity surveys, giving talks to local conservation groups etc. She was involved in local climate change groups, Landcare, the local Pilot Station educational programs, school educational planning on the Mid North Coast and its curriculum and much more. She had a constant stream of visitors (friends, colleagues, locals and business guests)—and the daily baking of cakes and soup making that she felt necessary (Mary's favourite occupation, like her grandmother and mother, was feeding people) made it impossible for her to focus on and settle down to write the major book on Antarctica that she had planned.

Richard and I visited *The Falls* a few times a year and spent time with Mary, drinking tea and eating cake on her veranda with her noisy, demanding galah and her gentle Major Mitchell cockatoo. We also did a lot of hard work hacking out weeds and lantana and opening up walking trails that had been totally overgrown. We explored widely and walked and climbed on the slopes and dry waterfalls on Middle Brother Mountain. The forests were beautiful, and I could understand Mary's total obsession with restoring and covenanting as much of the property as possible. As much as I loved the place I didn't like it being used by paying visitors when we were there—it somehow detracted from the peace and privacy of the place. Most of the guests were lovely people who appreciated what the place offered and what Mary was trying to do there. Mary charmed most of them and they left feeling that they were her best friends, as did Mary. There were, however, some difficult guests who freaked out about daddy-long-leg spiders in the room, or complained about some aspect of life in a rainforest environment. I recall one instance where an aggressive man shouted at Mary that as he was a descendant of Afghan cameleers he had more right to be in this country than she. I don't know what sparked this altercation but maybe he picked up on her deep-seated racism that lurked beneath some casual remark.

On one of our visits I had a very heavy fall when scrambling down a very steep, dry watercourse on Middle Brother. I landed on my backside, was winded and unable to walk for some time. There was no other way to get off the mountain, so as soon as I was able I scrambled down the rocky slope and limped the couple of kilometres back to Mary's, almost blinded by the tears that kept coming. In retrospect, I should have sat where I'd fallen for much longer as the fall onto the base of my spine was very hard and I obviously went into shock. I staggered into our accommodation and rested, then we drove back to Canberra, and I resumed work immediately.

A night or two later I suffered a neurological event that could only have been a delayed consequence of the fall. It left me disabled for over four years affecting my balance, eyesight, coordination, concentration—everything. I felt brain-damaged. Brain scans showed nothing, and it was never really diagnosed but I suspect it was a spinal concussion resulting from my spinal cord being rammed up into the base of my brain.

Mary wrote in **What it's like to be Eighty.**

**With a week to go to the 22.02.06, this is a time for taking stock, and looking back —**

It is surprising how long it has taken for the full realisation to dawn that I am officially old—that I look old, probably act old and often feel old. And it is fairly daunting to have been forced to confront my own mortality. The peace of that acceptance is disturbed with every death or major crisis of family or friends—and my generation are becoming thin on the ground.

If I had not left Forty Baskets and started a new life I might never have undergone the strangely rejuvenating mental changes that have been the result of moving out of my comfort zone, away from everything familiar and from a special place that I loved so deeply. Lately I have made the full mental transition (at least most of the time) so that the feeling of unreality and living inside someone else's head has gone, and I am me, in this unbelievably wondrous place that not only feels like, but is, home. From the moment when I first entered this valley, coming to see whether it could be the place of my dreams, it felt like coming home, and I have not wanted to be anywhere else.

I have been surprised to find that I did not miss the other home where so much of my living, nearly half my life, had been spent. Those were wonderful and happy family years with a husband and children whom I loved and who were my main interest and focus. And then I was so fortunate to find a new beginning and a 'career' as a writer when all that came to an end when Bill died and the family had gone to make lives of their own and I was alone.

The whole process of adaptation, mental and physical, that has been the result of the profound changes that the last 2½ years have brought, has been interesting when I was able to be a disconnected observer of how memory and other brain functions work. And I thought I should try to write down something of the journey, because, from speaking to others I have realised that most people, at some stage, will undergo similar emotional or cerebral upheavals and it is nice to know that they don't mean that one is heading for dementia or other horrors. I am one of the lucky ones, emerging as a different me in many ways and with a heightened appreciation of all the wonders of Life and the living Earth.

It is hard to describe states of mind and emotions and the nearest I can come to it all is to say that it is like a new awakening. The memory and experience bank that is processing the present is a younger one than the one that had evolved while I was on a familiar pathway and adding more of the same, within the same parameters (and, if truth be told, slowly running down). It is as though, at a time of upheaval, one's brain searches out all past similar experiences, in order to supply balance and to decide where to store the new stuff when all the usual connections have been severed. (The analogy of brains and computer hard drives is inevitable.) What is initially disturbing is that among all the disturbed memory material that comes up to colour one's days and dreams is all the baggage that was packed away as too difficult to deal with completely when it was happening, when one simply had to get on with things and wait for "time to heal".

One reads about how the ageing process makes one increasingly forgetful—short-term memory first, then down the years—so that all the old memories become clearer while the others fade. So, I suppose that when one shakes up the memory bank by making big changes of whatever sort, the process is accelerated and that I have really got nothing to write about here. But I am entitled to a little introspection as my next 'landmark' birthday approaches.

There have been other major changes in my life. The normal growing up and maturing in a stable and happy home with wise and loving parents and extended family have left pleasant memories and though these have become more accessible there was stability and no dramas—my sister, brothers and I were so fortunate — though with the self-centredness of youth we never knew it. The big change of going off to university (five days and four nights in a steam train across Africa) was a start of the excitement of growing up and finding the real joy of learning about the things that still interest me most. And that stage led naturally into marriage and children where again I have had such good fortune to have loved Bill always and to be so blessed in our children. (At the age of three, I had announced to the world that I was going to be a botanist just like my mom and I was going to find a really nice man and marry and have lots of children, so my main ambitions were easily achieved!)

The changes that came with marrying a geologist and going off into strange places in the early years were not emotionally or mentally difficult because I always knew that Bill would do what was best for me and the children. He had his role of providing for us, looking after us and loving us, and I had mine, clearly defined, of being the wife, homemaker and mother—all fulfilling and creative and not the dead end that so many, particularly in later generations, have made it out to be. Youth made everything feel like an adventure. My dad's death, which coincided with Zoe's birth in Northern Ireland when we were on leave from Somaliland, affected me greatly and I worried a lot about my mother after that and felt guilty for being so far away and unable to look after her and let her share the joy of my children.

When we left Somalia in 1955 and headed straight for Australia there was so much excitement about starting in a new continent with all its new wonders and opportunities and I was so busy with a young family that there was little time for introspection. There was no extended family and no friends, initially, for support — but we managed. I remember that I had recurrent dreams about looking for my mother who was lost in labyrinths of hotel corridors or other strange places and who was sick or in need of rescue. And I carried a heavy burden of guilt for having abandoned my parents by going off and making my own life so far away, from the time when we left southern Africa.

It was only when I was in my fifties and I had seen my own family move on, making their own lives, that I realised I should never have felt guilty because my parents would never have seen things in that way.

At that stage I was always confident, feeling secure and able to deal with life's ordinary problems, finding great happiness in ordinary family life. And on top of it all was an increasing interest and satisfaction in having the intellectual activities that my plant fossil work for the BMR and mining companies gave me—a

**half-profession / hobby that supplied an important escape from domesticity, particularly when Bill was away in the field so much and I was housebound with kids with measles or middle-ear infections!**

**I wonder, now that I know so much more about other people and their lives, how I could have been so fortunate that my first experience of real insecurity and knowing that things beyond my control could shape my life did not occur until I was forty.**

♠♠

(This was when Bill's cancer was diagnosed. It is probably from here on that Mary became a permanently anxious person.)

Mary turned eighty in February 2006 and the occasion was marked by a gathering of all her family—five children, their partners, her nine grandchildren and at that stage, one great-grandchild—at Falls Forest Retreat. Her feelings of peace contentment and satisfaction with life are expressed in her poem:

JACARANDA RAIN

I walk through jacaranda rain.
Lavender-blue confetti whispers down,
And rain-drop blossoms decorate my path.
The early sun makes palisades of shadows,
The summer breeze brings messages from roses.
Thanks for another new-washed morning,
This day a gift to do with as I will.

I know that life is the ordained succession
Of days on days till I run out
Of my allotted time.
Its river carries me along,
Sometimes through quiet reaches strewn with flowers
Where I may gather strength to face the challenge
Of rapids and white water,

# TO KNOW THE LOVELY NIGHT

Or stagnant and polluted swamps
Which lie across my journey to the sea.

I know a deep content.
The sun will rise and warm the opening flowers,
And birds will sing.
Black velvet night will be illuminated
By a myriad of stars.
The moon will sail serene above the sleeping Earth,
And owls will go about their night-time ways
Long after I have used up all the days
Donated for my use.

It warms my heart to know that others will be born
To see and know and love as I have loved,
That in my children's children are some genes
Which carry on my loving and my living.

A forested mountain with dark gullies behind me
Eucalyptus trees shedding their bark
And sheltering a friendly old house

# THE END OF THE GREAT DREAM

Around 2008 Mary was obviously giving some thought to how long she could continue living at *The Falls*. She had such a feeling of complete belonging in that little house in the valley below Middle Brother Mountain that her dream was to stay there for the rest of her days and be buried under the giant fig tree. She discussed this with various friends and in about 2008 a couple she'd met locally who were looking for a property on which they could develop a Buddhist retreat, made her an offer: they would buy her property but allow her to live out her days in her little house. Mary was absolutely thrilled with this plan—all her dreams were coming true! Who knows how firm an offer this was or whether it was just a vague plan. Mary truly believed it was a done deal. Sometime later however, the couple were visiting, and over a cup of tea and carrot cake, casually mentioned that they had bought a property elsewhere! Mary said she was so shocked she couldn't speak and that she felt her heart go stone cold. A couple of days later she had a heart attack and ended up being flown to St Vincent's hospital in Sydney where she had four stents inserted.

This whole event shook her seriously. She said she suffered from Post-Traumatic Stress Disorder for months afterwards and was shattered, deeply disappointed and hurt by the sudden change of plans. I accompanied her home from hospital, flying with her to Port Macquarie where Derek met us and drove us to *The Falls*. At the time I was still recovering from the spinal injury resulting from the fall I had when climbing on Middle Brother Mountain six months previously and was not really well enough to care for her but we battled on together and I wouldn't have been anywhere else. The second night at home Mary came out in an angry red rash all over her body and I had to take her in to Port Macquarie hospital where the doctors decided it was a side effect of one of the medications she had been put on.

Mary's confidence was rocked by her sudden health concerns and by having to face her own mortality, having never really been sick in her life (her only hospitalisations being related to child bearing). She told a number of people that she was worried about her failing memory but was assured that everyone had such problems and that it was only old age and nothing to worry about. Derek and Peter who saw her regularly were beginning to be concerned by her vagueness and erratic driving. When a routine eye test found that she had lost her peripheral vision, possibly from having a small stroke, she admitted defeat. Over the next couple of years she went through a grieving process, gradually accepting that she would have to sell *The Falls* and move in with Richard and me. We had recently moved from Canberra to Bundanoon where we had bought and renovated a house with a quadruple garage out the back that we turned into a granny flat.

In an open letter to friends, colleagues and contacts in 2013 she wrote:

**I have been the owner and custodian of Falls Forest Retreat for ten wonderful years, fulfilling my dream of creating a Private Rainforest and Biodiversity Sanctuary, covenanted and protected into the Future. The final documents have been signed by the Minister and new Title Deeds that record details of the up-to-date covenanting situation are expected soon. (A "Variation of Conservation Agreement" now includes the JVA Plantations that a Biodiversity Fund Grant enabled me to purchase from Forests NSW; some additional areas of prime natural vegetation; and parts of the Crown Land "Paper Road" that used to run through the valley until purchased by me in December 2008.)**

**My "Legacy to the Nation" — 73 hectares of wonderful covenanted forest on this 81- hectare property — is complete.**

Now advancing old age and the uncertainties that it brings have made me realise that I must put the property on the market now and let it be known that I am ready to sell whenever some-one decides to buy it. The continuing care of the property has to be a foremost consideration.

There will be deep sorrow for me when I leave but I know that my decision is right for me, my family and this place of peace and beauty that has so much potential for use and development in many different directions.

# NOT THE LIFE ENVISAGED

All Mary wanted was a peaceful place where she could write her autobiography which she had already started and live out her days in peace and quiet. However, the stress of trying to find a buyer, of packing and shedding stuff— she insisted on doing it all herself—and of leaving her beautiful home, took its toll and she apparently suffered a number of small strokes in the months, and possibly even days, before she moved. Some very good friends offered to drive her car with Mary and her beloved bird to Bundanoon, and they commented that she was behaving very strangely the previous night.

When she arrived in Bundanoon in February 2014 aged eighty-eight, she was a diminished, frail, totally confused and empty little old lady who bore no resemblance to Mary at all. She was pathetic and agitated beyond belief. Richard and I were totally shocked and attributed the change to her being tired and stressed and assumed that after a good sleep and a week to adjust to her new surroundings, she'd revert to the charming, charismatic and independent Mary she used to be. When this didn't happen, I had her checked by our doctor for the various complaints that can cause confusion in the elderly, then by specialists where she underwent brain scans, heart function tests etc. Scans showed that she had suffered a number of strokes and that she had advanced cardiovascular disease and vascular dementia. Mary received all this news like a condemned person, barely saying a word or showing any emotion. She didn't ask questions and didn't want to talk about it.

Mary was very distressed by what was happening to her brain. A few weeks after her diagnosis she said she felt that all the things that mattered most to her (*Falls Retreat* and her brain) were being taken away from her, that she was losing what made her who she was. She was devastated by it all. She tried to work on her autobiography, but it was beyond her. She tried gardening but didn't have the strength, so she spent a lot of her time watching News24 which, I'm sure, added to her depression. When she had visitors she managed to appear quite normal as she had a "loop" of conversation all about her work and herself that she stuck to.

I wonder if, when she wrote this poem for her close friend Cec, she had ever entertained the thought that one day she would be stricken with this cruel brain- and self-robbing disease.

CEC - VICTIM OF ALZHEIMERS DISEASE

She wanders restless, trapped in a limbo world
Where thoughts fly in as blurs and whirr away like frightened birds
Before they can be held to focus on.
Wandering, wondering, wanting, wishing—
Ever moving—to and fro, back and forth—
Ever seeking—walking aimlessly and lost
In a space where neither thought nor form has edges.
An archetype for gentle ghosts which in their different limbo,
Trapped between this life and life-hereafter
Walk back and forth along a corridor,
Wringing their feeble hands or pleating up a garment hem
With restless fingers, as babies stroke a comfort rag.

Her aura sweet, ethereal, sad.
Instinctively she reaches out for love and comfort.
And she is blessed for there are those who love and comfort her.
And in the end, so short a road to travel,
So tenuous her hold on life and living—
Her bonds with Earth already broken free,
She'll slip away and leave behind faint ripples
As dawn ruffles water as it goes.

Mary had trouble hearing me, despite her hearing aids and I had to shout to be heard at all. This made it impossible to have any sort of conversation and Richard had to relay what I said to her. She would get cross because I 'barked' commands at her and she would shrug off any attempt to take her by the arm to steer her across the road or steady her on uneven ground—she had been independent for so long she didn't want, or know how to accept, help.

As the months went by her needs became greater. She rarely cooked for herself and ate most evening meals with us. I cooked her breakfasts and morning teas as she would forget to eat and then get the shakes and she'd eat a couple of sweet biscuits whose instant but short-lived sugar hit made the problem worse in the long run. She now needed someone on standby all the time, when she showered, to dress her and toilet her etc.

We discovered that note writing had started in Mary's last few years at *The Falls*—she wrote everything down, reminders all over the place. While she was in her familiar surroundings and her daily routines she was able to function quite well and hide how bad her memory was becoming, and even drive into town. She told me once that she'd get into the car and couldn't think where she was going or how to get there, but as soon as she started it, the car knew where to go. This should have rung alarm bells!

Obviously in moving to her new home she lost the comfort of her routines and familiar surroundings and became very confused. Her dementia became apparent, and the recent small strokes compounded everything. She very bravely, outwardly at least, accepted what was happening and joined a Dementia Care group that got together on Thursday mornings. Once a week she had the company of a lovely lady, Meg from BaptistCare, who rapidly became a valued friend. Meg would spend a morning with her, take her shopping, do some cleaning or cooking, read to her, do jigsaws or whatever Mary wanted and it was a greatly appreciated respite for Rich and me. My friend Lorelei came in regularly to teach her Pilates and another, Pam, played Scrabble with her.

Mary's physical and mental health declined steadily over the first year and in 2015 she started having TIAs (Transient Ischaemic

Attacks or mini-strokes). We set up an intercom by my bed so she could call us when she felt a TIA coming on and we could be with her and comfort her until it passed. I lay awake at night, dreading a call from her and agonising over how best to manage her as things were obviously only going to get worse. My sleep that had always been poor, became even more disrupted and when I did doze off I'd wake with my heart pounding feeling sure I'd missed the intercom call.

Her care needs increased even further, and we bought her a commode chair beside her bed as she was too unsteady to make a trip to the loo in the night. She told everyone that she had the horrors of going into a nursing home and of being totally dependent, but that that was not going to happen as she was going to die peacefully in her sleep—she was totally convinced of that. Every day she said that tonight was going to be her last. This was all very distressing for us and our kids, and my mental health was deteriorating.

Then on 17 February 2016 Mary had what we thought was another TIA, but when she woke after a sleep after the shakes had subsided, we discovered she couldn't speak at all and was paralysed down her right side. Richard and I realised immediately that we couldn't lift her or give her the care she needed. There was no room for agonising about having to hand her over to institutionalised care: we had no choice. I was, however, still devastated that it had come to this, the scenario Mary had dreaded more than anything in life—being totally dependent and in a nursing home.

She went by ambulance to Bowral Hospital and was released into a nursing home in Bundanoon on her 90th birth-day on 22 February.

Mary regained a little bit of speech during the first six months but most of what she said was either nonsense, about going home, asking us not to leave her there, or unfinished bits of sentences. She then lost the ability to speak again and was unable to communicate in any way except by squirming and silently crying. She was utterly miserable and threw herself out of bed repeatedly, despite having rails on the bed, and from her high tub-chair—a bed that could be wheeled out to a common area where she was lined up in front of a TV with other occupants who all looked like corpses. Her mattress was put on the floor at one stage and her bed was surrounded by crash mats thereafter, until that phase passed. My siblings and my children too, couldn't bear to see Mary like this, and wanted to remember her as the full-of-life, adoring mother/grandmother that she used to be. So, they stopped coming to visit. I understood completely, but it meant that it was all left to Richard and me.

I'd never seen Mary cry in her whole life but now she often teared up, chin trembling and looking utterly miserable, pleading with me to help her. She often appeared to be in pain and was given morphine in increasing doses until she broke out in a massive rash. Her agitation appeared to be made worse by the drugs. She was then put on a morphine patch and pain medication was given as needed. We felt that whenever she was awake she was agitated and distressed—in mental or physical pain, or both. There were many hours in the day when she was unattended and staff did not react to her squirming and restlessness because they saw it as "what Mary did" rather than as the only way she could communicate her discomfort and misery.

We visited Mary almost every day and at all times of the day to begin with. More often than not, when we arrived at her room we'd find her slumped down in the bed, lying diagonally across it with her nightie hitched up around her waist, her pale legs and nappy displayed to all. She'd be squirming around, manoeuvring her paralysed leg with her good leg between the rails and the gap at the end of the bed until her legs hung out. With her head on the crash rail she was obviously very uncomfortable, she was red faced and distressed. We'd call the staff, and a carer would come and reposition her, whereupon she'd start squirming and trying to get out of bed or away from her misery all over again.

Another almost daily common behaviour involved pulling her bed apart. We'd arrive to find her sheets on the floor, the green waterproof mattress cover pulled off, her pillows all over the place and the covers on the bed rails literally torn off. She managed all this with only one functioning arm, and it would have taken considerable time to achieve such disarray. Staff obviously were not aware or considered it a harmless activity whereas we recognised it as a sign of agitation, frustration and/or distress from someone who had no other way of communicating her distress. Another less destructive behaviour which I still interpreted as an indication that she was not peaceful or comfortable, was a compulsive plucking and pulling at her blankets, nighties, or sometimes, Richard or me. A number of times she grabbed us with her frail old claw of a left hand and pulled and shook us with incredible strength and concentration. We both found these behaviours very distressing and would call the staff to help settle her either with medication or by changing her nappy, repositioning her or whatever was required. Even when Mary was asleep, her face was screwed up and she looked far from relaxed and peaceful.

We initiated numerous case conferences with the doctor and nursing staff who claimed that she was not suffering and that when she was, they addressed it adequately. My biggest complaint was that their actions were all reactive not proactive, and she suffered rather than being kept as pain free as possible, as she had requested in her Advanced Care Directive. We asked that her level of sedation be increased but were told that she would risk getting pneumonia if it were. My response was that pneumonia was the old person's friend and it would be a kind end, but the palliative care nurse said they'd do nothing that might hasten her death. We called in geriatric specialists, pain specialists, clinical psychologists, and a geriatric psychiatrist, who all recognised her agitation and suffering and recommended some medication changes, but very little change was made.

The clinical psychologist thought Mary was probably suffering neuropathic pain as a result of her stroke and suggested a drug that could help her. I relayed this suggestion to the doctor, but he dismissed it, whether because the suggestion came from me or from a psychologist (not a doctor), I'll never know.

We asked for a video camera to be set up in her room so we could get some idea of how often during the day and night Mary was displaying signs of agitation or suffering, but were told that it would be an invasion of her privacy and they would not allow it. We took a number of videos on our phone of her behaviours to try to convince the staff that she was often unsettled. You can imagine how awful I felt, standing there and filming her while she writhed around! The doctor agreed that she did look distressed but offered no solution or change to her management beyond monitoring her over the following week. It seemed odd to us that the monitoring showed that she was settled almost all of the time until we were eventually shown the charts and we could see that she was monitored after her personal care, after a meal, after her medication etc., in other words, at times when she was exhausted or doped up. She was rarely monitored in the late afternoon or evening.

We made a point of being there every evening as she was usually awake and agitated then and we could alert the staff and request pain medication. We also fed her her evening meal nearly every day. Mary often had to sit in a soiled nappy while she ate dinner as the carers were not allowed to change patients during meal times. She was often washed and had her nappies changed by male carers, something that must have distressed her enormously, and she found her personal care painful and undignified. The staff blamed her agitation (which they denied when it suited them) on me—my presence upset her. In some ways maybe it did, because it was me she wanted to express her misery to and me she wanted to ask to help her. It was never explained to us that there is a well-known phenomenon in dementia patients called 'Sundowning' in which they are often highly agitated and restless in the evening.

One evening I was there by myself and found her sobbing silently, shaking and thrashing around in bed. I called repeatedly for help and each time a carer came and told me the nurses would come soon. After the best part of an hour I pressed the emergency button —I should have done so much earlier! — and three nurses appeared instantly but I was in such an emotional state I couldn't explain that I suspected she was having a heart attack or had a bad attack of angina. Mary was exhausted and had settled slightly and I fled in a highly agitated state. When I got into my car I erupted—overwhelmed by a crying attack and beating my head and fists on the steering wheel. When I calmed down, I felt ashamed of 'losing it' and told no one about my breakdown.

By the end of 2017 Mary had pretty much stopped recognising us and she often ate her dinner with her eyes closed and barely conscious. Then like a beam of light through heavy clouds, there'd be odd moments when she seemed to recognise me, and she'd look at me with tears of utter desperation. I was finding this all very distressing and although I wouldn't admit it I was obviously depressed. Rich suggested a number of times that I should get some help, but I refused. Never once was I offered any support by the doctor or nursing home staff although my distress and emotional state was obvious at the many case conferences.

I felt fragile, irritable, hopeless and helpless and that I was failing Mary. I found myself bursting into tears in the shower and in the middle of the night. I was defeated by the smallest thing— not being able to open a jam jar had me raging and close to tears. I took a lot of my frustrations out on poor Richard with whom I'd barely ever fought or argued in our thirty-eight years of marriage. I dismissed him, hardly spoke to him and felt I didn't love him anymore and that my marriage was over. I was full of anger and resentment about everything, I lost all my creative inspiration and motivation and gave up doing anything and obsessed about Mary.

I was living in a cloud of despair, pain, guilt and confusion with no end in sight. I felt entangled with Mary—her suffering became mine. I didn't know where I ended, and she began, and I felt her utter desperation and frustration. When I looked in the mirror I saw her, when I looked at her I saw me. Watching her suffer was like watching myself die. I was overwhelmed by emotions. I didn't know where they came from, and I was frightened by their intensity and ashamed that I was not in control of myself.

Then at a case conference in July 2018, we were told by the doctor that there was nothing more they could do for Mary and that if we didn't like it we should take her elsewhere! We were absolutely speechless. Surely NO doctor should ever be able to say that! I felt abandoned, belittled, dismissed and betrayed, because he didn't believe Mary was suffering and he thought I wouldn't ever be satisfied with their management of her.

I started, almost manically, trying to find another facility to move her to. I was so distressed and admitted that I couldn't do this anymore. I started making plans for Mary to be transferred to a nursing home in Laurieton not far from *Falls Retreat*. I told myself that she'd be better off there. Her old friends could visit her and Derek and his wife, Janice, who were living in the area could oversee her care, even though they were away for four months of every year. We rushed up to investigate the nursing home and having agreed on a room, I sent out an email to my other siblings to inform them of the plans. Zoe, who had had no contact with Mary or us for four-and-a-half years, suggested that she'd find a room in a nursing home near her. I was too upset to argue.

So almost overnight, plans were made for an ambulance to take Mary to Sydney airport, a small plane to fly her to Coffs Harbour and another ambulance to drive her to the nursing home. I was not allowed to travel with her, and this distressed me greatly—having made the arrangements I suddenly realised that she would die, vomiting into a bucket, in a plane with complete strangers. I felt she was being packed off like a parcel, that I was abandoning her, had failed her and had let her suffer. I felt hopeless and helpless and could feel myself disintegrating, coming apart at the seams. I was racked by guilt and grief. The grief, along with anger and resentment at the universe for stealing my mother from me, had been a constant since Mary arrived in Bundanoon. I was grieving her loss and there was no closure—apparently a common feeling in relatives of those with dementia.

Mary was due to be moved on 7 August 2018 but died on 5 August with Richard and me at her bedside. Three days later I was arrested and charged with her murder.

# PART III

## THE AFTERMATH

# ARREST AND LIMBO

As Mary's move approached I felt increasingly disturbed, out of body and as though someone else was in my head controlling me. A few nights before the move, I decided to make sure she had a couple of peaceful, pain-free nights while she was still in my care. I crushed up and slipped a largish dose of Temazepam into her food at dinner. She obviously had a very peaceful sleep that night. I had a terrible night of fitful sleep punctuated with nightmares. In one particularly awful dream I was being attacked by terrifying 'things' that were coming at me from all directions. I was fending them off by grabbing them by their necks and trying to throttle them and when I turned to grab one I saw it wasn't one of 'them' but was Mary. She called out to me—BAR—and the sound of her voice woke me, and I was horrified that I had almost hurt her. I felt very disturbed and was haunted by the dream, her voice and the look in her eyes, throughout the rest of the night and all the following day.

The next evening before going to visit Mary, having no more Temazepam and stressing about wanting to help her, I suddenly had a clear vision of a little bottle of barbiturate I had in a bag of wildlife-care equipment tucked away in the top of my cupboard. In my disturbed and miserable state I decided to give her a dose of this and tipped a small quantity into her soup which I then fed her. She ate calmly and then seemed to fall into a deep sleep before becoming unconscious. Mary died peacefully four hours later.

When I fed her the barbiturate, I was literally beside myself—I felt I was outside my body, watching. When she gave a cough/snort and became unresponsive I panicked and ran to get help from the nursing staff. I had absolutely no recall of my actions and when she died shortly afterwards the floodgates opened and I thought I'd never stop crying. I sobbed out all the bottled-up misery, guilt, grief, desperation, longing and love for my mother until I was utterly empty and in a state of shock.

Still in a state of shock, the next morning at the funeral home we were told that the doctor had refused to sign the death certificate and that a police investigation into Mary's death was underway. My only thought was for my poor mother who had suffered so much and now had to undergo an autopsy and further indignities. It wasn't until the following night that the realisation of what had transpired hit me and I sat bolt upright in bed and said, "Oh my God, what have I done?" I honestly don't think I had intended to end her life but in the state I was in, I really don't know. My *only* concern for the two-and-a-half years since her major stroke had been for her and to relieve her suffering

I was in such a state in the morning—shaking and crying and unable to think straight— that I convinced Richard that I had to hand myself in to the police immediately. I thought he was going to have a heart attack on the spot when I told him what I had done. We didn't have a lawyer and I was adamant that I confess immediately as if we delayed long enough to find a lawyer the police would think Richard was involved too. I hadn't considered what would happen beyond confessing and I was shocked to be loudly (and gleefully) arrested by the Detective Senior Constable at the police station. I spent all day being interviewed and processed and finally charged with murder in a freezing cold police cell, without a lawyer and with no contact with Richard or anyone else. I was in shock, completely numb and it was a totally surreal experience. I felt like an observer and that it wasn't happening to me. To some extent this protected me throughout the next three years, although when I finally got home, I cried for days and was in a constantly heightened state of distress during those years, particularly early on. One cannot live in such a highly charged emotional state for long periods and fortunately, a process of adaptation occurs.

While I was being processed and charged our house was searched and all our electronic equipment was seized. The police were looking for evidence of planning or that someone else was involved. We were warned by our lawyers that our house may have been bugged so for months afterwards any discussions about strategies, or anything to do with the case, had to be held outside in the freezing cold (it was a cold August!). We felt violated and our home that should have been a safe haven and refuge felt far from safe.

Late that evening, I was handcuffed and stuffed unceremoniously into the back of a paddy wagon, in complete darkness and freezing cold and driven to Goulburn where I was put in a police cell for the night. Although the Corrective Services officers were, on the whole, pretty decent to me, the whole system is designed to totally dehumanise, demoralise and disempower a person, particularly when already devastated and broken by the circumstances leading to the arrest. I felt sullied and tainted and couldn't bear to be looked at, as I felt I must have the mark of a criminal on me.

A concrete slab with a thin vinyl mattress for a bed, no sheet or pillow, a blanket so stiff and thick there was no chance of strangling myself or of being warm or comfortable. No toothbrush, comb, face washer; something inedible thrust into my cell and a night of bright lights and the most incredible slamming of big metal doors all night. I now know why prison is referred to as "the slammer" in movies. Nothing edible for breakfast—I smeared a little Vegemite on a pat of butter (being gluten intolerant that was all I could eat). And then with no way to tidy myself, no shoelaces or belt and my coat that they finally allowed me to wear after I suggested they cut off the drawstring in the hood, I was cuffed and bundled into a paddy wagon again and disgorged into the cells under the Goulburn Courthouse to await my bail hearing.

The cells and the courthouse date back to convict days and were bitterly cold and incredibly uncomfortable—all concrete and metal. As I had no lawyer I was given the duty solicitor and I was handcuffed again and moved into a tiny ice-box of a concrete room with a small, barred window through which I could talk to him. The solicitor had been working on a case with a barrister who had previously appeared for a man charged with the murder of his dying partner and got him a two-year suspended sentence and he just happened to be in Goulburn that day. He agreed to represent me in my bail hearing but wanted to have time to prepare the case for bail thoroughly so asked for a deferment of the hearing until the next day. So after hanging around in the cold cell all day I was loaded handcuffed and shivering, into a large truck-paddy wagon that still contained all the smell and rubbish of the previous inhabitants and driven to the police cells in Queanbeyan for the night.

Queanbeyan was a 5-star hotel compared to the Goulburn establishment. I was given a towel, toothbrush and normal blanket and allowed to have a shower, and a tasteless chicken curry to eat. On the walls of the shower, scratched in the paint (probably with the toothbrush as nothing pointy was permitted) were the names and sentences given to previous inmates. It was almost as though they were proud of their achievements: - Johnno D. 10 months Long Bay! Davo Blogs 2 years! I was also greatly saddened to see a beautiful young Aboriginal girl in the lockup for the night and wondered whether she'd get caught up in the system (if she wasn't already) and waste her life behind bars.

I showered again in the morning just because it was such a luxury and other-worldly comfort and ate a banana for breakfast. Feeling almost human, I endured the trip back to Goulburn and the concrete cells again. When my time came I was handcuffed and led through a tunnel, surfacing inside the high wooden and metal railed dock in the middle of the courtroom. I shivered (with cold) and shook (with fear) throughout the bail hearing. The magistrate had the nickname No-bail-Bailey so I didn't have high hopes. I was so relieved when she granted bail even though it required me to report daily to the police in Moss Vale, 20 km away from home!

There was quite a gathering of TV cameras and press outside the courthouse after the hearing so with the help of some court officials and Corrective Service officers I was smuggled out the back and to the lawyer's office where Rich and son David (after running the gauntlet of the press) brought the car and took me home. We were met at home by a photographer, and I had to hide on the floor of the car and was driven around the back of the house.. For an hour or so I had to keep to the inside rooms as the persistent cameraman hung around, peering in the windows, hoping for a glimpse of me. I was in a very emotional state and this harassment by the press was the last straw.

I was swamped with love and concern from just about everyone I knew and from total strangers—many having their own story about how they had helped a parent die when life was utterly miserable and pointless for them. Many people with whom I'd lost contact over decades got in touch, offering their support and love and I am so grateful to everyone. Some friends even very generously contributed to the costs which were substantial (about $350 K all up).

When I heard from my sister that she had organised a funeral in her home town and that Mary had been cremated up there I was sitting on the floor in front of our woodfire on a very cold, miserable day. A wave of grief and misery swamped me, and I cried hysterically. The emotions were so powerful, I was racked with sobs and felt the need to bang my head on the floor and thrash my legs about in an attempt to make sense of the overwhelming pain, anguish and sorrow I was feeling. I have never in my life felt such utter desolation.

I had decided very early on that I would not let the ordeal define me or damage me or my family more than was unavoidable, and the generosity of so many people helped enormously. In addition, I always managed to hang onto the knowledge that my actions had possibly saved Mary more years of suffering and misery.

I was very grateful to the lawyers for securing my release, but they were firmly of the opinion that the DPP would change the charge from Murder to Manslaughter and that I would not have to go to trial, but rather appear before a judge in the District Court and plead Guilty to Manslaughter. Eventually, after much deliberation, we engaged Barrister Kieran Ginges and lawyer Adrian McKenna who felt we needed to take a much broader view and fight the charge on many fronts rather than just hope for a charge downgrade. I think our decision to change lawyers was the right move as we had more confidence in them, and they truly left no stone unturned and fought incredibly hard and with great skill.

Richard, my husband, with his incredible brain, compassion and understanding was (and still is), my rock. He fought just as hard as (or harder than) the lawyers. One of them said that they wouldn't want to be cross-examined by him, another said he should have been a lawyer. He kept them on their toes, wrote submissions to the DPP, and probably suffered more than I did as it felt all too real to him. I am so lucky to have such a decent, caring, loving partner—my soul-mate—who has stuck with me through everything.

I had to appear before the magistrate in the Goulburn court every couple of months so that she could be seen to be keeping things moving. There were huge delays however, and instead of the matter being dealt with within twelve to eighteen months it dragged on and on. The first long delay was waiting for the coroner's report. When it was presented to the court at last, the level of the barbiturate in Mary was reported to be below the toxic to lethal range and for a brief period it looked as if I hadn't caused her death. But then the DPP got the coroner to re-examine her findings and she determined it was in the toxic to lethal range although at the lowest end of the range. Hopes were dashed again, and another court appearance followed. We contacted a toxicologist to get our own opinion on what were toxic levels and what the readings really meant.

Within a couple of weeks of my arrest I underwent four two-hour sessions with a forensic psychiatrist in Macquarie Street, Sydney, one of the best in the business. It was very distressing having to relive events in minute detail and the tearful sessions left me totally drained and exhausted.

We engaged a pathologist to give his expert opinion on the pathology findings of the autopsy and were horrified at Mary's shocking state of health. There was hardly a blood vessel to her heart or brain that wasn't almost totally blocked and the stents she'd had inserted after her heart attack were crushed and almost impossible to identify. The verdict was that she could have died at any time.

The court appearances were very stressful and frustrating as they usually resulted in further adjournments as the DPP had not made progress on whatever the adjournment had been granted for in the first place. They all were preceded by meetings and/or conversations with our lawyers and great uncertainty and worry about what the DPP was planning or about to do next.

I was referred to a psychiatrist who I saw regularly for about 12 months, and put on antidepressants, and to a psychologist. Both were very gentle and sympathetic and helped me manage my fears and emotional state. At one point, when the frustration of the endless delays and court appearances was unbearable, I hacked down an overgrown hedge in our yard. When I saw the psychiatrist a couple of days later, covered in scratches and cuts, he was very concerned about my mental health. I suppose in a way I was self-harming. I had to vent my frustration some way and not being someone to smash and throw things I did something constructive and destroyed the hedge instead.

Our lives had a surreal feeling and we felt we were living in a very long, drawn-out Limbo or Purgatory. My bail reporting requirements were gradually reduced from every day to every second day, and eventually to Monday and Friday. If we wanted to travel to see family, or as when our daughter came out from New Zealand and we rented a house at the sea for us all, I had to arrange to report in at the nearest police station. When the bush-fires hit Bundanoon and I was traumatised by staying to defend our house and was neurotic about needing to stay at home where I could watch for the next approaching fire front, the police were not at all sympathetic. Bail is not supposed to be punitive, but it was used as such. It was only when Covid made it impossible for anyone to leave the country that I managed to get them to drop reporting requirements. Every change to such things required an appearance before the magistrate.

One morning I had a very touching encounter with a complete stranger (and I had many similar ones over the years). As we were leaving the cafe to go to the court, a woman stepped in front of me, blocking the exit. She put her hand on her heart and said she had been praying for me for two-and-a-half years and could she please give me a hug. It was people and encounters like this that kept me going.

Just after the bushfires in 2020 I had to be assessed by the Crown's forensic psychiatrist—by Zoom for less than an hour, some two years after Mary's death and when I was in a highly emotional state due to the fires. Once again, I found it very distressing and difficult as well as terrifying, as being a Crown witness, she was more likely to find in favour of the Crown. It could hardly compare with the thorough eight-hour examination within weeks of the event that I had undergone with our forensic psychiatrist.

In June 2020 I was supposed to appear in the Supreme Court in Sydney for an arraignment but, due to Covid restrictions, I appeared instead via Zoom from my Barrister's chambers. The charge against me was read from an indictment and I entered a plea of 'not guilty' and therefore, was committed for trial. This was yet another very stressful event, but far less intimidating than having to appear in the Supreme Court in person. While in Sydney we had a pleasant dinner and night in a hotel on Hyde Park and tried to forget things and make the time as relaxing as possible.

Around this time I bought myself a beautiful little Ragdoll kitten. I had been cat-less for about two years and I desperately needed a little animal to love and distract me from all my fears and uncertainties. It was the best thing I ever did and helped me survive everything.

Every day for almost three years I went to gaol in my head, worrying, imagining and I suppose, trying to prepare myself for what I thought was inevitable. I worried about ridiculous little things like how I'd be able to cut my nails when all sharp things were banned, what food I'd be able to eat, being gluten intolerant, (what I'd been offered in my three days and two nights in custody was not recognisable as food as far as I was concerned) and how I'd survive not being able to see the moon and stars or feel Bundanoon's clean, fresh air on my face. I was distraught at the thought of being separated from Richard, our children and grandchildren and all the special people in my life.

Part of the legal process involved "Case Conferencing" in which our lawyers met with the DPP and argued that the charge against me should be reduced from murder to manslaughter. I would then plead guilty to manslaughter and appear before a judge for sentencing and thus avoid a lengthy trial, the huge costs to the taxpayer (and us) and the associated stresses. The DPP's lawyers that our lawyers were working with were supportive and thought we had a good chance of success, however, our appeal was rejected, and the charge of murder remained.

Richard and our lawyers then put together a "No Bill" application, asking that the charge against me be dropped, or at least withdrawn and a lesser charge of manslaughter be substituted. This was based on the lawyers' legal arguments and Richard's research into similar court cases. However, when it went up to the Directors' chambers it was rejected— and that was it—I would go to trial in the Supreme Court. I was absolutely terrified and gutted as were Richard, our family and friends.

All in all this limbo lasted for almost three years with about thirteen court appearances, an arraignment in Sydney and then a four-week trial in the Supreme Court sitting in Goulburn.

# THE TRIAL

My brother David and his wife Chris came down from Queensland and stayed for the duration of the trial, driving us to and from Goulburn every day and helping with cooking and everything else. It was the most wonderful thing—having their love and support and time together, although I wish it had been under different circumstances. We got into a routine of leaving the house in the morning, discussing the trial on the way to Goulburn and having a coffee with them and our lawyers before the court proceedings started. On the way home we could debrief and discuss what had transpired during the day and then have a quiet dinner together talking about other things before going to bed. Derek and his wife Janice came down for a few days and other very special friends came from all over the country to support us during the trial. My lovely friend Dixie delivered a three-course meal to us once a week.

The whole trial process with its archaic rituals and routines was quite fascinating even though I was scared stiff every day. The jury empanelment was quite a different process to that in TV dramas. About 200 jurors were called up and then numbers were whittled down by drawing twenty or so names from a ballot box. A juror could then ask to be excused if they felt they couldn't be impartial or there was some conflict for them. We were told nothing about the background or character of the twelve selected jurors and based on sight alone our defence counsel, Kieran, was allowed a maximum of three challenges, as was the Crown. Anyone rejected was replaced from the jury pool. When a full panel was achieved the jurors were asked to take either an oath (swear to God) or an affirmation (promise to the court), not individually but as a group.

Every morning when we, the defence lawyers and those for the Crown, were assembled in the courtroom, the Judge's Associate would bang three times on the Judge's door with a special knocker, and we would all have to stand as he entered and seated himself. The court assistant was then sent off to bring the jury in and when she announced the jury, I had to stand until they were all seated. They filed in in front of me and due to Covid spacing requirements seated themselves on either side of the courtroom rather than in the designated jury box. Many of the jurors caught my eye and smiled shyly at me, while some of them never looked at me during the whole time. Once they were seated I sat down, and proceedings commenced. At the end of each day or any break in proceedings I had to stand as the jury departed or entered.

For the first two days we heard from the police officers and Corrective Services staff who had been on duty at the time of my arrest, and it was purely administrative. After that, Richard and my siblings were called to the stand, a couple of them by video link due to Covid restrictions on travel. Then the managerial staff of the nursing home and a couple of nurses were questioned. The video of the police interview was shown. I found it very distressing, seeing myself in such a defeated, shocked state, admitting to everything so that Richard wouldn't be arrested as well. I can't believe I didn't demand a lawyer before saying anything. I was in such a state it never crossed my mind. I had been allowed to make a call and the local solicitor I'd spoken to was unavailable. His only advice was to answer all the questions truthfully. No warnings about not saying a word until I had a lawyer with me!

The doctor who was looking after Mary at the nursing home admitted in his evidence that he had not been aware of the appalling state of health she was in, (it was all written in her medical history and file) and his claims that she was sitting up only a month prior to her death, eating turkey and drinking mulled wine were shown to be farcical and dangerously ignorant. He also admitted that he had never even heard of the phenomenon of "Sundowning" experienced by dementia patients until a couple of weeks before the trial—yet he was in charge of dementia patients!

Due to Covid all the expert witnesses except for the pathologist we engaged—the coroner, the Crown's and our toxicologists, both forensic psychiatrists—had to appear by video link. Their discussions of Mary's physical health, the toxicological evidence and arguments about causation were fascinating, even though my future depended on them. Our barrister Kieran became an expert on the physiology of embolisms (Mary had a fresh one on her vertebral artery), levels of substances in peripheral blood after death, palliative care and all sorts of things that were raised. He raised grave doubts that what I had given her had actually caused her death, but rather accelerated it, as she had apparently 'not been right' that afternoon and may have entered an 'active dying phase' coincidentally. The jury, however, didn't buy this idea apparently thinking it was too much of a coincidence. Had they accepted this I would have been acquitted and it would have ended there.

There were long discussions about my mental health that I found very painful, the Crown trying to prove that I'd killed my mother cold-heartedly to get out of having to care for her.

As my cross examination approached I had daily sessions with our lawyers after the day in court. These gentle, decent men turned into aggressive monsters and shouted questions at me, being as nasty as they could and trying to trip me up, to prepare me for the sort of questions the Crown would throw at me. I was grateful for this as the cross examination was not as bad as I had feared.

After almost four excruciatingly long weeks it was finished, and the jury retired to deliberate early on a Monday afternoon. We had to be at the court all the time the jury was out, within reach in case they returned. We sat in the park outside the courthouse all Tuesday and Wednesday and into the following morning. The tension was unbearable. We tried to read, wandered about and prayed to Mary's Gaia for a good outcome. As the time passed we lost hope that I'd be acquitted outright and focused on hoping that at least I'd be acquitted of murder which would entail a mandatory custodial sentence.

After two-and-a-half-days of deliberation the jury returned, and we were called into court. I stood shaking as the jury entered the room and my heart sank as they filed past and none of them looked at me. Kieran sat next to me, holding my hand as the foreman stood and delivered a verdict - Not Guilty to the charge of Murder, but Guilty of Manslaughter. There was a brief pause between 'Not Guilty' and 'Murder' and for a few seconds Kieran thought I'd been acquitted outright, and I felt a brief instance of absolute joy and relief. But it was not to be! I was just hugely relieved that there was still at least some hope of a non-custodial sentence. So back into limbo we went...

A month later—a long agonising wait—a sentencing hearing was held. Our daughter Rachel came over from NZ with her two little boys, to support us and see me just in case I was given a gaol sentence. We had a lovely dinner the night before with them and our other daughter Susanna who had come to be with the boys while we went to Goulburn. We had a real dilemma about what to tell the children if I didn't come home the next day. We didn't want to lie to the kids, but what do you tell three-to-seven-year-olds to whom things are so black and white. Cops and robbers, goodies and baddies and only baddies go to gaol. We never did work out how to tell them something that could be elaborated on as their understanding grew over time. And luckily we didn't have to. Maybe when they're old enough they can read this.

After a very long and detailed summation, during which my hopes were raised and then dashed many times, Justice Beech-Jones, a highly intelligent and compassionate man, sentenced me to a two-year Community Correction Order (CCO), requiring me to be of good behaviour and to continue getting treatment for my depression. My mental impairment was considered substantial enough to have clouded my judgement and diminished my control of my actions.

The judge told the court that it had been the most difficult of all the trials he had conducted. He concluded that I had acted out of love and desperation and "To compound the sad end to Mary White's remarkable life, by imprisoning a daughter who cared for her and loved her, would simply not be just". This was a huge relief as, due to changes in sentencing laws, a CCO was the **only** non-custodial option.

I think the whole court burst into tears simultaneously. I was swamped with hugs and tears and Rachel hugged me until we were both wet with tears of relief and joy. It was so special having her there. After the paperwork was completed we adjourned to the café which was crowded with my friends and supporters. Even the waitresses hugged me and expressed their relief.

So, after nearly three years of hell, I could at last begin to grieve properly for Mary and resume a normal life. I could also begin to process the trauma of the bush fires that had swept through the National Park and had come within 100 metres of our home the previous year, with the Covid 19 pandemic hot on their heels.

In what turned out to be a very therapeutic process that brought Mary back to life to me, I put together and self-published a book of her poems, illustrated with family photographs. And now I have had the honour of completing her autobiography. I trust it would have met with her approval.

# TO KNOW THE LOVELY NIGHT

SMOKE JOURNEYS Mary E. White

A trace of aromatic wood-smoke on the breeze
Immediately evocative.
Taking me back on instamatic journeys into the past..
....First to a crackling camp-fire,
Lamp-lit tent, black velvet African sky
Smouldering with stars.
Young red M'sasa leaves dancing in and out of darkness
In flickering firelight.
I feel again as I felt then,
Young and happy and very much in love

And the magic of the wide, wild veld is all around us,
Lapping like a sea at the fringes
Of our illuminated island.
The friendly night is not a sleeping presence -
Very much alive it sings its symphonies.
Tintintabulating frogs talk to the busy stream
Which chuckles, gurgling, among the reeds
And round-rolled pebbles.
Crickets chirrup;
A lonely night-bird's weird and wavering cry
Comes from afar.

Faintly I hear lilting, liquid music
Plucked on a Jew's harp by an African musician
Away in outer darkness.
The melody is endlessly repeated
Till it becomes the very heart-beat of the night.
The dry grass rustles and a tiny mouse
Scampers into the fire lit circle,
Picks up a crumb and darts away again,
Breaking the spell.

Or further back in time,
Another night, another place, but still the magic -
Watching the tracery of trees against the moon.
High white clouds scudding past,
A night breeze faintly stirring
Bringing wisps of smoky fragrance
From fires that are stoked all night,
To cure the golden leaves
Which hang in rows of glowing bunches
In a tobacco barn.

I hear again the haunting native music
Played by dark-skinned Rhodesians who believe
Their ancient tunes will keep at bay
The fearsome spirits of their night
While they, reluctant, tend their fires.
I seem to hear again the peaceful breathing
Of sleeping family around me.
I feel secure, and privileged to be alive,
To know the lovely night, and be a part
Of all creation.

# ACKNOWLEDGEMENTS

Many thanks to all my readers along the way, particularly Richard, my children, Dave and Chris White, Susan Varga, Peter Stanbury, Rosie Gray, Lorelei Tait, Bill Robins, Penny Stratton and Pamela Jane. ♥

I also want to thank my family and all the wonderful people who stood by me and were there for me during those dark years in limbo and my trial. I couldn't have survived without you. Thanks too, to all of you who were so good to Mary in her declining years. She appreciated your friendship and kindness. ♥

Thanks to Fiverr International freelancers for turning my cover design into a real cover, my maps into real maps and for interior design and layout.

Printed in Great Britain
by Amazon

41733450R00178